THE HOUSE OF SCINDIAS

'Rasheed has that rare skill, the discipline of a journalist and the brilliant flair of a storyteller, evident here in this riveting account of one of India's most intriguing political families. The book is fascinating and a must read.'
– Barkha Dutt, Mojo Story

'Rasheed Kidwai brings us the thick, complex history of one of India's most fascinating royals. Transitioning from parlaying with the Mughals and the British to democracy's dirt-road politics, Nehru to Jan Sangh, Kidwai's canvas is unenviably large – spanning history, politics, palace intrigue, a jailed queen, mother-son fall out, saas-bahu saazish, an unopened will, sibling turf wars and fighting over a leaking ship. And the Maharaja who died in Paris in 1925 setting aside money in his will to build a memorial for his dog Hussu.'
– Shekhar Gupta, Editor-in-Chief, The Print

'The Scindias are one of India's most charismatic political dynasties and this book captures their tryst with both royalty and democracy. And who better to tell their story than political historian Rasheed Kidwai? What stands out in Kidwai's books is how he places the contemporary in just the right historical context. His writings are a treasure trove of anecdotes that make his narration as accessible as an engaging conversation.'
– Priya Sahgal, Senior Executive Editor, NewsX

OTHER LOTUS TITLES

Anil Dharker	*Icons: Men & Women Who Shaped Today's India*
Aitzaz Ahsan	*The Indus Saga: The Making of Pakistan*
Ajay Mansingh	*Firaq Gorakhpuri: The Poet of Pain & Ecstasy*
Alam Srinivas	*Women of Vision: Nine Business Leaders in Conversation*
Amarinder Singh	*The Last Sunset: The Rise & Fall of the Lahore Durbar*
Aruna Roy	*The RTI Story: Power to the People*
Ashis Ray	*Laid to Rest: The Controversy of Subhas Chandra Bose's Death*
Bertil Falk	*Feroze: The Forgotten Gandhi*
Harinder Baweja (Ed.)	*26/11 Mumbai Attacked*
Harinder Baweja	*A Soldier's Diary: Kargil – The Inside Story*
Ian H. Magedera	*Indian Videshinis: European Women in India*
Jenny Housego	*A Woven Life*
Kunal Purandare	*Ramakant Achrekar: A Biography*
Maj. Gen. Ian Cardozo	*Param Vir: Our Heroes in Battle*
Maj. Gen. Ian Cardozo	*The Sinking of INS Khukri: What Happened in 1971*
Madhu Trehan	*Tehelka as Metaphor*
Moin Mir	*Surat: Fall of a Port, Rise of a Prince, Defeat of the East India Company in the House of Commons*
Monisha Rajesh	*Around India in 80 Trains*
Noorul Hasan	*Meena Kumari: The Poet*
Prateep K. Lahiri	*A Tide in the Affairs of Men: A Public Servant Remembers*
Rajika Bhandari	*The Raj on the Move: Story of the Dak Bungalow*
Ralph Russell	*The Famous Ghalib: The Sound of My Moving Pen*
Rahul Bedi	*The Last Word: Obituaries of 100 Indian Who Led Unusual Lives*
R.V. Smith	*Delhi: Unknown Tales of a City*
Salman Akthar	*The Book of Emotions*
Sharmishta Gooptu	*Bengali Cinema: An Other Nation*
Shrabani Basu	*Spy Princess: The Life of Noor Inayat Khan*
Shahrayar Khan	*Bhopal Connections: Vignettes of Royal Rule*
Shantanu Guha Ray	*Mahi: The Story of India's Most Successful Captain*
S. Hussain Zaidi	*Dongri to Dubai*
Thomas Weber	*Going Native: Gandhi's Relationship with Western Women*
Thomas Weber	*Gandhi at First Sight*
Vaibhav Purandare	*Sachin Tendulkar: A Definitive Biography*
Vappala Balachandran	*A Life in Shadow: The Secret Story of ACN Nambiar – A Forgotten Anti-Colonial Warrior*
Vir Sanghvi	*Men of Steel: India's Business Leaders in Candid Conversation*

FORTHCOMING TITLE

Narinder Singh Kapany	*The Man Who Bent Light*

THE HOUSE OF SCINDIAS

A SAGA OF POWER, POLITICS AND INTRIGUE

RASHEED KIDWAI

FOREWORD BY
SANKARSHAN THAKUR

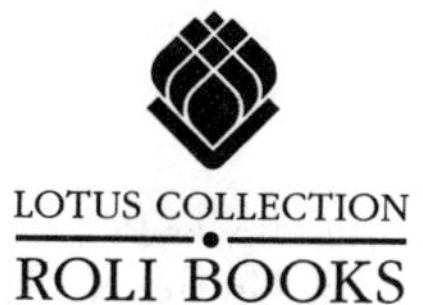

LOTUS COLLECTION
ROLI BOOKS

Lotus Collection

First published in 2021

The Lotus Collection
An imprint of
Roli Books Pvt. Ltd
M-75, Greater Kailash II Market, New Delhi 110 048
Phone: +91 (011) 40682000
E-mail: info@rolibooks.com
Website: www.rolibooks.com
Also at Bengaluru, Chennai & Mumbai

Cover Design: Sneha Pamneja
Cover Photographs (clockwise from top left): Vijaya Raje Scindia with husband Jiwajirao Scindia, Maharaja of Gwalior; Vasundhara Raje; Jyotiraditya Scindia; and Madhavrao Scindia. All photographs: Private Collection.
Layout Design: Bhagirath Kumar
Production: Lavinia Rao

ISBN: 978-81-951248-0-0

Typeset in Adobe Caslon Pro by Roli Books Pvt. Ltd
Printed at Saurabh Printers Pvt. Ltd., Greater Noida, India

Contents

Dedicated to

Prakash Patra and Rakesh Joshi
Inspirational and supportive figures in my life

Foreword

May I recount a short tale before you get into Rasheed Kidwai's altogether more elaborate and engrossing one?

It is a tale from the cataclysmic year of my formal baptism in journalism – Operation Bluestar; the toppling of Farooq Abdullah in Jammu and Kashmir in a remotely crafted coup; the assassination of Indira Gandhi; the unspeakable shame of the slaughter of Sikhs that followed; the horror of deathly spew in Bhopal. 1984. It seemed like we had been sentenced to live out a fangled variation of dark, Orwellian prophecy. It was in that year, too, that India cast her most one-sided vote ever and invested wholesomely in Rajiv Gandhi, the youngest to be elected prime minister, embodiment of the expectations of a shaken nation. This cameo is from that campaign.

I was a rookie, a little exhausted by the many directions in which the crackerbursts of 1984 had sent me as a reporter, but also breathlessly excited by the unstoppable drama of the stage I had landed myself on. One of the election datelines I was assigned to was Gwalior, and one morning I found myself in the courtrooms of the Jai Vilas Mahal, the elegant seat of the House of Scindias. I had received the grant of a seat to travel a stretch of the road with Madhavrao, Rajiv Gandhi's pick against the formidable Atal Bihari Vajpayee.

When I arrived – slightly early in the earnestness of a novice, and probably, too, because I may never have stepped into a lived palace before – the hall I had been motioned to was still empty. At one end of it sat a wooden throne on a pedestal, and if you sat in it you'd see in front of you, at a suitably lower level, row upon row of seating, like pews in a church. I felt a bit like a pea cast into a cauldron, utterly lost on where I should locate myself. Presently, the place began to fill up. Everybody that walked in came with palms folded around a garland. Soon enough the room became suffused with the redolence of marigolds.

Madhavrao arrived without preface (or perhaps, the marigolds were the preface) and seated himself on the throne with a swiftness of stride that barely afforded notice. Thereon, one by one, pew after pew, the gathered walked up, bowed in obeisance and garlanded the enthroned one. The hall echoed with singular enunciation: '*Maharaj ki Jai*!'

When I got into the back seat of the campaign car with Madhavrao (I can't remember what make it was but it was a cushioned and air-conditioned space; the kind of space journalists at the time were alien to) my prepped list of questions had already been superceded by the spectacle I had witnessed. 'How could you allow or afford yourself the trappings of royalty, how could you encourage feudatory mores,' I asked him, 'when you belong to a party that also calls itself socialist, and you are the citizen of a country that abolished the privy purse long ago? Do kings contest elections?'

Madhavrao looked out the window and brought on the charm of that signature smile to his lips, and then he turned to me and said: 'Well, if the woman leading the campaign against me is referred to as Rajmata by all and sundry, I must rightfully be Maharaj.'

I must confess that left me fumbling for a counter. Madhavrao was referring, of course, to his mother, Vijaya Raje Scindia, matriarch of the clan at the time and defacto campaign manager for Vajpayee, his arch rival in the contest for Gwalior.

There were at least two critical things to be understood about the Scindias in that one clipped sentence Madhavrao had responded with: that they had adopted to the ways of elected democracy smartly and seamlessly, and that they were astute about allocating their eggs to appointed baskets, even different baskets if that is what was required for the Scindia enterprise to remain a going enterprise.

Unwittingly or otherwise, we, as Indians, have telescoped our attention and understanding of dynasty as arbiters of democratic processes too narrowly. We think of political dynasty and we only think of the Nehru–Gandhis. Dynasty and democracy admittedly seem an anachronism, but they are our reality. The House of Scindias is proof we should expand our understanding of how, or why, dynasties have come to be intrinsic to our understanding of the dynamics of our democracy. The Nehru–Gandhis remain, for good reason, central to the alchemy of how dynasty alloys with democracy in our parts. The Scindias, though not comparable to the Nehru–Gandhis, make themselves singular after their own fashion. Do not omit to notice, for instance, their versatility, or dare I say, malleability of investment in ideology and party politics. Vijaya Raje began with the Congress, but turned, via a stint in the right-wing Swatantra Party, robustly to the Sangh and was one of the founding members of the BJP. Her son, Madhavrao, began in the Jana Sangh but became a sterling lead act of the Congress; heavens only know what summits he would have scaled because it was the heavens that cut him so tragically down. His son, Jyotiraditya, was born in the Congress cradle, and was a bubbling star of it, but, as it happens, he is back to where his family has been longest invested in: the Sangh. Call it atavism or opportunism, the youngest of the Scindias has returned to the precincts his aunts, Vasundhara Raje and Yashodhara Raje, have long inhabited.

Indian politics is replete with dynasties; the Nehru–Gandhis aren't alone in that alley, although they may still rivet most attention. Here, in this volume, lies the tale of what is arguably India's most successful transition of power from the assumptions and entitlements of royalty to the requirements of popular democracy. There is a lot that has been said, and will continue to the said, of the Scindias – none of that is likely to take away from how they have fashioned and sustained their fascinating, and very often dubiously achieved, alcove in power. Here is a work, painstakingly and punctiliously put together (Rasheed's talent for unearthing pearly anecdotes and golden personal nuggets is enviable) that tells us not merely about the Scindias but, in great measure, also about ourselves. This isn't where you must stop; this is where you must begin.

Sankarshan Thakur
April 2021

Acknowledgements

Andrew Rawnsley, the acclaimed British political journalist and author, was right when he said that writing about politics was far too important to be left to politicians. Most political autobiographies and authorized biographies are self-serving attempts to document a favourable history of the lives of politicians and events involving them.

However, writing an independent account of living politicians can be a hazardous enterprise. One, they can sue the author over real or perceived slights or something they feel might have an adverse impact on their career. Moreover, life in politics is a constantly evolving journey. Many politicians are also allergic to criticism or any attempt to peel off layers of protective armour they carefully build around their public persona. Personal details, gossip, scandals, indiscretions are no-go areas simply because of lack of access, information and facts.

The House of Scindias was a challenging assignment. Most living members of the Scindia family were courteous yet guarded, curious but reticent. I take this opportunity to thank the grace and courtesy extended by Jyotiraditya Scindia, Vasundhara Raje Scindia, Yashodhara Raje Scindia, Rana Dushyant Singh and others. Politically – and understandably – they may not want to endorse every word written in this book. But then, one need not agree with a political book to find it valuable.

What I have tried to do in this modest attempt is explain what the Scindias have stood for since 1731 when Ranoji Scindia, the founder of the dynasty, established his capital in Ujjain. Since then, for nearly 300 years now, they have received the adulation of their subjects: first as monarchs (representatives of God on earth) and then as humble *jan sewaks* (public servants) after Independence.

In purely electoral terms, the Scindias score over the Nehru–Gandhi family for their uninterrupted stint in Parliament or in a state assembly since 1957. Between 1991 and 1996, nobody from the Gandhi family was a member of parliament. Rajiv Gandhi was assassinated in May 1991 and Maneka Gandhi had lost as a Janata Dal candidate from Pilibhit in the general election that year.

The Scindias have been noble, kind-hearted and just, while being utterly human in their flesh-and-blood desires and aspirations. They remind of Henry David Thoreau's words: 'Every man is the builder of a temple, called his body, to the god he worships, after a style purely his own, nor can he get off by hammering marble instead. We are all sculptors and painters, and our material is our own flesh and blood and bones. Any nobleness begins at once to refine a man's features, any meanness or sensuality to imbrute them.' The story of the Scindias, too, is an account of a quest – towards a mix of benevolence and control, according to their perception of dharma. This subjectivity is fascinating, inspiring and has been a learning experience. Readers will decide whether I have even come close to capturing these drifts.

The continuation of dynastic culture in a democratic polity is illogical but not without its upside. For one, it has helped more women enter politics, which may not have been possible otherwise. About 25 to 40 per cent of women who have made it to Parliament are from dynastic families.

I owe this work largely to publisher Priya Kapoor. It was her idea and she believed that I was capable of writing it. I hope and pray that readers endorse Priya's trust, even if partially, as the book has certain limitations.

My friends Priya Sahgal and Sunetra Choudhury, both accomplished authors and two of the finest journalists around, are apparently guilty of recommending me to Priya Kapoor.

I can never thank my friend from *The Telegraph*, Ananda Sen, enough. He volunteered to read every word, cleaned up what I wrote and gave valuable suggestions. Even when he was critical, he was always lavish in his praise and encouragement. I have benefited immensely from Sen's perceptive approach and expertise in rewriting with minimum words, without tampering with the spirit and the context of the work.

Author and literacy consultant Atul K. Thakur, too, went through the manuscript and offered some valuable suggestions.

The list of friends, fellow journalists, authors, prominent citizens, bureaucrats and politicians who assisted me in this assignment is long. While some wish not to be named, I am hugely indebted to their help, perspective and insight.

I am grateful to Dr. Sunjay Joshi and Samir Saran of the Observer Research Foundation (ORF) for their support and encouragement.

A special word of thanks to Vir Sanghvi and Namita Bhandare. The writings of senior journalists N.K. Singh, Radhika Ramaseshan, Coomi Kapoor, Sheela Bhatt, Saba Naqvi, Rakesh Dixit, Vertul Singh, Amreesh Mishra, Anup Dutta, Brajesh Rajput, Dinesh Gupta, Deepak Tiwari and others are acknowledged in the bibliography but I wish to reiterate my sense of gratitude to them. Rafi Shabbir, a Bhopal-based librarian, author and playwright, handed me some rare books that gave fresh insight into the history of the Scindias. The India international Centre (IIC) library was most useful and its staff was ever helpful.

I am forever grateful to my wife, Dr. Farah Kidwai, for her patience and support through the COVID-19 lockdown, a testing period for everyone, including us; Abaan, Inaya and Falah for constantly making us laugh and smile, and Farhan–Saima, Saad–Ghazia, Shahab–Sadia, Saif–Farah, Shams–Shaista, Umar–Maryam, Samad, Sabur, Umair and Ayesha–Siddique for always being around.

Thank you Nirmal Pathak, Swaraj Thapa, Naghma Sahar, Rama Lakshmi, Sudeep Mukhia, Faisal Mohammad Ali, Avinash Dutt, Ravi Dubey, Avinash Kalla and Richa Sharma for being part of the journey.

I also profusely thank my household staff, Radha, Prem, Asha, Magan Dada and Rashid, who ensured that I had the time and space to remain focused on writing this book through the pandemic.

The always patient and candid Chirag Thakkar, my editor, gave his loving, professional, eagle-eyed care to the manuscript. A big thank you to him, and to Ekta Sharma, Ahana Singh, Neelam Narula and everyone at Roli Books as well as Binita Roy for her editorial contribution.

Rasheed Kidwai
May 2021
New Delhi

ONE

Scindias: A Brief History

Ranojirao, the Founder

The Scindias had migrated from Satara, in modern-day Maharashtra, to Gwalior over 300 years ago. Said to be Kshatriyas, they hailed from Kanherkhed, 15 km from Satara, and were locally known as Sendrak, one of the ninety-six *kulas* or clans into which all 'pure' Marathas are divided. Ranojirao Shinde, a personal aide to Peshwa Balaji Bajirao I, is acknowledged as the founder of the Gwalior dynasty. It is commonly believed that the word Scindia is derived from his Maratha surname 'Shinde'.

The Scindias were proud of their humble origins. They did not claim descent from the sun and the moon like the many feudal lords and royals who did and called themselves Suryavanshi or Chandravanshi. 'Unlike some princes who claim to be the descendants of the sun or the moon, I am proud of the fact that we had risen from being sons of the soil, peasants,' Charles Allen and Sharda Dwivedi have quoted the fifth maharaja of Gwalior,

Madho Rao Scindia (October 1876–June 1925), as saying in their book *Lives of the Indian Princes*.[1] 'Really just ordinary Maratha farmers who rose on their own sweat and blood.'

Sweat, blood and, possibly, a pair of slippers, too!

As the story goes, Ranojirao, who lived in the first half of the eighteenth century, had accompanied Balaji Bajirao I in the Peshwa's northern campaigns. In his book titled *The Great Maratha Mahadji Scindia*,[2] N.G. Rathod has narrated how Bajirao once returned late at night from a rendezvous to find Ranoji, his personal attendant, asleep but clutching his master's shoes close to his chest. In those days, a way of poisoning rivals was by pouring a toxic substance in their shoes; and thus, Ranoji had made sure that his master's shoes did not fall into the wrong hands. So impressed was Bajirao with Ranoji's sense of loyalty that he put him in charge of his stable. For the humble attendant, there would be no looking back from then on.

Sir John Malcolm (1769–1833), a Scottish soldier who served as an administrator and diplomat in central India, offers a slightly different version of this story in his lucid, two-volume account, *A Memoir of Central India: Including Malwa, and Adjoining Provinces*.[3] Malcolm describes the Scindias as belonging to an economically weaker caste, the Other Backward Class (OBC) Koombee or Kunbi cultivators. Relying on a letter written to him by Captain Stewart, who was the British Resident (political agent of the viceroy) at the Scindia court in 1819, Malcolm records Ranoji's rise from a low rank where his responsibility was to carry Bajirao's slippers in a box. One day, when Bajirao stepped out after a long audience with Chhatrapati Sahuji Maharaj, he saw Ranoji asleep clutching his master's slippers close to him. Bajirao then elevated Ranoji to the rank of *pagah* or bodyguard.

In 1728, when Bajirao successfully led the Malwa campaign against the Mughals, he appointed Ranoji the subedar of Malwa. This elevated position allowed Ranoji to collect taxes and keep

65 per cent of the proceeds as his remuneration. Later, he was presented with more fiefs. This period coincided with the decline in the power of the Chhatrapatis of Satara and the Peshwas of Pune, allowing Ranoji to declare himself an independent ruler in 1731 with Ujjain as his capital. It was at this time that Ranoji adopted the surname Scindia, dumping the family name of Shinde.[4]

Ranoji soon shifted his capital from Ujjain to Gwalior, a historical city that had been part of the Mughal empire till 1754. Abu'l Fazl, the court historian of Emperor Akbar, has recorded the history of Gwalior in his *Ain-i-Akbari*, a sixteenth-century detailed document recording the administration of the Mughal Empire. The town had an iron mine and a *taksal* (mint), from where copper coins were issued. The legendary musician Tansen, one of the *navratans* (nine jewels) of Akbar's court, also hailed from Gwalior. Some Scindia family historians claim that the family had come to the attention of Mughal rulers as possible allies during the time of the Bahmani Sultanate (which controlled the Deccan), their bitter rivals.

Ranoji turned out to be a benevolent ruler and enjoyed his newly established kingdom till his death in 1745. One of his most notable accomplishments was the building of a shrine at Beed for Mansoor Ali Shah, a saint of the Suhrawardi clan of Sufis, who had predicted the fame and greatness of the Scindias for generations to come. Ranoji and his wife, Chimna Bai, sought spiritual solace from the saint and often visited him. It is said that Ranoji's youngest son Mahadji (1730–1794) – who formed the Scindia dynasty in the real sense and expanded its sway – was able to ward off several ailments and threats to his life because of the benediction of Mansoor Shah, who used his supposed spiritual powers to help him.[5]

Mansoor Shah, the Patron Saint of Gwalior

The Scindias conferred every possible honour on Mansoor Shah. Although there are eighty-seven Sardar families who were once part of the Gwalior oligarchy – such as the Shitoles, Patankars, Phalkes, Angres, and Jadhavs – only Mansoor Shah was given the title 'Sardar Shree Saheb', which belongs to his successors even now. Mahadji even invited the saint to establish himself at Gwalior after the Scindia empire had been established there. The Sufi saint, in his late eighties then, declined the offer; but his son, Habib Shah, did acquiesce and received a *jagir* from Mahadji. Even today, the carefully preserved personal effects of Mansoor Shah, such as his *choga* (cloak), *khadao* (footwear) and utensils can be seen at Gorkhi near the Bada urs of the saint. The annual urs of Mansoor Shah now draws many thousands of visitors as the event is held with great pomp and show. During Muharram, an astonishingly large number of *tazias*[6] are taken out in processions where Hindus outnumber Muslims.

When Ranoji died in 1745, he left three sons, Jayappaji, Dattaji and Jyotiba, along with two illegitimate children, Tukaji and Mahadji. Jayappa was killed at Nagaur in 1759 and his son, Jankoji, was taken prisoner in the Third Battle of Panipat and put to death. It paved the way for Jankoji's uncle Mahadji as successor. But Mahadji faced resistance from various quarters. Sakhubai Shinde, the widow of Jayappa, and Raghunathrao, the uncle of Peshwa Madhavrao and acting regent, opposed his appointment. Mahadji, however, won the crown in 1768 when Madhavrao Peshwa declared Mahadji to be the true successor of the Scindia clan.[7]

Mahadji, Torchbearer and Statesman

Hazrat Mansoor Shah's blessings and spiritual guidance helped Mahadji time and again during his reign. One such episode is described in a popular legend: at the Third Battle of Panipat against the forces of Ahmad Shah Abdali in 1761, Mahadji was gravely wounded and his whereabouts could not be traced. His wife, a native of Beed, rushed to Hazrat Mansoor Shah at his shrine to seek help, and the saint, through his spiritual powers, is said to have guided her towards Rane Khan, a soldier whose duties were to carry water for the fighting forces.[8]

The story goes that Mahadji was driven out of the battleground by a pursuing Afghan soldier. Just as the pursuer was about to catch up with him, Mahadji's horse stumbled and the Scindia ruler fell into a ditch. The pursuer's horse also lost balance but the Afghan managed to inflict a crushing blow on Mahadji's knee. Because of the severity of the injury, Mahadji developed an infection that left a scar on his leg and a lifelong limp. Rane Khan is said to have carried the injured Mahadji from Panipat to the Deccan in a bullock cart, thereby saving his life. In 1765, when Mahadji won back Gwalior from the Raja of Gohad, he made Rane Khan a *jagirdar*[9] and declared him his brother.[10]

After recovering from his wounds suffered in the Third Battle of Panipat, Mahadji led campaigns against the Jats of Bharatpur, Berar, Rajputana, Malwa, Bundelkhand, Rohilkhand and around Delhi. At the age of twenty-five, he captured Mathura, became a devotee of Lord Krishna and rebuilt several dilapidated temples in the sacred city.

An astute man, he was quick to realize the advantages of having a European-trained army and sought the services of a French commander, Benoit de Boign, who was asked to raise battalions trained in European warfare. A gazetteer published in 1785 by the Scindias claimed that Mahadji had raised an army that eventually had sixteen battalions of regular infantry, 500 cannons and a cavalry that was over 100,000 strong.

By 1782, when the First Anglo-Maratha War ended, Mahadji had become a powerful Maratha ruler and an influential figure in contemporary affairs. In his *A Memoir of Central India*, Malcolm has described him as 'steel under velvet gloves' and given an extensive account of how the British were perturbed by Mahadji's acumen. So impossible it had become for the British to ignore Mahadji Scindia that he was declared an independent prince by the foreigners that same year. This was formalized by the Treaty of Salbai signed on 17 May 1782, in Salbai, Gwalior, between the British East India Company and the Marathas.

It was Mahadji's great political foresight that led him to side with the Mughals in the subsequent years. In their book *Madhavrao Scindia: A Life*,[11] journalists Vir Sanghvi and Namita Bhandare write that Mahadji had understood that he alone could not fight the British and thus needed the Mughals as his allies. 'It did not matter to him that Mughals were Muslims and he was a Hindu,' Sanghvi writes.

As a result of this alliance, Mahadji became indispensable to the Mughal emperor. In 1784, Shah Alam sought Mahadji's help after the Mughal ruler had been relegated to the position of a puppet by Afrasiab Khan, a minister at the court. Mahadji joined the emperor with a large force and restored him to full sovereignty. Afrasiab was soon murdered and Shah Alam conferred the title of Naib Vakil-ul-Mutlaq, Deputy Regent of the Empire, on Mahadji, virtually making him the master of the Mughal dominions.

This was not the last time when the Mughal emperor called on Mahadji for help. In 1788, Mahadji had to once again intervene in Delhi when the Mughals fell to a Rohilla adventurer, Ghulam Kadir, and emperor Shah Alam was imprisoned and blinded. Mahadji Scindia restored the throne to Shah Alam and, in return for his services, the emperor conferred on him the dignities of the Vakilul Mutlaq (Regent) and the order of Mahi Maratib (person to be granted the highest respect). At this time, the power and authority wielded by Mahadji was at such peak that he was instrumental in conferring the status of Vakil-ul-Mutlaq on

Peshwa Madhav Rao Bhatt II too. This was an incredibly astute political manoeuver on part of the Scindia: not only was Mahadji able to express a sense of gratitude towards the Peshwa, he was also successful in displaying his enormous clout with the Mughal emperor. All this at a time when both the Peshwa and the Mughal emperor were dependent upon him for their survival.

It was to the court of Peshwa Madhav Rao Bhatt II in Poona that Mahadji travelled in 1792, for the purposes of effecting a sort of unification of the southern Indian states at that time. Vir Sanghvi writes, 'Just as in north India, his policy was to establish a constitutional position of the Mughal Empire, in the South too. He wanted to achieve the unification by establishing the constitutional position of the Peshwa. Unfortunately, Nana Fadnavis, then in alliance with the British and the Nizam against Tipu Sultan, refused to cooperate and that dream was never realized.' But this trip did allow Mahadji to endear himself further to the Peshwa. When Mahadji reached the Poona court of Peshwa Madhav Rao Bhatt II, he made a dramatic yet powerful statement about his humble origins. Mahadji dismounted from an elephant at the gates of the Poona fort and placed himself lower than the positions of all the *Mankarries* (Sardars) or hereditary nobles. When Peshwa Madhav Rao II entered the court and asked him to be seated with nobles of high standing, Mahadji untied a bundle he was carrying. It contained a pair of old slippers that had belonged to Bajirao I. Mahadji said, 'This is my occupation; it was that of my father Ranoji.'

Peshwa Madhav Rao Bhatt II was visibly moved and is said to have personally escorted Mahadji to a high seat. According to General Malcolm, this was not the only time that Mahadji had proudly proclaimed his humble background. 'But he had, no doubt, other motives. These indeed are described in a common saying in India, Mahadji made himself the sovereign of an empire, by calling himself a Patel, or headman of a village.... His actions were suited to the constitution of the society he was born in, which had a just pride in his talent and energy, and esteemed him one of the ablest and most successful Maratha leaders. He was content with the substance of power and left others to wear its robes.'

Mahadji passed away in 1794. Had he lived longer, he might have been successful in bringing the Sikhs, the Afghans, the Nizam, Tipu Sultan and the Marathas together and the British, perhaps, would not have established their dominion in the subcontinent.

'Mahadji would have brought under one standard the horsemen and the French contingent of Tipu (Sultan), the powerful artillery of the Nizam, the whole force of Rajputs and every spur which Maratha influence could have collected from Poona, from Indore, from Baroda and from Nagpur,' George Bruce Malleson wrote in his book *An Historical Sketch of the Native States of India in Subsidiary Alliance with the British Government*.[12] 'Even if the final result might not have been attained, the great problem of contest between a united India and the English would have been fairly fought.'

It will not be far-fetched to say that the course of the country's history would have been different had Mahadji lived a few more years. He was a far-sighted statesman and recognized the need of an alliance with Tipu Sultan against the British. Mahadji's negotiations with the Peshwa also could not be completed before his death, else a common front against the British could have been organized. With Mahadji's death, the Marathas lost a remarkable personality and, perhaps, their greatest statesman.[13]

Woman in Power

Mahadji did not have a son. Towards the end of his life, he had adopted his nephew, Daulatrao (1779–1827), who ruled Gwalior till 1827. Daulatrao's wife, Baija Bai (1784–1863), served as his close aide and adviser and was the power behind the throne. Born in 1784 into the aristocratic Ghatge family of Kagal, Baija Bai was fourteen when she married Daulatrao. She could ride a horse, fire a gun and wield a sword or a spear. Fanny Parkes, a travel writer from Wales, met Baija Bai during her visit to India. While Baija did not speak English, she, like Parkes, had a passion for well-bred horses. When they met for the first time, Baija Bai expressed a desire to see an English lady ride a horse, because 'she could not comprehend how they could sit all crooked'. Maratha women, after all, sat astride like the men, never side-saddle. Parkes was asked by Baija's attendant to try the Indian style and she had accepted the challenge. She would later write in her diary: 'I thought of Queen Elizabeth and her stupidity in changing the style of riding for women (in Britain).' The way in which Maratha women rode, she added, 'appeared so safe… I could have jumped over the moon'.[14]

However, anti-British sentiment ran in Baija Bai's family. Her father, Sakharam Ghatge, a courtier to the maharaja of Gwalior, fell out of favour of the ruler because of his staunch anti-British stand. When Daulatrao signed a treaty with the East India Company in 1805, it explicitly required him to expel his father-in-law from positions of influence. Baija shared her father's contempt for the British. She was 'suspicious of the Company and capable of reckless bravery', Parkes would write of her. She also recorded a scene about Baija leading troops in battle 'with a lance in her hand, and her infant in her arms'. Baija Bai was also immensely wealthy and her personal fortune was estimated at Rs 3 crore. She was involved in moneylending, bills of exchange and speculation, and was the head of the banking firms Nathji Kishan Das and Nathji Bhagwan Das. By the 1810s, Baija had even become a banker to the British, extending and demanding back enormous loans to them.

However, by this time Gwalior under the Scindias had to become a British protectorate – Daulatrao had earlier tried to take on the British in military encounters but had lost. From 1803 onwards, he was obliged to come under the umbrella of British supremacy, which permitted him to retain his territory and capital at Gwalior but forced him to accept the status of a protected prince.

Not that Daulatrao's reign was only marked by resistance to the consolidation of British supremacy. The Gwalior ruler was also a man of taste and under his patronage the Gwalior gharana became a cradle of Hindustani classical music. Mohammed Khan, son of the legendary musician Shakkar Khan, migrated to Gwalior and became a court musician under Daulatrao's patronage. The king would also invite skilful and seductive dancing girls from all parts of the country to perform in his court.

When Daulatrao died, he had not named a successor. A young boy named Mugat Rao (1805–1843), who belonged to another branch of the family and was distantly related to Daulatrao, was adopted by Baija Bai and he succeeded to the throne as Jankojirao Scindia on 27 June 1827. But effectively Gwalior remained under a woman's rule as Baija Bai continued to wield power, with even the British acknowledging Baija Bai as a ruler of 'great ability'.

In order to strengthen her own position, Baija decided not to educate Mugat Rao, to ensure that he would never become a challenge. 'Her policy was to dwarf the growth of his mind' and develop in him a 'vague and indefinite fear of her, (so) that in future he might not shake off her thraldom,' wrote Pillai.[15] Baija Bai continued to issue coins in her name and passed orders under her own seal even after her adopted son had become the official ruler, till the British objected in 1829. She held out as long as possible paying no heed to their protestations declaring quite bluntly that 'during my lifetime, I should be allowed to retain supreme control of affairs'. But the British ensured that her troops mutinied and, by 1832, she was thrown out of power. Baija Bai fled Gwalior and took refuge in British-ruled territory. It was then that Fanny Parkes met her again and noted how 'she who once reigned… has now no roof to shelter her… (and) is forced to live in tents… (as) a state prisoner.'

With substantial amounts of cash and resources at her disposal, Baija continued plotting against the British and tried to unseat her adopted son, but failed every time. This also meant that the British confiscated large chunks of her fortune. However, Baija was able to buy peace with the British by striking a fine balance between the royal family, the rebels against the British and the British themselves. She eventually moved to Nasik with an annual pension of Rs 400,000 from the British government.

By 1843, her adopted son had died and Gwalior had a new ruler, Jayajirao (1834–1886). Baija Bai proposed that Jayajirao marry her brother's great-granddaughter Chimnabai and was able to forge an alliance with him. This move allowed her to stage a sort of a comeback and she returned to Gwalior. Since then till 1863, when she died, she ensured that she stayed on the side of the British, avoiding all clashes. During the turbulent times of 1857, Baija Bai acted deftly and shrewdly when the rebels approached her to side with them: first she sided with them and then handed over secret correspondence with Tantia Tope to the British.

Her obituary published in the *New York Times* in 1863 paid tribute to her with a degree of criticism: 'She was not the least remarkable of the many able and unscrupulous women who abound in Indian history, such as the Ranee Chunda of Lahore, the Ranee of Jhansi, who fell fighting against us in 1857; the Lucknow Begum, who is still a fugitive in Nepaul; the old Ranee of Nagpore, who kept the province faithful to us in 1857; and the present Begum of Bhopal, who kept her country quiet that year, and is now, like her Sovereign, decorated with the insignia of the most exalted Order of the Star of India. The Bhaesi-Bhae [Baija Bai] of Gwalior was fond of recalling the battle of Assaye.

When the wife of an officer who had been with her husband in the Crimea visited the old lady in 1857, she asked: 'Have you seen a battle between the English and the Ruski?' 'Ay,' she said, with glowing eyes. 'I too, have ridden in a battle. I rode when Wellesley Sahib drove us from the field, with nothing but the saddle on which we sat.' She was a true Asiatic despot, as we found to our cost. On one occasion, when on a journey, she applied to an oil-seller for oil for her torches. The man was out, and his wife refused the oil with a sneer at the Ranee, whom she believed to be an impostor. The poor wretch was seized, enveloped in a hundred yards of silk steeped in her own oil, and thus burnt to death. When the husband returned he was presented with a lac of rupees (£10,000) to enable him to marry a wife with better manners. Our Administration offers no career to such spirits, unless in the tame work of administration, to which the Begum of Bhopal has quietly settled down. What the native chiefs are not allowed by us to seek in war, cruelty and anarchy, they find in debauchery and petty intrigue.'

Aloof from Mutiny

Variously known as India's first war of independence, the Sepoy Mutiny, or the Indian Revolt, the 1857 clash between the East India Company and a confederacy of independent princely states forms a watershed moment in India's history. The Rani of Jhansi, Lakshmibai, was a rallying point for the various rebels in the Bundelkhand region after the revolt of 1857 began. Married to the maharaja of Jhansi, Gangadhar Rao, barely 70 km from Gwalior, Lakshmibai had become a widow without bearing a surviving heir to the throne. Just before his death, Gangadhar had adopted a boy as his heir, but Lord Dalhousie, the then British governor-general of India, refused to recognize the adopted heir and annexed Jhansi in accordance with the Doctrine of Lapse.

According to Hindu law and customs, an individual or a ruler without natural heirs could adopt a person who would then have all the personal and political rights of a son. Dalhousie asserted the British's right of approving such adoptions. In practice, the Doctrine of Lapse meant the rejection of last-minute adoptions to save the kingdom from getting annexed. Lakshmibai had refused to cede Jhansi to the British and became a force to reckon with in the 1857 war.[16]

While Rani Lakshmibai and others such as Tantia Tope were fighting against the British, Jayajirao, then twenty-two, remained in Agra and ordered his troops to remain idle and not to fight for or against the British. But many soldiers at Morar (belonging to the Scindia army) joined the Indian rebels and killed English officers at Lashkar, the capital of the erstwhile Madhya Bharat state. Many of the Maratha sardars had then pleaded with Jayajirao to take an open stand against the British but Jayajirao used a variety of pretexts to confine his mutinous soldiers to the territorial limits of his state. What was more significant was that Jayajirao kept communicating with Major Herbert MacPherson while staying in Agra. Madho Maharaj's biographers, Bull and Haksar, have sought to paint Gwalior's diwan (prime minister) Dinkar Rao as the villain of the piece and a British stooge during the turbulent period from 1857 to 1858. According to them, a young Jayajirao was caught between the British and the rebel forces and misguided by his diwan. For Bull and Haksar though, Jayajirao's decision was an act of effective subterfuge. 'The times demanded subterfuge rather than diplomacy – this was a product of his subtle brain,' they wrote four decades later. Jayajirao returned to Gwalior from Agra after the British general Sir Hugh Rose had routed Rani Lakshmibai hardly a kilometre away from Jai Vilas Palace in Gwalior. On 18 April 1859, Tantia Tope was hanged at Shivpuri, 70 miles south-west of Gwalior.[17]

Jayajirao's proximity to the British has been well documented since then. After the revolt of 1857 was quelled, the maharaja of Gwalior received many rewards from the British. In 1858, when the British crown took direct control of India, Jayajirao acted swiftly to show his loyalty to the new rulers. He abolished the *ijardari* system under which the East India Company had secured revenue rights.[18] New administrative measures were introduced in the hieratical order of the province, districts, tehsils and other administrative regions. New departments of police and judiciary were established.

In 1866, the Gwalior Fort, Morar Cantonment and a few villages, which had come under British possession in 1858, were restored to the Scindias. With a total area of 25,041 square miles and a population of over 300,000 – of whom 84 per cent were Hindus and 6 per cent were Muslims – Gwalior had an annual revenue of Rs 15 crore, derived largely from forest resources, opium cultivation and customs duties. A grateful maharaja thanked the British and claimed that the idleness of the Scindia troops during the mutiny and their not siding with the mutineers had achieved 'a political triumph without which India could hardly have been saved'. Thus, at this time, Gwalior was a shining star among the lesser moons of the British's friends in India. In 1966, the maharaja of Gwalior was made Knights Grand Commander of the Order of the Star of India. In the Imperial Durbar of 1877, Jayajirao was granted a personal salute of 21 guns and was made a Counsellor of the Empress. Later, he became a Civil Knight Grand Cross Star of the Most Honourable Order of the Bath (GCB) and a Counsellor of Indian Empire (CIE).

Jayajirao's Notable Works

Known as a progressive ruler, Jayajirao set up narrow gauge railway lines[19] in 1872 between Agra and Gwalior and between Gwalior and Sheopur (Madhya Pradesh). Jayajirao even drove the steam locomotive engine himself for nearly 2 miles on the tracks leading to Sussera, 18 km from Gwalior city.

Jayajirao also commissioned the Jai Vilas Palace, one of the grandest such structures in India, inspired by European architectural styles, in honour of the Prince of Wales, who visited Gwalior in 1875 during his tour of the subcontinent. The palace, built of sandstone and painted white, was designed by Lieutenant-Colonel Sir Michael Filose and was an amalgamation of Doric, Tuscan, Corinthian and Palladian elements. A major attraction of the palace, completed in 1874, is its Durbar Hall. It is said that elephants were made to climb to the roof to measure the strength of the structure.

The maharaja, it is said, also had immense wealth and treasure at his service. It is believed that he had the habit of stashing parts of his vast personal wealth in the secret chambers of Gwalior Fort. The secret chambers could only be accessed through a numerical code, referred to as *Beejak* or *Bijak*. Jayajirao's son Madho Maharaj supposedly lost the *Beejak* and, consequently, access to the hidden fortune. In 1886, the young Madho Maharaj reportedly sought the help of Colonel Bannerman to locate the accumulated but inaccessible riches. Bannerman conducted extensive searches and recovered gold coins worth Rs 6.2 crore, but this was thought to be only a part of what was buried inside the secret chambers. Madho Maharaj continued the search for the treasures but without success and had to look to other avenues of increasing his wealth. Acting on the advice of his financial accountant, F.E. Dinshaw, he invested in Tata Iron and Steel Company Limited (TISCO) in 1924 and, by the 1960s, the Scindias were a major shareholder in Tata Sons companies. Decades later, in 1975, when income tax and enforcement sleuths forced their way inside Jai Vilas Palace on the grounds of tax evasion, to look for the Scindias's hidden treasure, they were especially looking for the *Beejak* in the hope of recovering the lost fortune (see later chapters).

The Legacy of 'Betrayal'

In spite of, or perhaps because of, the prosperity experienced by Gwalior under the rule of the British crown, Jayajirao's descendants in Gwalior in post-Independence India were haunted by his pro-British stand and he was accused of siding with the British and not Rani Lakshmibai in 1857. Hindutva icon Vinayak Savarkar (1883–1966) in his book, *Indian War of Independence, 1857*, referred to Jayajirao as a 'cobra, traitor and a coward'. Referring to the relationship between Jayajirao and the Rani of Jhansi, Savarkar wrote, 'the cobra shows not such rage when it is trodden upon as Laxmi showed at the sight of this traitor.' Savarkar, a revered figure among the current ruling dispensation, including Prime Minister Narendra Modi, had also written, 'If Scindia is not for the country, drag him down from his throne.'[20]

In August 2006, the then Rajasthan chief minister, Vasundhara Raje, faced angry protests in Indore when she was invited to unveil a bust of Lakshmibai. Vasundhara, however, dismissed the charge and claimed that 'as a woman', she had the highest regard for Lakshmibai and considered her a 'role model'.

In 2010, a website of the BJP-ruled Gwalior Municipal Corporation had accused Jayajirao of having 'betrayed' Rani Lakshmibai by providing her with a 'weak horse'. At that time, Jyotiraditya Scindia was a Congress minister in Dr. Manmohan Singh's government, and his aunt Yashodhara Raje Scindia was a Bharatiya Janata Party (BJP) leader and member of parliament (MP) from Gwalior. The corporation website read, 'Rani (Queen) of Jhansi, Lakshmi Bai came to Gwalior when General Huroz of British army defeated Lakshmi Bai in Kalpi. Maharaja Scindia of Gwalior betrayed Lakshmi Bai. He gave her a weak horse. Sensing something fishy, Lakshmi Bai decided to leave Gwalior. She laid down her life, while fighting British, on 18th June 1858.'

Pramod Bhargava, a Shivpuri-based historian, had, however, questioned the website's claim. He insisted that Jayajirao did not have any functional ties with either Lakshmibai or any other leading lights of the 1857 revolt. 'I am a bit sceptical about Jayajirao giving a horse at all to Lakshmi Bai, weak or strong,' he said. Bhargava said that neither Savarkar nor Pandit Sunder Lal, who were among the first to describe the revolt as India's first war of independence, had referred to Jayajirao Scindia loaning a horse to Lakshmibai. But he added, 'Had the Scindias cooperated with the Rani or Tantya Tope, the history of India would have been different.'[21]

Madho Rao

The 1870s saw Jayajirao at the peak of his powers. But the king did not have a male heir who could succeed him. So, at the age of forty, he took a wife, a thirteen-year-old. Jayajirao's son from that marriage, Madho Rao (1876–1925), took over as maharaja in 1886, when he was barely ten.

Madho Rao was a truly modern maharaja. He was an LLD (Doctor of Laws) from Cambridge University, thus becoming the first Scindia to visit a foreign land. During his London days, he was fascinated by cars and decided to bring one of them – a single cylinder 6 HP De Dion – back home. Once back in Gwalior, Madho Maharaj created a separate civil engineering department to manufacture large storage tanks and dig canals for irrigation. He is also credited with strengthening the base of the Gwalior army, creating two cavalry and infantry regiments. *Jayaji Pratap*, a local bilingual weekly that started publication in January 1905, carried news and information about the maharaja's work and his views on public matters. A month later, in February 1905, the then Prince of Wales visited Gwalior where he stayed in Sipri (Shivpuri) for over two weeks. It was during this period under the rule of Madho Maharaj when the tracks of the Gwalior Light Railway were extended to Sheopur. The Gwalior Light Railway ran for about 185 km and cost the state Rs 4.4 million. Madho Maharaj built metalled roads, set up an elaborate postal system and distributed over Rs 14 lakh when a severe famine hit the state during 1899–1900.[22]

Although the maharaja was married earlier, the need for a male child made Madho Maharaj marry for a second time in 1912. A decade earlier, while he was studying in Britain, some newspapers there had made a mention about his friendship with a member of the royal family of Baroda. So when the time came to tying the knot again, the Gwalior royal's choice was the Baroda princess.[23] But just as the marriage was set to be solemnized, the Baroda princess called it off for an unexplained reason. Madho Maharaj was shattered and it took a toll on his health. He became diabetic, stopped participating in sports, refused to visit the Gwalior Gymkhana and other sports clubs or go hunting. The Gwalior durbar was concerned about the maharaja's well-being, and before long, the Maratha sardars prevailed upon him to marry a member of the Rane family of Goa. His new bride, Gajra Raje, brought five of her sisters with her to Gwalior. They married various sardars and nobles in the Scindia court. This was to be significant for the generations to come, including Madho Maharaj's son, daughter-in-law, grandchildren and great-grandchildren. One of Gajra Raje's sisters married Chandroji Angre, who became vice-chairman of the Regency Council when the maharaja died. Madho Maharaj's son Jiwajirao (1916–1961) was nine years old then. By the time Jiwajirao came of age, he realized that his powers had been reduced to that of a titular head, thanks to the palace intrigues. The British, on their part, reportedly used Angre to further their designs. When Jiwajirao gained the upper hand, he wasted no time in throwing out Angre. However, Angre's son Sambhajirao was to make a startling comeback in the fortunes of the Scindia family (we shall have much to say about him in subsequent chapters).

Madho Maharaj, the Military Man

Madho Maharaj tried to modernize his state troops but the British, while constantly applauding his loyalty, actively discouraged him from upgrading the arms and ammunition available to his army. An embarrassing consequence of this played out when Madho Maharaj sought to impress his people by blowing up the house of a dacoit, Baldeo Singh.[24] The cannons used by the Gwalior troopers failed to hit the target or dent even the plaster of Baldeo's house, situated on a hill. More than the cannons, the locally made black gunpowder was the reason that accurate shooting even from a distance of 100 yards was impossible. Among other things, it once again highlighted the British distrust of Indian rulers after the revolt of 1857. They did not want to arm any princely state with guns and ammunition.[25]

In his multi-volume *Darbar Policy*[26] Madho Maharaj had, from 1895, made a strong case for an efficient Scindia army but the British would neither allow state-of-the-art guns nor any increase in the number of state troops. The strength of the Scindia army, according to Bull and Haksar, was around 7,000 while the cost of its annual maintenance was over Rs 40 lakh. Madho Maharaj had argued that the British government should make a distinction between loyalists and those who used guns and ammunition for only ceremonial purposes. But the British, from the Viceroy to the political officer stationed in Gwalior, showed scant regard for Madho Maharaj's insistence on modernization of weapons. The polite but firm political officer could, perhaps, never tell the Maharaj that following the revolt of 1857, the British were opposed to the idea of giving weapons to Indian rulers regardless of their loyalty to the Raj.[27]

In 1901, Madho Maharaj had been appointed 'Honorary Aide-de-Camp' to King Edward VII in recognition of his support during the Boxer Rebellion in China. Thousands of men (some with their families) were sent to fight Chinese rebels during the Boxer Rebellion. The rebellion, which had broken out in response to China's national humiliation of losing wars to Japan and European imperial powers, was aimed at purifying China of foreign cultural, economic and political influence. Nine Indian princely states, including Alwar, Mysore, Gwalior, Bikaner, Jodhpur and Malerkotla, had provided units to the British for service in China. Madho Maharaj had himself led the campaign during this rebellion and gifted a state-of-the-art hospital ship to treat casualties in North China.[28] 'The Maharaja's support was made on the behalf of himself, his mother and his wife to testify their loyalty to Her Majesty the Queen Empress,' author Silbey J. David observed in his book, *The Boxer Rebellion and The Great Game in China: A History*,[29] adding that it reflected a kind of imperial reserve that could be drawn on in the times of crisis.

For fifty-five days, the Boxers laid siege to the heart of Beijing, keeping more than 400 foreigners holed up in the city's Foreign Legation Quarter in a dramatic denouement of months of anti-imperialist and anti-Christian sentiment that swept across China. The Gwalior army and the Patiala regiment guarded churches and Christian missionaries. The pleased Imperial Majesty later conferred upon Madho Rao the title 'Qaiser-e-Hind' and he was given an honorary LLD degree by the University of Cambridge.

However, according to Bull and Haksar, Madho Maharaj was not too happy with his China experience as, by the time he reached, most of the serious fighting was over. He did not like his formal staff appointment by the British and, in one of the dispatches, wrote that a post, even of non-commissioned rank, would have suited him more and given him some 'work' to do. Apparently, the only time Madho Maharaj faced a threat in China was when his boat came under hostile fire.

A subsequent report published in *The London Observer* in 1921 described Madho Maharaj in glowing terms. 'Scindia is a king and a statesman, financier and engineer, a mighty hunter of the big game and a captain of industry. He is as versatile as the Kaiser, as full of energy as Roosevelt. That he manages his own important state without a minister, is only the least of his activities. His great wealth is not locked away but put to reproductive uses, he is known to offer to an entire government loan on his own account. He is a man of vision and when he builds a railway, can show his people how to drive locomotive. Yet he is simple in his personal habit and those who have walked with him long hours in the moonlight, "beside the big gun" terrace before his glorious palace know the variety of his interests, piercing vision that lights his active brain. All the younger princes look to him for counsel and example.'

When the First World War broke out, the Gwalior Imperial Service Troops under Madho Maharaj helped the British fight in France, East Africa, Egypt, Salonika, Palestine and Mesopotamia. According to one estimate, the Gwalior state's expenditure during the war was Rs 25 million.[30]

The Aesthetic Side

Madho Maharaj had diverse interests apart from the military. Once, he paid for the tasteful decorations and mosaic work at Ireland's Timoleague's Protestant church. He bore all the expenses in the memory of Aylmer Martin Crofts, who had joined the Indian Medical Service and had served the Gwalior state.

Madho Rao was still a boy when Crofts was appointed resident surgeon at Gwalior in 1886. Crofts became Madho Rao's tutor and, years later, saved the life of the maharaja's son. As a token of appreciation, when Crofts died in 1915, Madho Maharaj decided to honour his mentor and benefactor in faraway Timoleague, the town from which Crofts hailed. On one wall of the church is a sepia photograph of the maharajah of Gwalior accompanied by Crofts. Jeremy Williams, an architect, wrote about the church, 'This building was a monument to a living friendship enshrined in a hidden masterpiece of the Arts and Crafts Movement in Ireland and that it transcended the sectarian divide between Irish Catholic and Protestant, the Indian Muslim and Hindu, personal friendship breaking up distinctions of caste and colour.'[31]

Madho Maharaj also set up the Gangajali Fund, which was reserved for development projects in Gwalior, such as for education, famine relief and irrigation. As a matter of principle, he deposited Rs 25 lakh in the fund every year. Often, he would disguise himself as a common man and wander the streets of Gwalior, unrecognized, to check how the administration was performing. He established the Scindia School in 1897 for the sons of the chieftains of the Gwalior state, to introduce them to modern, progressive education.[32]

But the maharaja was superstitious too and did not take it well when several unfortunate events occurred: first, his favourite elephant died while ferrying a cannon from the fort. Next, his sacred coat of arms, the Mahi Maratab, was found to have been damaged. The third incident that really rattled Madho Maharaj was a fire that burnt a Muharram *tazia* at Gwalior's Imam Bara, which was used in the procession that the Scindias had a tradition of leading. The fire, reportedly caused by a short circuit, was brought under control and alternative arrangements were made, but the maharaja remained traumatized. In the unpublished memoirs of Kaudikar Babuji,[33] a Gwalior palace insider, Madho Maharaj is described as saying that the '*tazia* is not burnt. I am burnt.'[34] Riding through the streets of Gwalior, Babuji records that tears kept rolling down the maharaja's cheeks. So upset was Madho Rao by these three incidents that he started smoking cigarettes against the advice of his hakim.

During the spring of 1925, the British king invited Madho Maharaj to England. Struggling with deteriorating health, the maharaja decided to go to Europe, handing the charge of the state to the senior maharani. On the afternoon of 5 June 1925, the maharaja asked for a cigarette while he was admitted in a hospital in Paris, where the doctors had operated on him to remove a diabetic carbuncle. A little later, when an attendant saw the maharaja in deep sleep, he took the cigarette from his fingers and noticed that the fingers had turned cold. The clock had struck 4 p.m. Madho Maharaj had passed away. His wife and two children, who had arrived a few days earlier, were also in Paris at that time. On the second floor of the Chateau De Madrid, arose piteous wailing. Below, at the back, there was a hotel (Office 49), where jazz music was being played for the foxtrot with the daily dansant (tea dance) as the usual opening.

~

Madho Maharaj lived and died an autocrat. He had no ministers or an organized bureaucracy and would often boast that a 'free life' in jungle camps kept his brain more active and helped him cope with the pressures of work. For Madho Maharaj, an organized bureaucratic set-up would have acted as a check on his initiatives and the rapidity of reforms. He feared that eventually, bureaucracy would become as bad as democracy, as he had a dim view of swaraj or self-rule and felt that constitutionalism was a slow and cumbersome method, fraught with danger in most emergencies. In an article, 'India Loquitor', published in the *Times of India* in September 1919, Madho Maharaj had expressed his views on government, justifying personal rule. For him, swaraj by passive resistance was just as destructive as swaraj by revolutionary methods. The royal could not believe that 'any jack' could be as good as him in administering the state.

An unsigned article in the journal *Jayaji Pratap* paid homage to Madho Rao after his death. 'His Highness set himself to the great task of reforming the administration', the article had observed. 'He had to cut his way through a tangled wood of vested interests, prejudice, tradition and insularity – such as might well defy the genius of a whole generation of administrators.'

But, the autocrat had a softer side too. Madho Maharaj had desired that a memorial be built to his favourite dog, Hussu, if the pet outlived its master. When Madho Maharaj fell ill in Paris in 1925, he is said to have asked senior maharani, Chinkoo Raje,[35] to take care of Hussu and set aside funds for the memorial in his will. After the maharaja's death in Paris, Hussu would visit its master's bedroom in Gwalior for five years, seven months and eighteen days. When Hussu's end came in November 1930, Chinkoo Raje built a befitting memorial in Gwalior. The dog was buried and a stone erected in its memory.

End of Kingdom

Madho Maharaj was succeeded by Jiwajirao Scindia, who became the sixth Maharaja of Gwalior on 5 June 1925, at the tender age of nine. Jiwajirao's reign, spreading over thirty-five years, saw some momentous developments that reduced the Scindias to ordinary citizens when Gwalior merged with the Union of India in 1947. Jiwajirao could sense that democracy was knocking at the country's door. A man ahead of his time, he tried making his administration more representative, revamping the Majlis-a-Aam (durbar) and Majlis-e-Kanoon (legislature). Like his father, he travelled across his state, stayed in tehsils and listened patiently to his people.

Before the country's independence, Jiwajirao had stated, 'Our earnest desire is that our administration should be responsive to the growing political consciousness of our people and that in the fullness of time, they should attain the progressive realization of their legitimate aspirations through peaceful and constitutional means.' Clearly, it was a significant departure from his father's world view as Madho Maharaj had described constitutionalism as slow and cumbersome while passive resistance, he thought, was destructive.

V.P. Menon, an Indian civil servant who played a crucial role in the integration of the princely states, generously acknowledged Jiwajirao's support in forming a free and united India. Menon observed in his book, *Integration of Indian States,*[36] that Jiwajirao was the first ruler of the big princely states – Hyderabad, Mysore, Kashmir, Baroda and Gwalior – to sign the Instrument of Accession. Menon wrote that Jiwajirao exercised a 'healthy influence' on other rulers to accede voluntarily. Jiwajirao also managed to get an agreement signed with the rulers of the neighbouring princely states to form Madhya Bharat. He was appointed the first *Rajya Pramukh* (governor) of the new state and served till October 1956, when the state was merged with the newly created Madhya Pradesh.

Jiwajirao's marriage with Lekha, a girl born to a branch of the Nepal royal family from her mother's side and who rose to become Rajmata Vijaya Raje Scindia, led to a formidable political legacy in independent India. This was a time when no woman in the royal family could step out of the palace, or out of the women's chambers, except when she was under *purdah* (veil). Jiwajirao was the first to do away with the *purdah* system when India gained independence. 'My husband was very broadminded and democratic in that sense,' the Rajmata would later write in her autobiography. 'In the presence of Sardar Patel,[37] we gave up our Purdahs because my husband said that since the kingdom didn't exist anymore, there was no need for that custom.'

The Rajmata records an incident when Sardar Patel had come to Gwalior to address a meeting. Patel, independent India's first home minister, had wanted Vijaya Raje to come on to the stage. '"If you call yourself the mother and sister of these people," he argued, "how can you bear to have a veil between them and you",' she recalled Patel as saying. For Vijaya Raje, the country's freedom coincided with freedom from *purdah*. 'That was how I came to give up purdah, and I have never worn a veil since then,' she would say later in her autobiography. It would also be the first time that Gwalior's residents got to see their maharani, something that amused Jiwajirao.

As the ruler of Gwalior, Jiwajirao owned vast properties, including zamindari villages outside Gwalior. The properties included Madhav Vilas Palace, Happy Vilas and George Castle (in Shivpuri), and Kaliadeh Palace (in Ujjain). In Delhi, the Scindias owned Gwalior House, a plot on Rajpur Road, and Scindia Villa. Jiwajirao also owned Padma Vilas Palace in Pune, Scindia Ghat in Varanasi and the Vithoba Temple, Sanquelim, in Goa. In addition, he controlled four *inaam* (gifted) villages and plots in ten other villages in the Deccan region. Jiwajirao had also acquired properties such as the Vasundhara building on Peddar Road in Bombay (now Mumbai). Another proud Scindia possession in Bombay was the Samudra Mahal, a sea-facing, 20-acre property in Worli that Jiwajirao's father Madho Maharaj had bought from Sir Aga Khan. According to a 2010 estimate, each flat built at Samudra Mahal was valued at Rs 100 crore. Madho Maharaj was so possessive about the Samudra Mahal Palace, considered the most fabulous private residence ever built in the city, that in a will dated 8 April 1925, he had directed all Scindia descendants to never sell the property. It was, however, sold off within a few years of Jiwajirao's death by his widow Vijaya Raje. Madhavrao Scindia's biographers, Vir Sanghvi and Namita Bhandare, have concluded that throughout the 1960s and 1970s, Vijaya Raje was the principal fundraiser for the Bharatiya Jana Sangh (the earlier avatar of the BJP). 'Some of that money could be traced but there was no way to substantiate the widely held view that she [Vijaya Raje] disposed of vast quantities of Scindia jewellery to raise the funds required to keep the party going.'[38]

Jiwajirao was not as consummate a ruler as his father. Faced with uncertain times and the growing nationalist movement prior to 1947, he left tricky matters of governance to his diwan and the sardars, and sought escape in Bombay and Pune where he could indulge his passion for horses and racing. But he did try to develop Gwalior industrially and invited his industrialist friends, such as Seth Ghanshyam Das Birla, to invest in Gwalior. Even today, Gwalior's rayon and silk mills have a brand called Jayaji, named after Jiwajirao's father.

Jiwajirao did not live long. At forty-five, he was afflicted by severe medical issues, particularly diabetes, which partially affected his vision. However, the maharaja remained resolute in not penning down his will. When his legal adviser, Kaka Tricomdas of Kanga and Co., reportedly suggested that he draw up a will, Jiwajirao flared up. 'Does he think I am going to die,' he said. 'I do not care if after my death, the government or someone else takes away my wealth, I will not write a will.' The remark would prove to be prophetic as abolition of the privy purse and legal disputes among the Scindias after Jiwajirao's death in July 1961 ensured that no Scindia descendant would enjoy the fabulous wealth of their ancestors.

Jiwajirao remained politically neutral even though he lived through one of the most turbulent periods in the Indian subcontinent. But his bid to stay apolitical did not entirely succeed as his wife, Vijaya Raje, was sucked into the politics of the times, setting the stage for a new Scindia legacy in post-Independence India that could match the history of the Nehru–Gandhi family.

Since 1957, the Scindias have been democratically elected representatives and, till date, there has not been a single day when a Scindia was not a member of a Legislative Assembly or Parliament.

TWO

The Rajmata of Gwalior

> 'Rajmata was tender as a flower but also tough like lightning. She never wavered in her resolve.'
> – Atal Bihari Vajpayee

Rajmata Vijaya Raje Scindia was only twenty-five steps away from the Nepal border – and immunity from Indira Gandhi's police – when she decided to turn around. Her 'political instincts', she would say later, had prevailed, even if that meant certain imprisonment in those days of the Emergency. It was this same resolve that would later see her side with her long-time adviser against her own son, capping an extraordinary family rift over politics. But then, life was probably never meant to be ordinary for someone born into a legacy of regicide, palace intrigue and political exile.

It would be against this backdrop of her birth and circumstances that her life would unfold, first as Lekha Divyeshwari Devi, a vivacious young lady with a college education – when pursuing higher studies for women in India was still the exception rather than the norm – and later as Vijaya Raje Scindia of the Gwalior royal family.

Lekha was born in 1919 to a branch of the Nepal royal family from her mother's side. Her maternal grandfather, Khadga Shamsher Bahadur Rana, had been taken off the roll of succession and exiled for plotting against the then prime minister and maharajah, Bir Shamsher. General Khadga Shamsher had earlier masterminded the assassination of Maharajah Ranaoddip Singh Kunwar Ranaji, which had resulted in Bir Shamsher being crowned maharajah. Khadga had been rewarded and made the commander-in-chief of Nepal, the second-most powerful post in the Rana regime. But, as the saying goes, 'uneasy lies the head that wears the crown'; Maharajah Bir started viewing Khadga, his ambitious younger half-brother, with suspicion, fearing that another coup d'état might be executed to finish him off.

Not much later, Khadga was indeed found plotting a palace intrigue to do away with Maharajah Bir during a wedding ceremony. Khadga was arrested and struck off the roll of succession. A decree was issued that even his descendants could no longer be on the roll. The British, who then controlled India and had deep interests in the affairs of the Himalayan kingdom, informally intervened to save Khadga's life and advised him not to stay anywhere close to the Nepal border. He was offered Sagar, in what was then the Central Provinces, as a safe sanctuary. The terrain and environment of the area often reminded Khadga of Nepal.

When Khadga's daughter, Chuda Devashwari Devi, came of age, she was married locally to Thakur Mahendra Singh, a Maratha government administrator whose rank was equivalent to that of a deputy director in the Scindia administrative service. She died soon after giving birth to a girl in 1919.

Mahendra remarried, much against the wishes of Khadga, who then asked his son-in-law to hand over to him his granddaughter, Lekha. Young Lekha was brought up by her maternal grandparents and had no contact with her father till she turned eighteen in 1937.

Mahendra, who lived in Jhansi, would play a significant role in Lekha's higher education although her maternal grandmother, Rani Dhan Kumari, a deeply religious and orthodox person, did not approve. Khadga had passed away by this time and Rani Dhan Kumari had a lot of influence on the young Lekha. Storytelling sessions were an integral part of her childhood as Rani Dhan Kumari would enthrall her with tales steeped in India's culture, tradition and faith, allowing Lekha to widen her imagination.

Life in 'Nepal Palace' at Sagar was comfortable but not one of opulence. The palace had a car, two horse carriages, riding horses and a tennis court, and it also hosted seasonal parties. The outhouses had *darzis* (tailors), butlers, syces, mashalchis (torchbearers), pujaris (priests) and a compounder of Western medicine. Lekha's grandparents were careful that she did not miss the best formal education but, in keeping with the times, were opposed to higher education for girls. However, she was sent to Lucknow to study at Isabella Thoburn Women's College, where she realized that she was different from other girls of her age. After her school education, when her grandmother opposed her going to college, Lekha sought help of her father and stepmother to move to Lucknow.[1]

In her memoirs, she recalls an incident from her college days. '...I went to class dressed in one of my silk saris and wearing my everyday jewellery, which included a rather showy nose-ring made of a diamond solitaire. More and more of my fellow students turned their heads to glance at me, whispering among themselves. Surely, something was wrong. Slowly it dawned on me that nearly all of them were wearing plain cotton saris and no jewellery.'

When Lekha was studying at the prestigious Isabella Thoburn or IT College in Lucknow, the year was 1941, and the country was in the throes of the struggle for freedom from the British. Influenced by the Swadeshi movement, Lekha abandoned her chiffons and took to wearing coarse, hand-spun cotton saris.

In her autobiography, the Rajmata has confessed that as a student, she did not think much of Mahatma Gandhi's non-violent methods to achieve freedom. Instead, her role model was Netaji Subhas Chandra Bose. 'Either I was unable to understand the true meaning of *ahimsa* or being a Kshatriya (warrior race), my value system did not help me accept that. In my views, *ahimsa* stands for keeping your calm in the face of torture.'

Young Lekha's first suitor was Brij Bihari Singh, an Indian Civil Service officer under whom Mahendra had served. Lekha had gone to Lucknow with her father and stepmother when she met Singh. Oblivious of Singh's interest in her, Lekha had kept talking passionately about various exhibits that were on display at the exhibition held in a park. By Lekha's own admission, Singh was so enamoured of her that he told Mahendra, 'I have seldom come across such a bright girl among Rajputs who is knowledgeable and keeping pace with the times.'

Singh is said to have offered to marry Lekha but her father had gently told him to speak directly to her. Instead, Singh wrote a seven-page letter addressed to Lekha, listing her qualities and expressing his desire to spend the rest of his life with her. However, the alliance did not progress.

In her memoirs, Lekha, who was later given the name Vijaya Raje, indicated that the marriage proposal did not fructify though she and her father were interested. For some reason, Singh had not pursued the proposal.

In 1943, Lucknow would be scandalized when Singh, working as secretary to the United Province's (UP's) local self-government was charged with the murder of his eighteen-year-old maidservant, Bilasia. She was reportedly in love with Samuel, a bearer of the household. Singh's ayah, Mussamat Halliman, testified that Singh was obsessed with strict moral notions and expected his young maidservant to adhere to them. Singh had reportedly found Bilasia and Samuel in a compromising position and kept hitting the young girl with a stick till it broke, leaving her dead. He was jailed for six years, for culpable homicide not amounting to murder, though his sentence was later reduced.

Lekha's next suitor was an army officer, Lieutenant Dushyant Chouhan, who was based in Sagar. Horoscopes were exchanged and the wedding was fixed for 8 May 1940. But destiny had other designs for the twenty-one-year-old girl. The Second World War had broken out and Lieutenant Chouhan was called to go to Europe to fight Britain's war. Instead of postponing the marriage, he called it off.

Next, the family identified Rajkumar Durjey Kishore Dev Burman of the Manikya dynasty of Tripura as an ideal match for Lekha. Spread over 10,000 km, the Tripura princely state had a recorded history of monarchy since 1400 AD. The British had given the rulers of Tripura the title of Maharajah and honoured them with a 13-gun salute. Durjey was said to be the 180th ruler of the Manikya dynasty.

The two families met in Calcutta where Durjey's family had a palace that hosted the British. Calcutta was chosen as the venue as the journey to Agartala, Tripura's capital, was fraught with danger because of the Kuki insurgency. In any case, the custom was not to visit the groom's house before the marriage alliance was confirmed.

Before long, however, Lekha's family discovered that the young prince had unsavoury pastimes, such as gambling, drinking and a fondness for the high life.

Meanwhile, the magazine *Illustrated Weekly* published photographs of Gwalior Maharaja Jiwajirao with the princess of Tripura, Kamal Prabha, sister of Durjey, speculating about a possible marriage alliance. It led to vehement protests from influential sardars (nobles) in Maharaja Jiwajirao's court who opposed inter-caste marriage and upheld caste-based endogamy for the court and the nobility. These nobles petitioned Queen Mother Gajra Raje that Jiwajirao, twenty-four then, should marry only a Maratha princess. The proposed wedding was abruptly called off amid widespread opposition in the court.

This incident left the young Lekha deeply upset. It was not that Jiwajirao was in love with Kamal Prabha; what she couldn't get over was his failure to stand by her.

It's true that Gwalior was a much larger princely state than Tripura in terms of area, population and in the British pecking order. While the Scindias were granted 21-gun salutes on ceremonial occasions, Tripura was placed several notches below at 13. In terms of the privy purse, too, Tripura received an annual grant of Rs 330,000 in the initial years after India's Independence, as against the Scindias's Rs 1 million. But matrimonial alliances among princely states were common despite the disparity in 'status'. For instance, the last Nawab of Bhopal, who used to draw a privy purse of Rs 620,000, married off his daughter, Begum Sajida Sultan, to Nawab Iftikhar Ali Khan Pataudi, who received a mere Rs 48,000 a year.

The Tripura royals commanded a lot of respect for their long unbroken line of succession and their formidable reputation as protectors of Hindu shrines. According to *Rajmala*, a chronicle of the kings of Tripura, Tripura's royals traced their origin to the celebrated 'lunar' dynasty, following in the footsteps of their counterparts in the Hindu royal houses of the rest of India who claimed to have originated from the 'lunar' or 'solar' dynasty.

As a young monarch of twenty-four, Jiwajirao led a carefree and extravagant life. He was fond of horseracing and frequently travelled to Bombay. A part of the Gwalior court would shift while he was there to Samudra Mahal (the palace by the sea), one of the finest properties in the metropolis, which spread over 20 acres of sea-facing land and had been tastefully built by his father, Madho Maharaj. While Maharaja Jiwajirao would fly down to Bombay in his personal aircraft, a vast army of staff would be dispatched by road and train. Nearly fifty cars would be sent from Gwalior carrying provisions sufficient for four months. The staff that moved from Gwalior to Bombay included typists, clerks, cooks, waiters, physicians, compounders, dressing boys, drivers and even dog boys to attend to the maharaja's dogs. This retinue was in addition to the permanent staff based at Samudra Mahal. For a few months, this part of Worli would turn into a mini-Gwalior with all the paraphernalia of a princely court.

Jiwajirao's inability to marry Kamal Prabha made him adamant about not marrying any Maratha princess. Everyone followed this doomed love story with interest, including the young Lekha. She would later write, 'Being her age, I could empathize with Kamal Prabha that she was being subjected to injustice. We were all peeved. Our sympathy with Kamal Prabha was natural. We were so agitated that if Gwalior Maharaja would have come to our college those days, none of us would have ventured to welcome him.'

In Gwalior, the Queen Mother and some nobles came up with a suggestion that a Nepalese girl of a Rajput origin should be considered as a prospective bride for the unhappy Jiwajirao. Krishnarao Mahadik, a noble, was given the task of identifying a suitable girl. Mahadik then asked Lekha's maternal uncle, Chandan Singh, who served in the Gwalior court, to visit Nepal. Two months passed but a suitable match could not be found. Chandan finally wrote to Mahadik suggesting Lekha's name as a likely candidate. Her photograph was shown to Jiwajirao, who agreed to meet her in Bombay.

In her memoirs, Lekha has said she was not comfortable about marrying Jiwajirao. 'Do not you know how callously he broke off (sic) Tripura engagement? How can you even think of marrying me off to someone so fickle-minded – agreeing to marry a girl and, when the preparations are nearly complete, breaking it off?' she would write. However, under pressure from her family, Lekha agreed to meet Jiwajirao at Bombay's plush Taj Mahal Hotel, where many such marital alliances have been forged. After the initial meeting, the two families met at Samudra Palace. Apparently, at the first meeting itself, Lekha had left a lingering impression on her future husband. Soon, Jiwajirao invited Lekha and her family members to visit the race course. And it was there that a subtle change of heart would take place for the young lady. If Jiwajirao was smitten by her at the Taj, Lekha was deeply impressed by Jiwajirao's ability to accurately bet on the horse that won the race. What left a bigger mark on her was the fact that the maharaja did not place any money on a horse or gamble even though he owned 278 horses in Bombay.

A firm indication of the maharaja accepting Lekha as his soon-to-be maharani came when his aide-de-camp (ADC), Captain Lad, greeted her with a ceremonial *mujra*, a traditional courtly salute with a slight bow followed by a deferential gesture of the right hand in front of the chest three times. This was how courtiers in the Maratha princely states greeted the maharaja, maharani, their children and other members of the royal family. It was performed with a good deal of flourish and style, and outsiders were seldom greeted that way. This is how Lekha's family learnt that Jiwajirao had made up his mind to marry her.

On 19 February 1941, at 10:31 p.m. to be precise, Jiwajirao and Lekha became man and wife at the Usha Kiran Palace which had originally been built to welcome the King and Queen of England. For days, the palace, with its artistic stone carvings, magnificent courtyards and delicate filigree work, would be lit up, highlighting its landscaped gardens where lunches and dinners were hosted. In the wedding photographs, Lekha can be seen decked in expensive clothes and wearing iconic royal jewellery.

Jiwajirao is seen wearing a pagri (turban) studded with gems. The pagri, one learns, was a 60-metre-long cloth, while the gems weighed over 5 kg.

On their wedding night, Lekha, given the royal title Vijaya Raje, or the victorious one, was taken to the royal *tosha khana* (treasury), the storehouse of the Scindias' enormous wealth, where diamonds, rubies, pearls, emeralds, gold bars, silver bricks, currencies from across the world, clothes, watches and countless gifts were stored. The maharaja also asked her to pick some saris of her choice from among French chiffon, American georgette, Japanese silk, Dhaka mulmul, Banarasis and many more. When Vijaya Raje said she would wear only cotton or handloom saris, Jiwajirao was a tad disappointed. The *tosha khana* did not have a single cotton sari. But he presented a blue sapphire necklace to her. The sheer beauty of the necklace, made by Phillips Brothers & Sons, took Vijaya Raje's breath away.

Jiwajirao gifted her another gold necklace, with a central section made of diamonds, suspended pearls, polished ruby and emerald drops. The London-based jewellers Philips Brothers & Sons had mounted the foil-backed diamonds and rubies to preserve the original Indian style of setting known as kundan (pure gold).[2] But more than these expensive gifts, Vijaya Raje was pleasantly surprised when Jiwajirao, during their honeymoon in Bombay, took her to a khadi store and bought her some simple, cotton saris. The gesture cemented an instant bond between the newly-weds.

Life for the young couple was easy and carefree. Within a year, they were blessed with a daughter, Padmavatiraje. In October 1943, another daughter, Usha Raje, was born. On 10 March 1945, they were blessed with a son, born in Bombay. The arrival of a male heir was greeted with great joy which Gwalior had not seen when Padmavatiraje and Usha Raje were born. Prisoners were freed liberally and thousands were fed. The fort was lit up and sweets were distributed throughout Gwalior. The baby, Madhavrao, was brought to Gwalior by a special train from Bombay. The celebrations and the public jubilation reminded C. Rajagopalachari, a veteran freedom fighter who had translated the epic Ramayana into English, of an age 'long gone by, in Ayodhya, when Kausalya gave birth to Rama'.

Integration into the Union

But the royal idyll was about to change, although it would be still some years before the family was pulled into the politics of a new India.

The freedom struggle was at its peak and most Indian princely states were anxiously courting the Congress or the British to maintain status quo. Under British rule, about 60 per cent of Indian territory was directly ruled by the colonial masters while the remaining 40 per cent was governed by 584 native rulers, or princely states, that enjoyed a degree of internal autonomy under the British. At the time of Independence, the British left it to each of these states to choose whether to join either of the two newly independent countries, India and Pakistan, or remain outside them. For a while, some of these rulers explored the possibility of a federation of states separate from either, but their efforts came to naught.

Jiwajirao was an exception to this. A carefree soul, he remained busy in Bombay's race course. The new government of India, headed by Jawaharlal Nehru, made Jiwajirao a titular head or *Rajya Pramukh* of Madhya Bharat from May 1948 to October 1956. Special provisions were added to the Constitution under Article 366 in Part B of the First Schedule that gave formal gubernatorial status to the erstwhile rulers of Hyderabad, Saurashtra, Mysore, Travancore-Cochin, Madhya Bharat, Vindhya Pradesh, Patiala and East Punjab States Union (PEPSU), and Rajasthan.

Jiwajirao donated Rs 17 crore (a fortune then and easily over Rs 20,000 crore at today's value) from his personal funds to the new country. This was in addition to the Rs 3.09 crore given from the state's exchequer at the time of the merger of the Gwalior state with the Union of India. The ease with which Gwalior merged with India was noted and appreciated by V.P. Menon, the secretary in the ministry of states. In his book, *Integration of Indian States*, Menon observed that Jiwajirao had 'a healthy influence on several rulers in persuading them to accede'. For a while after India's Independence, Jiwajirao remained aloof from politics – he never contested any election – but Delhi was concerned about the maharaja and his wife's leanings towards the ultra-right Hindu Mahasabha that had emerged as the Congress's principal opposition in India's first general election in 1951–1952.[3]

An interesting side story to the saga of the Scindias is that while their ancestors had always been staunch followers of the Hindu faith, their seat of power had been known as the Mussalman *gaddi*, or Muslim Throne, as the earlier kings used to rule in the name of the Mughal dynasty until 1858. The Scindias' goodwill for Muslims remained until the 1930s before the princely state turned into a 'bastion' of the Mahasabha. The transformation was influenced by Sardar Chandrojirao Angre, the father of Sardar Sambhaji Angre, who would eventually become Vijaya Raje's adviser.

Speculation about the Scindias' proximity to the Mahasabha had been gaining ground since Mahatma Gandhi's assassination in 1948 brought adverse attention on the family. First, Vijaya Raje, by her own admission, had always been drawn to revolutionaries such as Subhas Chandra Bose and others who opposed Gandhi's pacifist ideology. Then, it was alleged that the Italian-made revolver that was used to kill Gandhi had been brought to India from Ethiopia by a colonel from the Gwalior Regiment who fought in the British regiment in the Second World War. This officer had later become the ADC to the maharaja of Gwalior. According to Tushar A. Gandhi, the great-grandson of the Mahatma, Gandhi's killer Nathuram Godse had on 28 January 1948, two days before the assassination, gone to Gwalior along with Dattatreya S. Parchure (another accused in the case) to purchase the revolver. The Italian pistol of the ADC was available with a gun trader named Jagdish Prasad Goyal in Gwalior.

Tushar Gandhi wondered why there was no further investigation to find out how the gun under the custody of the ADC of the Gwalior maharaja reached the gun trader's hands, and then Godse's. 'Nathuram had no experience in handling such a gun and 36 hours before the assassination of Gandhi, he got hold of that with requisite number of bullets. How he got it is still the weakest link in the Gandhi murder investigation,' Tushar Gandhi said in an interview with *Open* magazine in May 2019.[4]

In the 1950s, Delhi's suspicions – that the maharaja of Gwalior and his wife were actively patronizing the right-wing outfit – were getting stronger, its concerns exacerbated by the Mahasabha's performance in the elections. The Mahasabha won two Lok Sabha seats in the 1951–1952 general election and eleven assembly seats in the Madhya Bharat Assembly to emerge as a challenger to the ruling Congress. By then, however, Jiwajirao had been diagnosed with diabetes. Worried about Gwalior's deteriorating ties with the Jawaharlal Nehru government, Vijaya Raje decided to pay a courtesy visit to the prime minister in New Delhi to clear the air. She did not consult her husband, who was in Bombay then. In her autobiography, Vijaya Raje has gone at lengths to explain that telephones line were down and she could not communicate with her husband.

Vijaya Raje says in her memoirs that when she told Nehru that neither she nor the maharaja were against the Congress, the prime minister suggested that Jiwajirao contest the 1957 Lok Sabha polls as a Congress nominee. This was like a bolt from the blue. Vijaya Raje insisted that Jiwajirao was not politically inclined but Nehru would not relent. Nehru then suggested that Vijaya Raje meet Govind Ballabh Pant and Lal Bahadur Shastri, both senior ministers and towering Congress personalities. Later, in the presence of Indira Gandhi, Pant and Shastri urged Vijaya Raje to contest as a Congress nominee instead of Jiwajirao.

When Vijaya Raje returned from Delhi, Jiwajirao was not happy with the developments but relented. But he insisted that as a parliamentarian in Delhi in 1957, she should be accompanied by Sardar Sambhajirao Angre, the maharaja's first cousin and one of the nobles in the Gwalior court. The Angre family had served the royal family of Gwalior for eight generations as prime ministers or commanders-in-chief.

Congress Nominee

Vijaya Raje won the 1957 Lok Sabha seat from Guna as a Congress nominee, defeating the Hindu Mahasabha's V.G. Deshpande. She polled 118,578 votes, or 66.95 per cent of the votes cast, against Deshpande's 58,521 votes. Jiwajirao largely stayed away from campaigning. He directed Sardar Angre to act as Vijaya Raje's campaign manager. Angre, a self-declared Mahasabhai, joined the Congress. Vijaya Raje did not campaign much. Instead, it was Angre who held meetings and sought votes for the 'Mahal'.

This was a time when the States Reorganisation Act, 1956, had been implemented, ending the erstwhile Gwalior empire's notional identity as Madhya Bharat and enabling the creation of Madhya Pradesh as a new state. Madhya Bharat was incorporated into the newly created Madhya Pradesh and Jiwajirao ceased to be the *Rajya Pramukh*.

Vijaya Raje was not an 'active' parliamentarian. Her attendance in the Lok Sabha was less than 50 per cent, mainly because of issues related to Jiwajirao's health and her complete dedication to the school she had set up, Scindia Kanya Vidyalaya (SKV), in Gwalior. The school had been established to inculcate a sense of Indian values, religion and culture among girls and embodied her dream of providing progressive education. 'I believe in the old adage, "the hand that rocks the cradle rules the world". I wanted a school to strengthen those hands. My dream was to start a school which would serve both these ends,' Vijaya Raje said at the inauguration of the school. SKV, she said, tried to develop in its students the ability to 'create', as against 'copy', by providing an experiential learning curriculum in their formative years.

Early in 1960, Vijaya Raje's eldest daughter, Padmavatiraje, nineteen, was married to the last and 185th ruler of Tripura, Kirti Deb Burman (nephew of Vijaya Raje's suitor Durjey Kishore Dev Burman), forcing her to neglect both the 1959 winter session and the 1960 budget session of Parliament. Padma's wedding at Bombay's Samudra Mahal was a grand affair. Over 10,000 people were invited and virtually every hotel in the metropolis was booked. The marriage did not last long. Four years later, Padma was found dead, apparently after an overdose of sleeping pills.

The year 1960 also saw Jiwajirao's health take a serious turn for the worse. Jiwajirao passed away on 9 July 1961. He was only forty-five. As their son Madhavrao was barely sixteen, Vijaya Raje, who was then Lok Sabha MP from Guna, was given the title of Rajmata (Queen Mother).

By the time the dates for the third Lok Sabha polls of 1962 were announced, she was already in a year-long mourning period. Nehru reportedly sent Madhya Pradesh chief minister, Kailash Nath Katju, to persuade her to contest. Shastri, too, called her up. But the Rajmata was reluctant to contest and pointed to her inability to campaign. A call from Nehru, however, sealed the deal as the prime minister offered to campaign for her. The Rajmata filed her nomination, this time from Gwalior, and Angre took charge to ensure her victory. She won, with over 76 per cent of the votes. Her Hindu Mahasabha rival, Manik Chandra, polled barely 10 per cent of the votes cast.

But by now the Rajmata was beginning to get disillusioned with the Congress. She was unhappy with the way Nehru had handled the 1962 Indo-China conflict. She was also resentful of a government scheme under which gold was sought from the public to fund the war against China. Prime Minister Nehru had addressed the nation, calling upon the women of India to donate their jewellery to the cause. Nehru also asked people to donate money and woollens. The Rajmata, in her memoirs, claimed that she donated 1,000 *tolas* worth of gold but somehow government agencies were not satisfied.

According to one estimate, more than US$220 million were collected in cash for the Defence of India Fund. The prime minister's daughter, Indira Gandhi, herself donated gold to the effort. In an article written for *Scroll*, Manoj Joshi, a Distinguished Fellow of the Observer Research Foundation, has said that many gold ornaments and jewellery donated then to the Defence of India Fund lie forgotten in the vaults of the Reserve Bank of India even today.[5]

The Rajmata, who had over the years developed right-wing economic and political leanings, also disagreed with the Nehruvian socialist model and resented the government's quest to unearth and tax money stashed away by former royals, businessmen and traders.

Moreover, this was a time when Sardar Sambhajirao Angre began crafting Vijaya Raje's political career. Angre, about the same age as Vijaya Raje and a staunch Hindu Mahasabhai and Bharatiya Jana Sangh supporter, had become a central figure in Gwalior and in the Rajmata's political life, earning the tag of a Machiavellian 'Uncle' and master of palace intrigue. After Jiwajirao's death he was always by her side, in tweeds and carrying a gun. Angre fancied himself to be a Grigori Rasputin, a Russian mystic who had served as adviser in the court of Czar Nicholas II of Russia. It has also been claimed that Rasputin was Empress Alexandra's paramour. 'He [Angre] was much more than a secretary,' a source close to the Scindia family was quoted as saying in *The Guardian* on 10 February 2001. 'I would not go so far as to talk about a physical relationship but there is no doubt he had a great influence over her [Vijaya Raje].'[6]

In her autobiography, Vijaya Raje writes, 'Sambhajirao (Angre) came to my husband to offer his services in the spirit of the historical ties between our families. From that day on, he became my husband's most trusted confidant. He was, after all, from the same fold, brought up on the same orthodoxies. I, too, soon began to call him by his nickname "Bal", while the children, by instinct, began calling him uncle.' According to Vijaya Raje, Angre had strong Hindu Mahasabha leanings but joined the Congress in 1957 in order to serve her and Gwalior. Angre's influence on her resulted in the Rajmata's renewed interest in politics. Vijaya Raje was always quick to shower praise on Angre: 'He had, since my husband's death, made himself indispensable. There was a close affinity between my political beliefs and his, as well as in our concern for the Hindu faith. He'd become a financial advisor of unquestionable integrity, trusted confidant, guide and troubleshooter. I don't believe his position can have many parallels among non-feudal families, no decision is made without him.'

The Rajmata must have been lonely too. Apart from losing her husband, she had sent her son, Madhavrao, to study at Winchester and then to New College, Oxford.

In 1962, D.P. Mishra, a seasoned politician, became chief minister of Madhya Pradesh. When Prime Minister Lal Bahadur Shastri died in Tashkent in January 1966, Mishra played a pivotal role in Indira Gandhi checkmating the Congress old guard to become the prime minister. The Rajmata, who had started nursing a grudge against the Nehru–Gandhi family, did not see eye to eye with Mishra.

On one occasion in 1966, Mishra had used a Youth Congress convention at Pachmarhi to target the erstwhile rulers of Gwalior, terming them parasites and misfits in a democracy. A month later, a student agitation in Ujjain and Gwalior saw the Rajmata backing student bodies while the Mishra regime used strong-arm tactics such as baton-charge and police firing to quell the stir.

The 'Bastar massacre' of March 1966 was the flashpoint. Pravirchandra Bhanjdev, former ruler of the Bastar tribal area, was opposed to the Congress and intensely disliked by Mishra. On 26 March, when Indira Gandhi was the prime minister, local police reportedly surrounded Pravirchandra's palace in Jagdalpur where the deposed ruler and a group of tribals were said to have barricaded themselves in. Following a bloody 'night-long encounter', the bullet-riddled bodies of the former raja and seven of his supporters were found the next morning, triggering outrage. Atal Bihari Vajpayee, then a senior Jana Sangh leader and an MP, rose in the Lok Sabha to lodge a protest. Vajpayee quoted Pravirchandra's brother as saying that the police had tricked the former ruler into coming out of the palace where he was holed up, and then shot him. The police performed the last rites of the slain men without waiting for the raja's wife, who was then in Delhi.

The Rajmata was outraged. Pravirchandra had sought her help but she could do little, with Indira being in power at the Centre. 'What happened in Bastar shocked one. But the indifference of the party's leadership [read Indira] shocked one even more,' she has said in her memoirs.

Switch to Jana Sangh

By the time the dates for the 1967 general election were announced, the Rajmata had made up her mind to quit the Congress. The

Rajmata contested for the Madhya Pradesh Assembly from the Jana Sangh and on a Swatantra Party ticket for the Lok Sabha in the simultaneous elections held that year. Both the Jana Sangh and Swatantra Party were opposed to Indira-led Congress. The Rajmata's son, Madhavrao, back from England, teamed up with Angre to supervise her campaigns and together they made a formidable team. She won both the contests and decided to hold on to her assembly seat but later joined the Jana Sangh, ending her ties with the Swatantra Party.

By the Rajmata's own admission, she was torn between the Swatantra Party and the Jana Sangh. The Swatantra Party had been formed in 1959 by Rajagopalachari, also fondly known as Rajaji, along with other dissident and liberal Congress leaders who were opposed to Nehru and Indira's obsession with what they described as 'foible socialism' – the Nehruvian brand of mixed economy that tried to achieve social justice in the garb of socialism. The outfit projected itself as a 'party with a difference', a slogan later adopted by the BJP, which would be co-founded in 1980 by the Rajmata, A.B. Vajpayee, L.K. Advani, Sikander Bakht, Bhairon Singh Shekhawat and others.

The Rajmata's entry into the Madhya Pradesh Assembly paved the way for a major political twist. Soon, thirty-six Congress members of the legislative assembly (MLAs) defected to the opposition ranks, with the Rajmata seen as the brain behind Mishra's ouster as chief minister. For the first time in central India, a non-Congress party, the Samyukta Vidhayak Dal (SVD), formed the government. The Rajmata's memoirs offer a detailed account of her antipathy toward defections but she sought to justify it on the ground of 'teaching a lesson to an arrogant Congress'. Vijaya Raje, however, declined to be chief minister and did not provide any reason for her decision. Later, in the 1980s, when she would be asked to head the BJP, she told Advani – according to the veteran's book, *My Country, My Life*

– that she had been advised against accepting any public post by the chief priest of Pitambara Peeth, Pujyapad Swamiji Maharaj.

With the Rajmata opting out, former Congress leader Govind Narayan Singh was made the chief minister of Madhya Pradesh. Twenty months later, Govind Narayan would break the alliance and return to the Congress fold.

Under the Rajmata's leadership, the Jana Sangh locally defied the Indira wave in the 1971 Lok Sabha polls, when the Congress walked away with an overwhelming 352 seats in the House. The Jana Sangh won three seats in the Gwalior region – the Rajmata from Bhind, her son Madhavrao from Guna and Vajpayee from Gwalior. But the war with Pakistan that resulted in the creation of Bangladesh in 1971 had made Indira both popular and powerful. The Congress, which had swept the 1971 general election, won the subsequent assembly polls in 1972, riding high on Indira's G*aribi Hatao* slogan.

Earlier, on the eve of Independence Day in 1970, Indira Gandhi had visited the All India Congress Committee office and consulted colleagues about the objective of achieving a socialistic society. 'There must be a steady narrowing of inequalities and enlargement of income-earning opportunities for the weaker sections of society,' she had said, adding, 'We need to enlarge the area of socialism.' It was this era that saw the radicalization of Congress policies, programmes and leadership. Indira also displayed her extraordinary political acumen and sense of realpolitik, pitting one Congress leader against another to deal a body blow to the conservatives during the nationalization of banks and the abolition of the privy purse.

The privy purse was the payment made to the 565 royal families of princely states as part of their agreement to integrate with India in 1947. Indira wondered why the culture of gun salutes and titles should continue in independent India. The feudal princes, on the other hand, took these ornamental and illusory titles very seriously. Among them were the Scindias, one of the four most illustrious Indian royal families; the others being those of Baroda, Hyderabad and Mysore, who also merited a 21-gun salute during the British Raj. Indira felt it was scandalous that about a billion rupees of taxpayers' money should be paid (tax free) to a few hundred 'parasitical puppets' more than two decades after Independence as part of the privy-purse arrangement. The Nizam of Hyderabad was the biggest recipient with a tax-free pension of over Rs 80 million a year. The Scindias used to get Rs 25 lakh a year.

When Indira moved the 24th Constitutional Amendment Bill on 22 July 1971 in the Lok Sabha, it led to uproar. Jana Sangh leader Vajpayee alleged that Indira was acting under pressure from communists. In reply, Indira spoke not like a political strategist but as a compassionate social philosopher with an original mind. She admitted that while the abolition of privy purses and princely privileges were not going to solve poverty, unemployment or any other problem, it was a step in the right direction. 'If we do not take (such a step), we will be swept aside,' she said. Incidentally, the Congress's old guard which had formed the Congress (O) voted against the bill along with the Swatantra Party and the Jana Sangh.

Beyond the contentious privileges – that ranged from reserved pastures for horses to immunity from legal prosecution – Indira had to take the final call on the official recognition of India's maharajas. And that day had come. For the first time, the Scindias, along with the other royals, had to file income tax returns.

The Rajmata, in her memoirs, has written about this sudden change of status. 'Money was never a consideration. When you are young, you don't think too much about poverty, or other people. So, I used to enjoy myself. Like, if I went out shopping, I'd buy saris by the dozen, or jewellery – not just one article, but 6 to 10 pieces at a time.' But not anymore. After the abolition of the privy purses, the Scindias had to think twice before buying anything expensive. But blessed with the ability to laugh at herself amid adversity, the Rajmata would say, 'Now we don't buy, we are the sellers.'

The Rajmata and her family felt socially embarrassed. The Gwalior royals had dozens of elephants which would be pressed into service for ceremonial occasions. The Rajmata was reluctant to sell them off but running the big fat, indulgent household became difficult.

Indira's initial attempt of abolishing the privy purses had failed due to a stay order from the Supreme Court of India. The prime minister remained unfazed and amended the Constitution to discard the provision for privy purses. According to historian-author Manu S. Pillai, the debate on privy purses had begun much before and that, by 1967, there had been considerable sparring on the topic in the Parliament. 'The Bengali Communist leader, Bhupesh Gupta, for instance, described privy purses as "blood money" to feed a "parasitic class", thundering that the Indian state was not an instrument to subsidize royal harems,' Pillai has said.[7]

The already strained relations between the Rajmata and the prime minister worsened when the former was removed as chancellor of Hari Singh Gaur University in Sagar in 1969. The Rajmata believed that chief minister of Madhya Pradesh, Shyama Charan Shukla, had acted on instructions from Indira. She thought that the sole objective of amending a state law (to debar an elected member from becoming the chancellor) was to deprive her from continuing as chancellor of the university even though the varsity's academic council and senate had nominated her for the coveted post.

The Rajmata had annoyed Indira by supporting newspaper baron Ramnath Goenka and ensuring his electoral victory from Vidisha, which was part of the erstwhile Gwalior state. A rank outsider and contesting as an independent, Goenka's victory was all the more spectacular as it came in the middle of an Indira wave in 1971. The Rajmata was a key campaigner for Goenka, whose newspaper (*The Indian Express*) had an anti-establishment reputation.

On her part, Indira had stepped up a campaign against former royals. At a public meeting in Jaipur, she hit out at former royals and took on Maharani Gayatri Devi, who had won the 1962 Lok Sabha polls by a mammoth margin, getting 192,909 votes out of the 246,516 that were cast. Gayatri Devi, a glamorous queen, had also fancied herself as Indira's rival and worked hard to bring the Swatantra Party, which believed in free enterprise and closer ties with the West, close to the right-wing Jana Sangh. Indira asked the voters 'to go ask the maharajas and maharanis how much they had done for the people in their states when they ruled them and what they did to fight the British while they lived in luxury at the cost of the people.'

Emergency Years

The period between 1969 and 1973 also saw the emergence of Jayaprakash Narayan (JP). JP, who had met Nehru in 1930 and joined the Congress, had been imprisoned many times during the independence movement. But soon after 1947, he had developed differences with Nehru and, by 1952, had joined the Praja Socialist Party. He, however, belonged to a rare breed of politicians who did not contest any election.

In 1973, JP wrote to several MPs seeking to protect individuals' rights and democratic values as a mark of protest against Indira's growing cult. This was the time when many 'backward castes', such as the Yadavs, Jats, Reddys, Patels and the Marathas, were becoming disillusioned with the Indira-led Congress.

But Indira's star was still in the ascendancy. The Pokhran nuclear tests in 1974, which made India the world's sixth nuclear power, had further enhanced her stature, both at home and abroad. The annexation of Sikkim in 1975 further boosted her image as a towering leader who could do no wrong and the personality cult around her continued to grow.

Conscious of her bitter experience with the Congress's old guard, Indira tried to take total control of her party's organization. Many powerful chief ministers were shunted out and replaced by her favourites. Among them were Barkatullah Khan, who replaced Mohanlal Sukhadia in Rajasthan; and P.C. Sethi, who replaced S.C. Shukla in Madhya Pradesh. Indira also made deliberate attempts to control the party funds that were crucial for elections and all other political activities, making the party and the government dependent upon her for survival.

Indira's younger son, Sanjay, had returned from England, where he had trained at the Rolls Royce factory at Crewe. Sanjay, then twenty-three, applied for a licence to manufacture a small and cheap car. When he turned out to be the lone applicant to have been granted a licence, allegations of nepotism started doing the rounds. The matter was raised in the Parliament and the House saw the prime minister purse her lips and shrug off the criticism. There was more to follow. The Haryana government under Bansi Lal handed over 300 acres of land for Sanjay's car factory, for which some 15,000 peasants were evicted. P.N. Haksar, who was principal secretary to Indira till 1973, was fired for opposing Sanjay's project.

To counter Indira, JP formed a body called Citizens for Democracy and became a sort of patriarch for disgruntled elements. His followers multiplied quickly in number. In June 1975, the Allahabad High Court held Indira accountable for electoral malpractices. Her private assistant, the burly Yashpal Kapoor, was caught acting as her electoral agent, even though his resignation from government service was yet to be accepted. Indira refused to step down. Her refusal to accept the court's verdict stunned the nation and there was a sudden rise in civil unrest. JP appealed to the police and the armed forces to 'disobey' any illegal order their conscience did not approve of. On 25 June 1975, a cabinet meeting was called. Moving away from the established custom of discussion and consultations, Indira merely informed the ministers that an Emergency was being imposed under Article 352 of the Constitution. The Emergency effectively bestowed upon Indira the power to rule by decree, suspending elections and civil liberties.

The Indira government also decided to detain all top-ranking opposition leaders likely to oppose the Emergency. Rajmata Vijaya Raje, then firmly in the Jana Sangh, was among the top ten on the list. Her son, Madhavrao, also a Jana Sangh MP, feared arrest and fled to Kathmandu where his wife's family members were influential Ranas of Nepal. The Rajmata was in Delhi celebrating her youngest daughter Yashodhararaje's birthday (more details in Chapter 5) when she got a message. It was from Madhavrao, asking his mother and three sisters to join him in Nepal. The Rajmata was caught in a bind. 'My son's concern for my protection made me very happy,' she would write in her memoirs. But then she had second thoughts after Angre stoked her political ambitions. He called Madhavrao a coward. The Rajmata managed to avoid the police for a while and, at one point, was only twenty-five steps away from the Nepal border. But Angre and her 'political instincts' prevailed, pulling her back to Gwalior where a surrender was staged.

For the rest of her life, she would side with Angre, counting on his assessment and advice, while nursing a life-long grudge against Madhavrao. The mother-son rift would be irrevocable, with Angre dubbing Madhavrao as somewhat weak-willed and lacking in courage.

After her surrender in Gwalior, the Rajmata was whisked away to Pachmarhi and kept in isolation. This was not a jail as she was lodged in the picturesque 'Bison Lodge' forest resort. The weather too was salubrious, when the rest of north and central India was under the spell of a hot and humid summer. Taroon Coomar Bhaduri, the author-journalist, was then posted in Bhopal as the state correspondent of *The Statesman*. The father-in-law of megastar Amitabh Bachchan wrote in his book, *Off the Records,* that when Indira came to know about the Rajmata's comfortable incarceration, she was furious and ordered her to be shifted to Delhi's Tihar Jail.

Around the same time, income-tax officers and several other agencies raided the Jai Vilas Palace, the seat of the Scindias in Gwalior. A report published in *India Today* on 30 September 1991 claimed that during the 1975 Emergency raid, taxmen had unearthed silver articles weighing 53 quintals and trunks full of jewellery from Jai Vilas Palace. The Scindias were charged with economic offences, including gold smuggling, an allegation vehemently contested by the Rajmata and her daughters. The tax officials did not merely find silver and jewellery during the raid. They also took away with them notations for a new raga that Ustad Allauddin Khan had composed and named after Vijaya Raje, thinking it was some secret code. The grateful maestro had composed the raga – perhaps within the first five years of Vijaya Raje's marriage to Jiwajirao – for sponsoring a surgery in Gwalior.

Yashodhararaje, the Rajmata's youngest daughter, barely twenty-one then, was the sole representative of the Scindias at the palace when the law enforcement officials carried out the raid. The Rajmata's eldest surviving daughter, Usha Raje, married in Nepal, was away, and Vasundhara Raje was at Dholpur, Rajasthan, battling to save her marriage.

When the Rajmata arrived at Tihar, she was appalled by the prison conditions. She was brought to Tihar on 3 September, and, like any other criminal and prisoner, was identified with a number – 2265. Here, she met another high-profile prisoner, Maharani

Gayatri Devi of Jaipur, who had been put in dingy barracks with petty thieves and prostitutes.

In her book *The Emergency: A Personal History*,[8] journalist-author Coomi Kapoor has given a graphic account of how these maharanis coped with imprisonment. Gayatri Devi had developed a mouth ulcer but jail authorities waited for three weeks before granting permission to her personal dental surgeon to visit her. Kapoor's account has perhaps relied heavily on husband and fellow journalist Virender, who was in Tihar when the Rajmata and Gayatri Devi were interned. Kapoor quotes him seeing both the maharanis in Tihar. 'There was a glow on her [the Rajmata's] face. The Rajmata of Jaipur, on the other hand, looked haggard and shell shocked,' Coomi has written, quoting Virender Kapoor. The living conditions at Tihar were appalling. Coomi remembers Vijaya Raje's cell being at the edge of the women's ward. 'It was a small, narrow room with high, barred windows. The common bathroom had no tap. A hole in the ground, covered with a plank, served as a toilet and a sweeper came twice a day to flush it with a bucket of water. There was an all-pervading stench, ever present flies and mosquitoes, and perpetual noise. The location of her cell was between the women and men's wards. She got to hear the sounds from both sides. The women inmates were engaged in frequent slanging matches, with their children constantly howling. From the other side of the wall came the sounds of political slogans and patriotic songs as well as demented screams and maniacal laughter.'

Housed in ward no. 3, the Rajmata, however, found a way to interact with Nanaji Deshmukh, a Jana Sangh veteran who was in prison along with Arun Jaitley, George Fernandes, Parkash Singh Badal, Choudhury Charan Singh, Lala Hansraj and others, charged under the Maintenance of Internal Security Act (MISA).

The Rajmata's doctor had prescribed her yoga. In Tihar, Deshmukh held yoga classes in the men's ward and the jail authorities permitted him to teach yoga to the Rajmata also. In their bestseller *Black Warrant*, jailer Sunil Gupta narrated to co-author Sunetra Choudhury, 'I do not know how much yoga they did, but these deliberations were the seeds of the Janata Party.'[9]

For Gupta, then a young officer, it was fascinating to witness how Badal acted as a facilitator between the Hindu right and Indian communist leaders to form a broad platform against Indira. Badal first drew these ideologically hostile leaders into carom and, when some rapport had been developed, plans to overthrow the Indira regime through democratic means were contemplated. Gupta often saw Jaitley playing badminton with jail staff, Fernandes writing with a flourish and Charan Singh performing yagna (ritual sacrifice).

The Rajmata, Deshmukh, Jaitley and other political prisoners had engaged so much of the attention of the jail authorities – from the warder to the superintendent, effectively six ranks and over 500 personnel – that a group of thirteen facing life imprisonment plotted and carried out a successful jailbreak on 16 March 1976. They dug a tunnel from their barracks to escape. Not a single political prisoner joined them.

Within three months of her arrival in Tihar, the Rajmata was diagnosed with diabetes. After much lobbying by Madhavrao (who was in Nepal), Usha, whose husband was a minister in the Nepalese kingdom, Vasundhara and Yashodhara, the Rajmata was finally released on parole on medical grounds. The Rajmata was against opting for parole but reluctantly agreed after her spiritual guru, Pujyapad Swamiji Maharaj, instructed her to avail herself of the relief. In all, she spent six months in jail where she faced rigorous imprisonment.

In her book, the Rajmata has admitted that her daughters, Usha and Vasundhara, tried reaching out to Indira for some sort of a 'solution' and get her released. The Rajmata claimed that a person close to Indira spoke in double entendre, wondering what all Vasundhara was ready to sacrifice in order to secure her mother's release. In political circles, the man (now dead) who tried to make a pass at Vasundhara was quickly identified but was seldom named due to lack of evidence. He was known to have inflicted hardship to media and Bollywood bigwigs during the Emergency and was linked to several women.

On his part, Madhavrao, whose brother-in-law had risen to become a minister in the Nepal cabinet, had also tried to reach out to Indira and Sanjay. He was told to return to India and remain apolitical. Indira and Sanjay viewed Madhavrao with great political interest. The former maharaja was seen as someone who could dismantle the Jana Sangh's influence in Madhya Bharat and effectively neutralize the Rajmata and her party.

In retrospect, it appears that the 'solution' that helped the Rajmata escape another year in jail till the end of the twenty-one-month Emergency was an informal assurance that she would turn 'apolitical'. R.K. Dhawan, Indira's close aide, would talk about it in private conversations while admitting that there was no 'paper trail' to it. Both N.K. Singh, a Bhopal-based veteran journalist who worked for *India Today*, and Taroon Coomar Bhaduri see some merit in Dhawan's claim.[10]

The Emergency was lifted in March 1977. A few months later, on 1 July, Taroon Coomar Bhaduri met the Rajmata in Bhopal. Indira had by then been voted out and the Janata Party, a rainbow coalition of opposition parties, had come to power. When Bhaduri asked the Rajmata about her future role, she had replied rather impatiently, 'No, no, no, I am not in politics anymore. I am not disenchanted, but disgusted with politics and the politicians. I never thought they could stoop so low. Politics is not for me.' Bhaduri had asked her if there was 'pressure' on her to renounce politics, leading to her release on parole. To this she said, 'No, that is not true. I was rotting in jail. I was a physical wreck. The world outside was a silent spectator and did not even raise a little finger. What was the point? I renounced politics and came out.' For Bhaduri, this was an admission that the Rajmata had indeed given an undertaking – a precondition for her release.

The Rajmata did not stay out of politics for long. She decided to contest against Indira from Raebareli, Uttar Pradesh, in the 1980 general election and later founded the BJP with Vajpayee, Advani and others. From 1977 onwards, she also mentored a large number of party leaders. One of her successful protégés was Sadhvi Uma Bharti, a fiery orator who would become a parliamentarian, union minister and chief minister.

Bhaduri had his own doubts about the Rajmata's resolve to stay out of politics. She was in Bhopal the day the Janata Party legislators were meeting to elect a new chief minister. A number of newly elected MLAs were meeting her one-to-one or in small groups. In Bhaduri's presence, a local journalist had asked the Rajmata if she was becoming the centre of an 'extra-constitutional authority' in the selection of a new chief minister. The Rajmata reportedly thumped the arm of her sofa and then said in a raised voice, 'I am neither extra, nor centre, nor a constitutional authority.' The correspondent persisted and asked her if she would advise her son, who had won a Lok Sabha election as an independent candidate with the support of the Congress, to join the Janata Party. 'No,' the Rajmata replied, cool and impassive. 'He is a big boy and he can take his own decisions. The days of a mother advising the son or vice versa are gone. Previous results have been disastrous.' She then stood up, as if in a hurry to end the conversation that was turning painful.

Mother–Son Rift

So, when did the mother and son split? There are many dates and versions. N.K. Singh remembers Madhavrao telling him in 1991 that his rift with the Rajmata could be traced back to 1972, the year he wanted to opt out of his mother's party, the Jana Sangh, and join the Congress instead. In fact, joining the Jana Sangh after returning from Oxford was 'a colossal mistake', Madhavrao had insisted. But Sardar Angre, addressed by his friends as 'Baldy', had a different take. 'He [Madhavrao] chickened out because the Jana Sangh did not do so well in the 1972 Vidhan Sabha elections,' Angre had told Singh.[11]

Some of the surviving members of the Scindia family accept that the rift between the Rajmata and Madhavrao dates back to before the June 1975 declaration of the Emergency. Madhavrao deeply resented Angre's influence on his mother and felt strongly that the Scindias's wealth was being spent 'recklessly' on politics. He had differences with his mother over money and her funding of the Jana Sangh, the political arm of the right-wing Rashtriya Swayamsevak Sangh (RSS) and the earlier avatar of the BJP. Close friends of Madhavrao have claimed that the young maharaja was shocked to see money and jewellery disappearing from Jai Vilas Palace. 'There were supposedly wells full of gold, silver and precious metals. Madhavrao was stunned to see these "wells" depleted,' one of them has said.

In Madhavrao's assessment, his mother had 'zero business sense' and that, often, prime properties in Bombay and elsewhere were 'disposed of' at a throwaway price when the market value was much higher. On many occasions, Angre was said to have facilitated these sales and allegedly received a 'cut'. On top of this, the Rajmata, it has been claimed, would invariably hand over a part of the money from the sales proceeds to Angre as a sign of her 'gratitude'. Angre increasingly became the man who stood between Vijaya Raje and her son.[12]

Madhavrao had initially agreed with his mother's assessment of Angre's acumen and devotion towards the house of the Scindias but increasingly grew wary of him. Madhavrao's childhood friend,

Balendu Shukla, recalls a conversation he had one day with the titular maharaja of Gwalior. 'What do you think of Angre?' Madhavrao had asked his friend, after a game of squash. 'There is something about him I do not quite like,' Shukla had responded.[13]

On 30 September 1991, while speaking to N.K. Singh, Madhavrao had described his mother as a dominating woman who had used emotional blackmail to keep him in her political party. He also described her as being in thrall of Angre. 'Angre is a vicious man making a complete fool of my mother, siphoning off her money,' Madhavrao had told the *India Today* journalist. 'He has some strange hold over her. Sometimes I think he has performed some sort of black magic on her.' In the interview, Madhavrao made some sharp comments about the Rajmata, too. 'She made her choice in 1977. I did not want Angre to interfere in our household affairs. So I asked her to make a choice. She chose Angre. I was very hurt,' he said. Madhavrao also described his mother as a 'highly strung' person. 'She is very dominating. When she was with my father, that was the situation. The same when she was with us. She can become totally hysterical. There is so much more peace in the family, now that she is staying separately,' he had said. 'The sort of things she says about me, make the parting much more painful,' he had added ruefully. 'Once she said that I should have been trampled under the foot of an elephant.'[14]

But there was a time when Madhavrao was exceptionally close to his mother, to the extent that he discussed his girlfriends with her. Singh had interviewed the Rajmata and her comments appeared in the same issue of the magazine. 'Bhaiya [the Rajmata addressed Madhavrao as that] and I were like friends. One night he came to my hotel room and lay down on the carpet. He was feeling lonely, and talked till 2 a.m. He was so free with me, he even used to discuss his girlfriends,' the Rajmata told the journalist, according to a passage quoted by *India Today*.[15]

The Rajmata, while speaking to Singh, had blamed Madhavrao's wife, Madhviraje, for the family rift. 'He was a sterling boy. He used to pick up my shoes in front of everybody. But his wife could not bear his proximity to me. So she caused the rift. She is extremely greedy and ambitious. People hate her. Find out what her own staff says about her,' the Rajmata had said. 'My bahu's mother has taken my place,' she added, blaming Madhavrao's in-laws who, like her, hailed from Nepal. The Rajmata looked composed but broke down twice as she spoke to him, Singh recalls.

Singh remembered that Angre, who was present during the interview, had intervened to say, 'She [the Rajmata] is reacting like a mother by trying to shift the blame on to her daughter-in-law.' To Angre, Madhavrao's most reprehensible action was 'fleeing' to Nepal during the Emergency. 'While the Rajmata was in jail, being treated extremely badly and kept with mad women and criminals, he was in Nepal and then to England,' Angre told Singh. 'He [Madhavrao] ran away. This upset the lady. She was a very emotional person.'

Angre would often narrate an anecdote related to the legendary Maratha queen, Ahilyabai Holkar. According to him, Ahilyabai had established a custom of making charitable donations to her subjects every morning. One day, she discovered that her only son, still a boy, was putting poisonous scorpions inside the shoes of those who came to seek her benevolence. An angry Ahilyabai ordered her son's execution – he was crushed to death under the foot of an elephant – and made Yashwant Rao Holkar, her general, the next maharaja. Angre viewed Ahilyabai as a heroine and often compared Vijaya Raje with her for disinheriting her son and leaving much of her fortune under the control of a trust. Angre was both a trustee and the executor of Vijaya Raje's will.

Author-journalist Saba Naqvi, who closely tracked the BJP, had claimed in an article in *Outlook* magazine that Angre's influence turned the Rajmata against her son. She quoted a close friend of Rajmata as saying, 'I told her that you should make up with Madhavrao. After all, you are called Rajmata [queen mother] because you are the mother of your son, the Maharaja.' In response, Vijaya Raje had reportedly said, 'It was Bal's [Angre's] influence over me which gave my political beliefs their rigidity. That is why he [Madhavrao] has taken special trouble to subject "Bal" to a host of major harassments such as getting his staff to file criminal cases.'[16]

Before the mother and son parted ways, an angry showdown was said to have taken place at Jai Vilas Palace where Madhavrao had questioned Angre's dominance on the Rajmata's life. 'Amma, this can't go on. You simply have to choose. It's either Angre or me,' Sanghvi has quoted Madhavrao as saying. To his horror, the Rajmata had made the choice with no apparent difficulty. 'I cannot leave Angre. He has stood by me through some of my worst times,' she had reportedly said. 'You will not leave Angre even if it means alienating your only son?' a shocked Madhavrao is said to have replied. The Rajmata apparently shrugged her shoulders and an angry Madhavrao had stormed out of the room.

Soon, word was out that the Scindia family was on opposite sides on most issues – two separate political parties; two separate palaces; two separate courts; and two separate sets of assets. The formal split took place on 12 October 1980, the Rajmata's sixtieth birthday. It was both dramatic and unfortunate.

Madhavrao and Madhviraje had organized a party for the Rajmata in Bombay's Samudra Mahal. According to Sanghvi, the Rajmata, accompanied by Sardar Angre, arrived late and left within minutes. While leaving she asked Madhavrao to sit in her car and told the driver to take them to D.M. Harish, the tax consultant for the Scindias. Harish had played a pivotal role in enabling Madhavrao's escape from India when the Emergency was imposed. The Rajmata's instruction to Harish to work out a partition of the Scindias' assets had put the lawyer in a difficult position as he was caught between the Queen Mother and the erstwhile maharaja. Harish had enormous respect for the Rajmata but shared an emotional bond with Madhavrao.

Sanghvi narrates the battle over the Scindia *shivling* (an abstract or aniconic representation of Lord Shiva), supposedly a flawless emerald the size of an egg. Legend has it that Mahadji Scindia would wear it under his turban when the Gwalior army went off to battle because it always brought good luck and victory. It had also become an essential part of the customary puja ritual performed by every reigning maharaja and maharani. While the emerald's monetary value was said to be incalculable, for the Scindias it had always been a symbol of the family's good fortune. Soon after the split, the Rajmata wanted the emerald back from her son. The otherwise timid wife of Madhavrao, Madhavi Raje, intervened to say that as the maharani of Gwalior, it was her duty to worship the *shivling*. Madhavi pointed out that ceremonial puja was considered auspicious only when it was done by a married woman, deeply upsetting her widowed mother-in-law. The Rajmata announced a fast unto death until the *shivling* was handed back to her. Madhavrao panicked and asked his reluctant wife to return it. Since the Rajmata's death, the shivling has been in the possession of her eldest daughter Usha Raje in Nepal.

The bitter split with her son made the Rajmata more dependent on Angre and his family. Ugly spats followed. During the Emergency, Hiranvan Mahal, located near Gwalior's Jai Vilas Palace, was taken over by Angre's family while the Rajmata was still in prison and Madhavrao was hiding in Nepal. It was alleged that Angre's wife, Manu, raided Jai Vilas Palace and ripped apart gold-plated taps, chandeliers and carpets to decorate her house. Later, when the Congress government came to power, Madhavrao tried to recover his property. Recalls a family source:

'When Madhavrao's men went to raid Hiranvan, the Angres set their Rottweiler on them. So they shot the dog.' In February 2005, three years before Angre's death, the maverick won a legal case getting control over Hiravan in the Gwalior estate.

Angre's influence over the Rajmata was an important factor in Madhavrao's decision to join the Congress. By the time the 1980 general election was announced, Madhavrao had made up his mind to join the party. However, as part of a well-thought out political strategy, he preferred to contest the 1980 Lok Sabha election from Gwalior as an independent candidate. The Rajmata was pitted against Indira Gandhi in Raebareli.

Jai Vilas Palace saw a vertical split. Angre openly called Madhavrao a coward. Torn between her politics and maternal affection, Rajmata still issued an appeal to residents of Gwalior to vote for the 'Mahal' (Jai Vilas Palace). This was a clever tactic. The Scindias may have been divided but they did not wish anyone from the house of the Scindias to lose an electoral battle. This practice of issuing an appeal on their royal insignia in favour of 'Mahal' candidates, regardless of the party they represented, continued for decades till Narendra Modi's arrival on the political scene in 2014. Modi made it clear that regardless of family ties, the primary loyalty of BJP leaders should be with the party. Six years later, in 2020, all politically inclined Scindias were in one party: the BJP (more of it in Chapter 6).

Madhavrao won by a huge margin from Gwalior but the Rajmata suffered a humiliating defeat in Raebareli. As a Janata Party nominee, she lost an election for the first time, that too by a margin of 173,654 votes. The Rajmata admitted that she was wrong in her assessment that the people would punish Indira for sending her to prison. But that was not the only wrong assessment she made. Inherent contradictions, clash of ideologies and one-upmanship within the Janata Party brought Indira back to power in less than three years after being voted out. It was an emphatic return: the Congress won 352 seats, eighty more than the required majority.

Indira's return to power stunned a beleaguered and divided opposition. The Janata Party split into many factions. The socialist members of the Janata Party wanted Jana Sangh members to completely disassociate themselves from the RSS. But RSS leaders and Jana Sangh workers of the allied groups of the Sangh Parivar felt it was time to break away because the Janata Party had no future. The Rajmata came to the forefront, advocating that the RSS ideology of Hindutva needed a strong and open political face.

Birth of the BJP

Five prime objectives led to the formation of the BJP. The first was cultural nationalism. The Rajmata, Vajpayee, Advani, Kushabhau Thakre, Jaganthrao Joshi, Sunder Singh Bhandari, J.P. Mathur, Nanaji Deshmukh, Sikander Bakht and others felt that there was an urgent need to practise a brand of politics that would push this concept. Although the RSS was never overtly religious in the sense of asking its followers to go to temples, perform pujas or observe fasts, it firmly believed in enthusiastic practising of a religion that accorded primacy to the concepts of *matribhoomi* (motherland) and Bharat Mata (Mother India).

Linked to this was the idea of cultural and religious revivalism. The RSS felt that the pivotal role played by deities such as Lord Ram and Lord Krishna in the growth of civilization needed to be re-emphasized. Others who were revered included Sri Aurobindo, Lokmanya Tilak, Ramakrishna Paramahamsa and, due to political exigencies, Mahatma Gandhi, too.

The RSS had a reluctant admiration for Gandhi's belief in grassroots-level activism but privately detested his politics and posture at the time of the country's Independence and the creation of Pakistan, as well as his accommodating attitude toward Muslims. So, when Gandhian socialism was made a cornerstone of the new party 'with a difference', the Rajmata, the founder vice president, opposed it bitterly. She was supported by Bhairon Singh Shekhawat, who later rose to become the vice president of India.

Dr. Hari Desai, who was present at the BJP's inaugural meet as a political correspondent of the *Hindusthan Samachar*, a Hindi national news agency backed by the RSS, had interviewed the Rajmata, who recorded her protest against Gandhian socialism. She kept emphasizing the themes of Hindutva and cultural nationalism, clarifying that the BJP's conception of Hindutva was nationalist, not religious or theocratic.

The second objective behind the formation of the BJP was to pursue value-based politics. Commitment to democracy was the third pillar in the context of Indira's draconian measures to suspend civil rights and curb free speech during the Emergency. The BJP believed in 'positive secularism' or equal treatment for all, instead of what it described as the Congress's appeasement of minorities (read Muslims). The last and final objective of the BJP was to break caste barriers and establish *samata* (equality) in Indian society.

On 6 April 1980, the BJP was born in New Delhi where its name, Bharatiya Janata Party, and symbol, the lotus, were chosen. Madhu Deolekar, a member of the Jana Sangh since 1952 and the new party's general secretary, recalled that the lotus was selected as the party symbol because it represented the Hindu ethos. 'It's a holy symbol. Everyone in rural India understands what it stands for. It is symbolic. It blooms in dirty waters but it is pure in itself. Like the lotus, we thought we would be in politics without getting mired in the corruption around us,' Deolekar had said.

Deolekar and some others have claimed that the Rajmata was considered for party presidentship to pit her against Indira. But a section of the RSS and BJP leaders felt that the move might reek of feudalism. 'So, the core group dropped her name. Advani was not a big enough leader to be considered for the historic nomination.... To many of us, Vajpayee's commitment to Hindutva was a little feeble. During the Janata rule, when he was a minister, he had written an article criticizing the RSS's approach to national issues. But there was no alternative to Vajpayee. He was the most popular face of the party and a great orator,' Deolekar reminisced.

A month later, in May 1980, a BJP conclave was held in Bombay, where Deolekar recalls the presence of Mohammad Ali Currimbhai Chagla, an eminent jurist and former union minister who had served under both Nehru and Shastri. Chagla had made a stirring speech, saying he saw a miniature India gathered at the conclave and predicted that the BJP would one day come to power and Vajpayee would be India's prime minister.

Perhaps, as a counter, Indira started pandering to the religious sentiments of Hindus. Much to the surprise of many, she accepted an invitation to launch the Vishwa Hindu Parishad's (VHP's) 'Ekatmata Yatra' in 1981, also called the 'Ganga Jal Yatra'. This was the VHP's first mass-contact programme that gave a glimpse into how Hindu rituals and symbols could be effectively utilized for popular and political mobilization. By 1982–1983, Indira could be seen warming up to a 'Hindu Vote Bank'. Her loyalist, C.M. Stephen, declared in 1983: 'The wave-length of Hindu culture and the Congress culture is the same.'[17]

Indira's solicitude for Hindu sensitivity was significant in the context of the formation of the BJP. She was bitterly opposed to the creation of a Punjab state on linguistic lines as she used to closely identify with her minority Hindu supporters in the state. Barely six months before her assassination in October 1984, Indira had sought to assure the majority community that 'if there is injustice to them or if they did not get their rights, then it would be dangerous to the integrity of the Country'.[18]

On 31 October 1984, Indira Gandhi was assassinated by her Sikh bodyguards. Her son Rajiv took over as prime minister and quickly called for Lok Sabha elections. Much to the dismay of the Rajmata, Vajpayee, Advani and other BJP leaders, the Congress under Rajiv's leadership swept the polls. Prior to the polls, there was talk that Rajiv had a secret meeting with RSS chief Balasaheb Deoras, resulting in Sangh cadres supporting the Congress in the elections despite the presence of the BJP on the political scene.

Rajiv had met Bhaurau Deoras, the younger brother of Balasaheb Deoras, at least half a dozen times at different locations, including at Delhi's 46 Pusa Road residence of family friend and alcohol baron, Kapil Mohan. Close Rajiv associate Arun Singh, Delhi mayor Subash Arya and liaison man Anil Bali were among those who were present at these meetings. It was widely believed that the RSS wanted Rajiv to open the locks of the Babri Masjid–Ramjanmabhoomi site and give clearance for the *Ramayana,* Ramanand Sagar's television adaptation of the epic, to be aired on the state-run Doordarshan.

Having lost the 1980 polls against Indira, the Rajmata, who was the BJP vice president in 1984, had opted out of the electoral fray, ostensibly to campaign for the nascent party. But some felt that the Rajmata, sensing the sympathy for Rajiv, did not want to lose another election, particularly from a constituency that was part of the erstwhile Scindia empire.

Gwalior witnessed a titanic battle between Madhavrao and Vajpayee, who had no idea that the former royal would contest from the constituency. Madhavrao had switched his seat from Guna to Gwalior at the eleventh hour, under instructions from Rajiv. Vajpayee was taken aback as he had never wanted to contest against anyone from the Scindia family. In his book, *Na Dainyam, Na Palayanam* (a shloka from the Gita that means neither will I beg, nor quit), Vajpayee has written that he was cornered by certain political leaders within the BJP who wanted him to remain occupied in Gwalior so that he could not campaign for others elsewhere in the country. Was it the Rajmata or Advani, or both?

Gwalior, however, witnessed a graceful Vajpayee fighting against Madhavrao. The BJP supremo did not utter a single word which was disrespectful toward Madhavrao or his family. In his book, Vajpayee revealed the reason for this: his higher education in 1945 would not have been possible had the Scindia family not supported him. 'Jiwajirao Scindia, the Maharaja of Gwalior, knew me since my school days. When the question of my higher education was looming large on the family, which was already burdened under the marriage of my two sisters, and having limited resources after the retirement of my father, the royal family sanctioned me monthly scholarship of Rs 75,' Vajpayee said. Vajpayee always acknowledged the contribution of the Scindia family toward his personal life and party. When the Rajmata and Madhavrao were embroiled in an ugly family dispute, Vajpayee had declined to take sides.

In spite of the BJP's electoral setback, the Rajmata remained active and optimistic. In 1987, when the eighteen-year-old, convent-educated Roop Kanwar reportedly committed sati in Deorala village of Rajasthan, decked up in bridal finery, the Rajmata had supported this act. She was reportedly escorted to the cremation ground in a procession, with the active connivance of Kanwar's in-laws and the dominant families and community in Deorala. There were conflicting reports in the media on how the end came. Some villagers of Deorala had claimed that the sati was forced and they had heard Kanwar crying out for her father and even trying to escape. There were also reports that she did not live with her husband, Maal Singh Shekhawat, and had come to Deorala just before his death.

The sati created nationwide outrage. While the Rajput community and conservative sections of upper caste Hindus in Rajasthan closed ranks to defend and glorify sati, liberals and women's rights groups were aghast at the revival of a social evil that had been banned. The Rajiv Gandhi government was forced to enact a central law. The Representation of the People Act, 1951, was amended to disqualify any person convicted under the Sati Prevention Act from standing for election to Parliament or any state legislature during the period of conviction and for a period of five years after their release. The propagation of an act of sati or its glorification by a candidate at such an election would also be deemed as a corrupt practice under Section 123 of this Act.

Under pressure from her party colleagues as well as women's rights groups, the Rajmata had to modify her stance on sati. She publicly said that immolation of a widow should not be termed as sati. Some sections of the BJP, however, kept glorifying the custom of sati as something pure and pious. The BJP opposed the Rajasthan government's Commission of Sati (Prevention) Act, 1987, which reflected its thinking at that point of time.

Ayodhya

The Rajmata's next big political move came with the launch of an agitation for building a Ram temple in Ayodhya, a long legal dispute that would finally end in November 2019. The mosque, built in 1528 during Mughal emperor Babur's rule, was considered the birthplace of Lord Ram. In 1859, too, communal clashes over the possession of the site had reportedly taken place, prompting the then British administration to erect a fence: the inner court was to be used by Muslims and the outer court by Hindus. It became a potent political issue for the BJP when a Faizabad district judge in 1986 ruled that the gates of the mosque should be opened and Hindus allowed to pray inside. The lock of the Babri Masjid was opened with the tacit approval of Rajiv Gandhi.

In 1990, Advani, heading the BJP, and with the Rajmata as his deputy, embarked on a rath yatra (procession or pilgrimage).

The starting point of the rath yatra was Somnath, Gujarat, and it was to end in Ayodhya. The yatra ended abruptly when Lalu Prasad, who was chief minister of Bihar then, ordered Advani's arrest in Samastipur. By then, however, the rath yatra had served its purpose, arousing the passions of even moderate Hindus in the northern, central and western parts of India.

The Rajmata was present on the dais at the rally in Ayodhya on 6 December 1992, along with Advani, Murli Manohar Joshi and Uma Bharti, when the domes of the Babri mosque were demolished and the entire structure of the sixteenth-century mosque was pulled down. The BJP leadership were subsequently accused of having made inflammatory remarks at the rally and were said to have encouraged *kar sevaks* (a devotee who offers voluntary service to a religious cause) to go on the rampage. The demolition triggered massive riots across the country, causing death and destruction.

Noted journalist Swapan Dasgupta, who later became a Rajya Sabha MP for the BJP, was present in Ayodhya on that day. In an article for *Open* magazine,[19] Dasgupta, however, offered a different take on the events when the domes of the mosque came under attack. 'I recall seeing Advani walking off in a huff and an incensed Rajmata Vijaya Raje Scindia telling some of the VHP functionaries to yank people off the domes by their trousers. Indeed, there were numerous appeals on the public address system asking people to keep the peace and desist from doing their own thing. Someone asked Ashok Singhal, arguably the real head of the Ram Janmabhoomi movement, to go to the site – about 100 metres from the place where the leaders had assembled – and calm things down.'

Author-historian William Dalrymple wrote in his book, *The Age of Kali* (1998), that the Rajmata was among those cheering from the viewing platform as the three domes fell. He recalled her telling him after the event that she could die without regret, now that her dream had come true. And though she was a maharani, she lived simply, if elegantly: her vegetarian meals were served on a silver thali and her puja paraphernalia were always carried in a Gucci tote bag.

Following the demolition, the BJP emerged as a major political force, consolidating its hold on national politics. In several states, it developed strong footprints but, somehow, the Rajmata remained out of the loop. She retained the Guna Lok Sabha seat in 1996 and made it a win four times in a row in 1998, when Vajpayee formed the government for the first time for thirteen days, but her name was missing from the cabinet. In 1999, she retired from active politics because of failing health.

This was a period when the Scindia family was embroiled in litigation, some of which continue today. One involved a family dispute over Scindia Villa, a 32-acre prime property near the Hyatt Regency hotel in New Delhi. Then there was the curious case of Dr. J.K. Jain, a leader of the Jana Sangh and then the BJP, who had once partnered with Angre to buy *Surya*, the magazine run by Indira's daughter-in-law, Maneka Gandhi. Dr. Jain, with the help of Angre, set up his Jain TV studio in Scindia Villa despite protests from Madhavrao's sisters, Vasundhara and Yashodhara. The channel shut down in a year but Jain could not be evicted.

The family bitterness turned into murky legal battles that ran into crores of rupees and continued even after the death of both Vijaya Raje Scindia and Madhavrao within a span of eight months in 2001. According to an estimate by the newspaper *Business Standard*, the Scindia family litigation was worth Rs 20,000 crore.

Final Years

Months before the Rajmata's death, Madhavrao had moved close to his mother but she had remained apparently oblivious because of her complex medical condition. Madhavrao would often visit her at the hospital, sit by her bedside, hold her hand and read the *Hanuman Chalisa.* Vasundhara would later recall that the Rajmata's eyes lit up hearing Madhavrao's voice. Yashodhara, Madhavrao's youngest sister, said she often saw tears in the eyes of both her mother and brother.[20]

Thirteen days after the Rajmata died on 25 January 2001, her embittered relationship with son Madhavrao exploded into the open with the dramatic disclosure of her last will and testament. In her handwritten will, she had described Madhavrao as the 'most painful part of my life'. 'I have not disinherited him though my bequest may show I have done it. But the hard and true fact is that he has disentitled himself and rendered himself unfit even to the right to cremate his mother's dead body and do the last rites (*Kriyas*), which is the religious duty of every son,' she wrote.[21]

Copies of the twelve-page will, drawn up on 20 September 1985, were given to the press by her private secretary and four-decade-long confidant, Sardar Angre. The copies circulated had the names of two witnesses, Prema Vasudevan and A. Janakiraman. Angre and swadeshi ideologue S. Gurumurthy were mentioned as executors. The statement said copies of the will had been sent in sealed envelopes to her solicitors in London, Lovell, White and King, and two others.

Her will read like a political chargesheet: 'He [Madhavrao] just did not stop with merely surrendering to his political masters, but actually became their tool in order to harass me and my supporters. He foisted, by his power and money, false criminal cases on my loyal friends and relations merely because they were loyal to me, locked me out of my own house, got my private living apartments raided by the help of the police and his own staff in my absence under the allegation of theft, with the sole objective of humiliating me, his mother.'

But Madhavrao did perform his mother's last rites. When

asked, Sardar Angre said: 'This was not in my hands. It [the will] came after the cremation.' Apparently, the Rajmata had told Angre's wife to hand over the envelope to him after her death. But the family retainer came to know of his designation as one of the executors only after he opened the envelope following the cremation. Asked why the envelope was not opened immediately after the Rajmata's death, as she had desired, Angre said: 'It's never done. It is against human conduct. I got a copy of the will in my hands only after the cremation.'

'Apart from the unalloyed support I received from Sardar S.C. Angre in my public life, as a person I am greatly indebted to him for his unquestioned loyalty to me and to my family at all critical and testing times and the ease and smile with which he suffered all insinuations and hostilities of my own son who (afraid to hit me although willing to) made him and his family special target and used all his official and muscle power to harass and persecute this most loyal man of the Scindia Royalty,' her will read.

In her will, the Rajmata had nominated Angre as a trustee of the Rajmata Vijaya Raje Scindia Trust, which also included her daughters Usha Raje, Vasundhara Raje and Yashodhara Raje, S. Gurumurthy, the late N.K. Shejwalkar, a former Lok Sabha MP from Madhya Pradesh, and Appa Ghatate, a close friend of the then prime minister, A.B. Vajpayee. The Rajmata's three daughters found fleeting mention in her will and inherited only a part of her jewellery. Unlike Madhavrao, Vasundhara and Yashodhara were of the same political persuasion as their mother.

Madhavrao contested this will and produced another one, reportedly written in February 1999 by the Rajmata, claiming it to be legally validated as compared to the 1985 will flaunted by Angre.

Eight months later, Madhavrao died in an air crash, bringing a pause in the Scindia versus Scindia saga. Vasundhara and Yashodhara became more accommodating towards their nephew

Jyotiraditya, Madhavrao's son, who continued to fight legal battles with them.

Angre died in March 2008, leaving behind a son, a house in Delhi, another on the Scindias' Gwalior estate, a flat in Mumbai, a mango plantation, a stud farm and ancestral property near Indore.

Jyotiraditya's subsequent move to join the BJP in March 2020 brought the Scindias on the same side of the political spectrum. The 'reunion' rekindled the BJP's affection for the Scindias.

Prime Minister Modi paid tribute to the Rajmata in September 2020 during one of his *Mann Ki Baat* programmes, sharing an anecdote from the 1990s that gave an insight into her maternal side. Modi, in his radio address, recalled a rally that the Rajmata had participated in. The rally, from Kanyakumari to Kashmir, had been organized by Murli Manohar Joshi and, as Modi narrates, they had reached Shivpuri late in the night, around 2 a.m. The prime minister said that he was startled to see the Rajmata standing outside his door with a glass of hot turmeric milk. He later found out that she had done this for everyone in the yatra, Modi added. 'She hailed from a Royal Family and devoted herself to public service. She was blessed with compassion,' the Prime Minister's Office added in a tweet. As a mark of respect, Modi released a commemorative 100-rupee coin in the Rajmata's honour on 12 October 2020, celebrating her birth centenary.

Hours after Jyotiraditya joined the BJP in March 2020, Yashodhara tweeted crediting the Rajmata for Jyotiraditya's 'bold decision' to switch sides. 'Rajmata's blood took the decision in the national interest; a new country will be formed; every distance is now removed,' she said in her tweet.

Rajmata's prodigal son Madhavrao had always remained reluctant to switch sides or unite the house of scindias. His reluctance was overturned by the grandson's indulgence. Jyotiraditya's stride towards the BJP was also a step towards fulfilling his grandmother's dream of uniting the House of Scindia on one saffron platform. But there are political commentators like Priya Sahgal who viewed Jyotiraditya's actions more like a bridge than a breach. For Priya, both the bridge and the breach were interlinked (the former as a means across what is impassable otherwise, the latter as an opening allowing passage through those walls built by ideology, political practices, religion, and cultural and economic values).

THREE

Madhavrao Scindia: In Retrospection

Madhavrao Scindia, like Sardar Vallabhbhai Patel and Pranab Mukherjee, was probably one of the best prime ministers India never had. His rise was cruelly cut short by fate – at the same time as when the Congress was on the trail of a comeback.

He died in a tragic plane crash on 30 September 2001, just eight months after the death of his mother, Vijaya Raje Scindia. But while the ailing Rajmata was in her eighties and had the satisfaction of seeing her party, the BJP, firmly on the seat of power, Madhavrao was just fifty-six, in the prime of his political life.

Less than three years later, in 2004, a Congress-led coalition would come to power at the Centre and remain at the helm for the next ten years. '...Madhavrao Scindia would have been Prime Minister if he had lived,' K. Natwar Singh, eighty-nine, diplomat turned politician, insists even today. In other words, according to Singh, Madhavrao would have been Sonia Gandhi's first choice as prime minister in the United Progressive Alliance (UPA) government instead of Dr. Manmohan Singh.[1]

While that will always remain in the realm of conjecture,

there is little doubt that within the Congress, Madhavrao was much more popular as a leader than Manmohan Singh, who is by nature a reticent man. A measure of Madhavrao's popularity can be estimated from the fact that he would win every Congress Working Committee election he contested by a huge margin, without even being part of the 'informal panel' that would be formed as a quid pro quo to garner votes from delegates.

He also shared a unique understanding with Sonia Gandhi. In private conversations, Madhavrao was perhaps alone in a league of Congress leaders addressing politician Sonia on a first name basis. He would however, address her as 'Sonia ji' in the presence of others and at formal party forums. Sonia used to address him as Madhav and often invited him for a cup of tea or coffee at a rather short notice too. They had known each other from the time of her arrival in India and her marriage to Rajiv Gandhi in 1968.

Madhavrao was aware of the Italian-born party president's inner conflict on opting for the 'big chair' of the country's prime ministership whenever such a situation may come to pass. It was not that Sonia had discussed this hypothetical scenario with him, but political events in 1999 had given Madhavrao an insight into the matter. It was at this time that the BJP-led National Democratic Alliance (NDA) regime failed a no-confidence motion by a single vote and an attempt – an unsuccessful one – was made by the opposition to stitch together an alternative coalition. Sonia Gandhi was to be the leader of this alternative, but it was at this time that Madhavrao was able to assess that she was in search of a person who could be trusted with the prime ministership.[2]

And Madhavrao had the credentials to aspire for the job. Apart from his own comfort level with Sonia, he had also amassed a huge following among the great Indian middle classes through his previous stints as minister for railways, civil aviation and human resource development (HRD).

'People's Maharaja'

This is not to say that Madhavrao was not without his detractors. M.L. Fotedar, a Nehru-Gandhi family retainer, who had served both Indira and Rajiv Gandhi as a political aide, gives his readers a glimpse of his antipathy towards Madhavrao in his autobiography, *Chinar Leaves*, where he claimed that a few days before her assassination on 31 October 1984, Indira had summoned him, Rajiv (who was All India Congress Committee [AICC] general secretary then) and Arun Nehru, a member of the Nehru–Gandhi family. 'During the course of conversation regarding parliamentary elections, she categorically told her son two things he should never do in future,' Fotedar writes, adding, 'she said: Do not ever bring Teji's son – Amitabh Bachchan – into electoral politics and do not induct Madhavrao Scindia in your cabinet if you ever become the prime minister.' Fotedar, the so-called Indira loyalist, did not bother to substantiate or offer any evidence to back up his claims. However, it seems Indira's advice did not stop Madhavrao from becoming a minister in Rajiv Gandhi's cabinet in 1984. As the minister of railways under Rajiv Gandhi, Madhavrao became a hero of sorts for the growing Indian middle classes by introducing fast and comfortable trains, such as the Shatabdi Express between Delhi and many state capitals, and for installing a computerized reservation system that reduced the serpentine queues at ticket counters.[3]

Madhavrao had been in the reckoning for the top job when Rajiv Gandhi was assassinated in Sriperumbudur on 21 May 1991. There were many who, in that hour of grief, had felt that Madhavrao would carry forward the young Rajiv's vision and legacy. The buzz around Madhavrao's candidature as Rajiv's possible successor led to a chain reaction. Rajesh Pilot, a former air force squadron leader, also joined the fray, projecting himself as a young leader best suited to step into Rajiv's shoes. But unlike Madhavrao, Arjun Singh or Sharad Pawar (others in the running), Pilot had no locus standi in terms of experience in the organization. Sonia was too shell-shocked to intervene in party wrangling and the old guard manipulated the Congress Working Committee and other decision-making bodies to bring in at the helm a rather listless Narasimha Rao, who, prior to the 1991 general election, had in fact already opted out of active politics and retired. Rao was the most unlikeliest of candidates but it was on him that the mantle of leadership would fall.

After Rao had officially taken over as the prime minister in June 1991, he inducted Madhavrao into his cabinet as civil aviation minister. Within a year, the accountability-conscious Madhavrao resigned, when an aircraft, leased from Uzbekistan Airways during a domestic pilots' strike, crash-landed – thankfully without loss of life – at Delhi airport. Rao subsequently inducted him into the cabinet again in 1995 as the HRD minister, as successor to Arjun Singh, who had at that time quit the Congress to form a breakaway outfit.

Such was Madhavrao's popularity at this time that his personal staff at Shastri Bhawan, New Delhi, would regularly receive letters and gifts such as bottles of perfume, flowers and handkerchiefs – all addressed to the 'People's Maharaja'. A file that documented these items was marked 'Confidential' and shown to the minister, who made it a point to thank every sender.

This was also the period when the ties strengthened between Madhavrao and Sonia Gandhi, who was already wary of Rao and was looking for a political role. Madhavrao went out of the way to help Sonia continue as the head of the Indira Gandhi National Centre for the Arts (IGNCA), the country's premier and wealthiest cultural institution. It was Madhavrao's machinations that Sonia was made life trustee of the IGNCA.

According to the original deed of 19 March 1987, the IGNCA's trustees were to have ten-year terms. The founder trustees were Rajiv Gandhi, R. Venkataraman, P.V. Narasimha Rao, Pupul Jayakar, H.Y. Sharada Prasad and Dr. Kapila Vatsyayan. Rajiv headed the trust, which was given 23 acres of prime land in New Delhi's central vista area (near the India Gate lawns). Rajiv had continued to head the IGNCA even when he ceased to be the prime minister in 1989. In May 1995, Madhavrao, as the HRD minister, introduced amendments to the IGNCA's original deed without getting the cabinet's approval. Vatsyayan, a former secretary-level officer in the ministry and the director of the Centre, wrote in the agenda papers that 'the minutes of this meeting have been approved by Sonia Gandhi, President of the IGNCA Trust'. Significantly, the IGNCA trust was converted from a public to a private body and the rights of the president of India as 'Visitor' to review the functioning of the Centre were abrogated. Sonia Gandhi, who had stepped in to head the IGNCA in 1991, weeks after Rajiv's assassination, was made the trust's president for life, and the entire original deed was subjected to fundamental alterations. Under the new system, the government had no control over the trust any more even though huge amount of public money and government resources were used. According to those familiar with government rules and procedures, this was highly abnormal and unusual.

This was also a tumultuous time for Narasimha Rao, when he was waging battles on several fronts. Apart from the fallout of the Babri demolition and subsequent communal tensions and riots, his government was facing serious allegations of corruption, including accusations of engineering a political defection to survive a no-confidence motion in the Lok Sabha.

Congress veterans such as Arjun Singh, Narain Dutt Tiwari, Sheila Dikshit and a number of other senior leaders had left the party that same month to float a breakaway group, the All India Indira Congress (Tiwari). Arjun Singh and the other rebels were counting heavily on Sonia Gandhi's support but she failed to show up at Talkatora Stadium on 19 May 1995, giving Narasimha Rao sort of new a lease of life.

Madhavrao approved the IGNCA deed without consulting the cabinet or the departments concerned, thinking that the move would please Sonia. But when the Vajpayee government took over, HRD minister Murli Manohar Joshi forced Sonia to step down as the trust's life-president, causing her acute embarrassment.

Madhavrao remained popular even after he had fallen out with the then Congress president and outgoing prime minister P.V. Narasimha Rao over the Hawala scandal (discussed later in the chapter). Subsequently, during the 1996 elections, he would be called upon by many contestants to campaign for them. One of them was Natwar Singh, who was contesting from Bharatpur, Rajasthan, as a nominee of the breakaway faction All India Indira Congress (Tiwari). When Madhavrao went to Bharatpur to campaign for him, Natwar said while addressing a gathering: 'Maharaj, when you become the Prime Minister of the country, please remember to avail my services as your foreign minister.' The entire gathering burst into laughter.

Madhavrao himself contested as an independent candidate from Gwalior that same year. P. Chidambaram, who was in the breakaway party the Tamil Maanila Congress, led by G.K. Moopanar, campaigned for Madhavrao, projecting him as a 'future prime minister'.

But eight years later, in 2004, when the Congress's chance came to form the government, Madhavrao was no more, and Sonia chose to bestow the prime ministership on Manmohan Singh. In fact, Sonia had started to give more responsibilities to Singh since September 2001, since Madhavrao's untimely demise. Singh and Gandhi turned out to be a well-functioning team. Both shared some common traits: they were reticent, uncomfortable with too much media attention and had a strong dislike for the culture of flattery and false promises. However, one can conjecture that this understanding might not have had a chance to develop had Madhavrao been around.

Conscientious Politician

For Madhavrao, probity in public life was paramount. But just before the 1996 general election, he became a victim of a political plot that forced him to quit the Congress and opt for a brief spell of being without a political party's backing. Madhavrao was trying to marginalize Arjun Singh in Madhya Pradesh – his as well as the rebel leader's home state – when he found himself embroiled in the Jain hawala scandal. The Hawala case was based on diary entries made by two Jain brothers who hailed from Madhya Pradesh and were alleged to have bribed several top politicians in return for favours. The diary entries carried the names of these leaders and the amounts, running into several lakhs of rupees, paid to them. The Hawala probe sent shock waves across party lines. It was the first time in the history of India that so many political leaders had been booked under the Prevention of Corruption Act, 1988.

Madhavrao was the first to resign under the burden of this scandal. Vir Sanghvi, a personal friend of Madhavrao, says a sense of 'honour' was the most important thing for the Gwalior royal, above everything else. 'He was always worried about being misrepresented, especially during the Emergency and the Hawala scandal. His honour was most important to him,' said Sanghvi, a former editor of the *Hindustan Times*. Two other union ministers, V.C. Shukla and Balram Jakhar; two governors, Motilal Vora and Shiv Shankar; and the leader of the opposition, L.K. Advani, resigned too.[4]

Although badly affected, Madhavrao shunned Rao's emissaries who requested him to field his wife, Madhavi Raje, to contest the polls as his proxy just as Kamal Nath's wife, Alka, had contested from Chhindwara. Madhavrao bluntly refused the offer; Madhavi Raje, too, was totally averse to the idea.

In fact, following the scandal, Madhavrao refused to have anything to do with Rao, who, according to him, had acted like a cunning Machiavellian politician. In happier times, Rao was known to often tell Madhavrao that he saw him as his successor post 1996, once Rao stepped down from active political life. In the sympathetic biography titled *Madhavrao Scindia: A Life*,[5] noted journalists Vir Sanghvi and Namita Bhandare claimed that Prime Minister Rao had once telephoned Madhavrao to assure him that he regarded him as his successor. This was the time when Madhavrao had resigned as civil aviation and tourism minister, owning moral responsibility for the plane mishap mentioned earlier. 'Rao called Scindia one day out of the blue to assure him that he regarded him as his successor. He was getting on, he said he certainly had no interest in the second term. After Rao, the field was open for such leaders as Scindia.' Sanghvi and Bhandare, however, insist in their work that despite such assurances, Rao saw Madhavrao as a potential threat to his future political career from the time he became prime minister in 1991.

After December 1995, when the Hawala case started hitting headlines, Madhavrao had reportedly called on the prime minister twice, asking him about the rumours relating to his alleged involvement. At one point Rao is said to have told him, 'The case against you is built on foundations of sand, Madhavraoji.'[6] Years later, Margaret Alva, in her memoir, *Courage and Commitment*,[7] confirmed that it was Rao himself who had ordered the Hawala probe to 'fix' the careers of many leaders cutting across parties. 'Many of those chargesheeted were denied tickets in the 1996 elections. The Hawala case dragged on – despite a change of governments. On April 8, 1997, the Delhi High Court Judge, Mohammad Shamim, acquitted Madhavrao Scindia, L.K. Advani and V.C. Shukla, saying that there was no clinching evidence – only coded entries in private dairies that proved no trail of payments. After this, there was one common intent and resolve across all parties – to bury the Jain Hawala case.'

Madhavrao formed the Madhya Pradesh Vikas Party in 1996, as a part of the United Front coalition, revolting against Rao for denying him a seat to contest on the grounds that he had been implicated in the Hawala case. He won from Gwalior, as an independent, by a margin of 223,000 votes. Madhavrao returned to the Congress in November 1996 even though the Deve Gowda-led United Front government at that time was keen to have him as a senior minister. When Madhavrao returned to the Congress fold, he received a warm welcome: the then AICC chief, Sitaram Kesri, was there to receive him at the portico of 24 Akbar Road. Kesri addressed the press conference and described his ties with Madhavrao as that of Ram and Lakshman. When laddoos were brought in, Kesri could not resist and planted a kiss on a rather sheepish Madhavrao.

Madhavrao relished a sort of a victory when Narasimha Rao was subsequently booked in the Lakhubhai Pathak cheating case. Strolling in the front lawn of his Safdarjung Road residence, Madhavrao appeared to be introspective. He looked up at the sky and mumbled something like: 'There's a natural law of karma that vindictive people, who go out of their way to hurt others, will end up broke and alone....'

Although Madhavrao was eventually acquitted in the Hawala case, the controversy had a tremendous bearing on his career. The country's politics moved on, paving the way for Vajpayee, a man Madhavrao had defeated in 1984 at Gwalior, to become prime minister. Madhavrao, one of the most senior and promising faces of the Congress – a leader who never lost an election in his life, a record unblemished till the end – became yesterday's man.

Madhavrao versus Vajpayee

The 1984 Lok Sabha contest between Madhavrao Scindia and

A.B. Vajpayee in Gwalior, home turf for both, was a titanic battle – one of the most memorable and closely watched elections in the history of independent India. The elections had been advanced in the wake of Indira Gandhi's assassination. The opposition had sensed an opportunity to edge out the Congress, and leaders, including Vajpayee, had calculated that sympathy over the prime minister's assassination would soon die down. They also viewed Indira's successor Rajiv Gandhi as a bit of novice and a greenhorn.

Vajpayee decided to contest from Gwalior – the city of his birth and a seat he had previously won in 1971. He was counting heavily on support from Rajmata Scindia. Vajpayee had old association with the Scindia family as his father had served the state. Vajpayee, throughout his life, kept expressing a sense of gratitude over the generous grants to fund his education under Jiwajirao Scindia's rule.

Rajiv Gandhi, on the other hand, was hot on his heels. His advisor, Arun Nehru, came up with an idea to pit young and dashing faces against established opposition faces. Kept as a closely guarded secret till the last date of nomination, the Congress fielded Madhavrao against Vajpayee, actor Amitabh Bachchan against Hemvati Nandan Bahugana, and actor Sunil Dutt against veteran lawyer Ram Jethmalani in other key constituencies.

When Rajiv Gandhi confided in Madhavrao about his plan, the former maharaja of Gwalior was immediately on board. He reportedly told Rajiv that if Vajpayee gets wind of this strategy, the BJP leader would possibly shift to another constituency. This was the time when Madhavrao's relationship with mother Rajmata was at an all-time low. Perhaps Madhavrao wanted to prove a point to the Queen Mother by putting to test which way the voters in Gwalior would sway; he possibly hoped that the people would choose Scindia over Vajpayee.

As part of Rajiv Gandhi's strategy, Madhavrao first filed his nomination from Guna, which was widely expected and anticipated. From the Congress side, Vidya Razdan, a political lightweight, was fielded as a dummy against Vajpayee. However, on the last date for filing nominations, an hour and a half before the deadline for filing nominations lapsed, Madhavrao dramatically turned up in the office of the returning officer in Gwalior and filed his papers. Vajpayee simply had no time to react. While Vajpayee was stunned, Rajmata, for the first time, decided to campaign against a Scindia and her son. As history is witness, her campaigning was inconsequential. Vajpayee lost Gwalior by 175,000 votes. He was so badly stung by the defeat that he did not return to the city of his birth for political validation ever again. To Vajpayee's credit, he did not hold his 1984 Gwalior defeat against anyone, including Madhavrao. The poet seemed sure that no defeat could deny him what was his destiny: to become prime minister one day.

Thus, it was ironical that at a time when Vajpayee became prime minister (though for a mere thirteen days) in 1996, Madhavrao had to leave the Congress in a huff and, till his death, harboured a profound dislike for Narasimha Rao.

Deputy Leader in House

Despite his royal inheritance, Madhavrao had taken to the grime of electoral politics with ease, while retaining the mystique of his distinct identity. Madhavrao was often asked if he would become the prime minister of India. His response would always be: 'I am not manipulative enough.' This lack of 'killer instinct', however, did not come in the way of his becoming one of the most sought-after leaders of the Congress. Between 1996 and 2001, when the party was out of power at the Centre, Madhavrao emerged as the most modern, progressive and dynamic face of the party; a leader who possessed the qualities that could potentially propel it out of its moribund state.[8]

In March 1998, Sonia Gandhi staged a coup of sorts to

dethrone Sitaram Kesri from the AICC. It was then that Madhavrao became her close adviser and troubleshooter. However, a bit of a surprise was in store for Madhavrao when Sonia herself became leader of the Congress Party in Parliament without being a parliamentarian in 1998 through an extraordinary amendment in the party constitution. She also appointed Sharad Pawar as the leader of opposition in 1998 much to the disappointment of Madhavrao who had fancied himself as a contender. He, however, concealed his sense of disappointment. This sequence of event showed how Sonia became a politician among politicians, surprising even those who considered themselves close to her. A year later, when Sonia became MP from Amethi, she herself took the job of the leader of the opposition. Consequently, Pawar revolted against her on grounds of her foreign origins. She fell back on Madhavrao and appointed him as deputy leader of the Congress in the Lok Sabha.

Pawar formed the breakaway Nationalist Congress Party (NCP) in Maharashtra, where it fought a bitter assembly election against the Congress in September–October 1999. However, the voters threw up a fractured mandate in which neither the Congress nor the NCP independently had enough seats to keep the coalition of the BJP and Shiv Sena at bay; there was no other way but for Congress and NCP to join hands. As the AICC's point man for Maharashtra, Madhavrao had a major role to play in this situation. He deftly convinced Sonia Gandhi and reached out to Pawar to form a coalition government in the state. This was a rare feat in real-politick as the two leaders – Sonia Gandhi and Sharad Pawar – had to keep aside their personal disagreements and forget their past humiliation. As if practising the dictum 'no one ever choked to death swallowing his pride', Gandhi and Pawar maintained functional ties in Maharashtra and even came together later when the UPA government at the centre was formed under Dr. Manmohan Singh.

By 1999, Sonia was elected to the Lok Sabha and took on the role of the leader of the opposition herself. With Pawar out of the fray and virtually nobody else remaining as a claimant, Sonia made Madhavrao the deputy leader of the party in the Lok Sabha, which lacked political gravitas and any official recognition.[9] Madhavrao would follow Sonia like a shadow inside the parliament. Shy, reticent, not very comfortable in speaking Hindi at public forums, Sonia often had to rely on 'friend Madhavrao' to assist her in discharging her parliamentary responsibilities.

Madhavrao kept helping Sonia reach out to many other opposition leaders. As deputy leader of the Congress in the Lok Sabha, Madhavrao would handle day-to-day party affairs, both inside and outside the parliament. He also frequently represented the Congress at all-party meetings and those of the business advisory committee when parliament was in session. All this was bringing him into closer contact with the party cadre and a bigger role beckoned. But alas that was not to be.

In some of the most significant debates in Parliament during 1998–2001, it was Madhavrao and not Sonia who led the charge against the Vajpayee government. His fluency in both Hindi and English and skill in articulating a point often rendered the ruling party members' benches speechless, while his effective floor coordination strategy in the Lok Sabha earned him the admiration of politicians across parties.

Madhavrao was among the astute few to realize that the BJP's brand of Hindutva politics was gaining ground in the country, and he also understood that the Congress would not be able to counter this by acting alone. He, therefore, consciously started coordinating strategies with the other opposition parties, especially the Left. His impeccable secular credentials, which had even led to strained relations with his own mother and sisters, had earned him the respect of the Left parties.[10]

Democratic pluralism was a matter of faith with him and his belief in the principle of secularism went far beyond the clichés that are often the currency of political exchange. Madhavrao was visibly moved when he presented a report to Sonia Gandhi on the brutal murder of Australian missionary Graham Staines and his two young children in Manoharpur, Odisha (Orissa then), on 23 January 1999. Madhavrao was the AICC general secretary looking after the state when the incident occurred and he flew to Odisha to prepare a detailed report. Timothy, six, Philip, ten, and their father, Staines, fifty-seven, were burnt alive in their station wagon by a mob on the rumoured suspicion that the missionary was forcing tribals to convert to Christianity. The national outrage over the murders, however, failed to jolt the Vajpayee-led union government out of its slumber. Vajpayee commented that his head hung in shame but he failed to act against the extremists who had committed the crime in the name of Hindutva. Under Congress pressure, the Vajpayee government ordered a judicial probe but attacks on Christians in Odisha, Madhya Pradesh and Gujarat continued. To salvage his battered image, Vajpayee announced a fast for communal harmony on 30 January that year, on the death anniversary of Mahatma Gandhi.

Unfortunately, Madhavrao's end came too soon after this. In 2009, while speaking at a book release in New Delhi, Sonia lavished praised on the late Madhavrao. 'Adversity brings out the best in people, and at a time when we seemed confident in public but inwardly wondered if we could achieve the impossible... that's when we met Madhavrao,' she said. 'What impressed me was that he never gave up or took the easy way out. His answers were straight and advice always good. When I came to Parliament for the first time, he stood by as a deputy leader, sharing a great deal of the burden.'[11]

Man of Many Interests

Madhavrao was not just a well-loved Congress leader but wore many other hats. Even as a full-time politician, Madhavrao would take time off for a round of golf or don a pair of flannels to play cricket, his greatest passion. He would also captain his side in the friendly cricket matches played by MPs in Delhi. As president of the Madhya Pradesh Cricket Board and the Board of Control for Cricket in India (BCCI), he did much to improve the status of the game.

Madhavrao headed the BCCI in 1990. The presidential contest, fought in Kolkata (Calcutta then), had more to do with politics than sports. Madhavrao was pitted against the incumbent, B.N. Dutt, who enjoyed the backing of businessman and cricket administrator, Jagmohan Dalmiya. In order to checkmate Dutt and Dalmiya, Madhavrao made politician Amar Singh his strategist.[12] The outcome of the contest went in his favour, 16 votes to 15, even though Dutt chose to exercise his prerogative to vote for himself. According to Ali Bacher, a South African cricket administrator, Madhavrao's back-channel diplomacy in organizing the 1996 World Cup, jointly hosted by India, Pakistan and Sri Lanka, had made him a leading contender to take over as the next president of the International Cricket Council.

Madhavrao's passion for cricket began at an early age. Encouraged by his schoolteacher and coach Sharief Ahmed, Madhavrao had set up a palace cricket team that played against various sides. Ahmed felt that cricket could teach the young Madhavrao lessons on how to lead a team, on and off the field, and accept victory and defeat in everyday life.

Madhavrao's passion for cricket even came in way for his imperial lifestyle sometimes. In Gwalior, once a young lad shouted at him for a cheeky single saying, 'Chal, chal [run, run]'. The brusque address had almost Madhavrao run himself out.

After the match, the lad went up to him apologizing, 'Maharaj, I am sorry I couldn't address you as shrimant or maharaj in the heat of the moment!' Madhavrao laughed it off.[13]

Senior Congress leader Ahmed Patel used to recall how he himself got bowled out, short of a century, just because Madhavrao wanted the strike. This had happened in winter afternoon of 1980–1981 when a friendly cricket match among parliamentarians was on. Patel, a young Congress MP from Gujarat, was batting with flourish when Madhavrao walked in to join him at the other end.

The Print journalist D.K. Singh recounted while writing Patel's obituary: 'Patel was on a roll, nearing the century mark, leaving Scindia at the non-striker's end most of the time. Frustrated, the scion of the erstwhile royal family of Gwalior walked up to him and said, "You have done your part. You can let others take it from here."' Patel, second time Lok Sabha MP from Bharuch, Gujarat, got himself bowled, short of a century. D.K. Singh remembered impatiently asking Patel why he did not complete the century and walked out, and Patel's response, 'Arre, how could I? He was Madhavrao Scindia and I was a nobody in Delhi.'[14]

There were also stories that bowlers often bowled slowly and inaccurately when Madhavrao was batting as part of MPs Eleven or for the Railways when he was a minister. To be fair to him, Madhavrao was often not aware of the flattery in this form as he took cricket, particularly batting, rather seriously, always relishing a good score with pride and satisfaction.

Madhavrao loved playing pranks. Once, several notable cricketers, including Mansoor Ali Khan Pataudi, a family friend, had been invited to Gwalior to play an exhibition match. On a 'rest' day, Madhavrao decided to take Pataudi, Sunil Gavaskar, Erapalli Prasanna, Gundappa Viswanath and a few others to Shivpuri for a shikar trip (yes, hunting was permitted then). At midnight, when the players had gone to bed, they heard gunshots and found themselves surrounded by 'dacoits' who said they would 'kidnap' them. All the members of the party were asked to get inside jeeps and hand over their belongings. Viswanath and Prasanna were in particular petrified and started howling, saying they were part of the Indian Test cricket team and the country needed them. The 'dacoits', however, pretended they had never heard of cricket. The drama went a bit too far and the guests were not amused when they were told that the 'dacoits' were, in fact, Madhavrao's employees and that the whole incident had been staged.

However, despite such varied and light-hearted interests, many of Madhavrao's contemporaries cutting across the party lines felt the former maharaja of Gwalior was not a 'frivolous' or carefree sort of politician. 'He gave an impression of being man of many interests but his heart was in politics and he was extremely ambitious too. After 1998–1999, he had sensed that prime minister's chair was within his sight. Madhavrao was craftily working towards it,' a close associate of Madhavrao said while requesting anonymity. Interestingly, around 1998–2001 Madhavrao started resenting Manmohan Singh's proximity to Sonia and viewed the economist as some sort of a challenger. While like rest of his Congress colleagues, Madhavrao had regard for Singh's sense of decency and credentials as an economist, he always considered Manmohan Singh as Narasimha Rao's man. Since Rao was responsible for setting up many political hurdles posed before Madhavrao, he considered Singh to belong to the hostile camp. At another level, the senior Congress leader had reportedly been alarmed by a buzz that Manmohan Singh was Sonia Gandhi' s choice to be the prime minister in future.

Madhavrao was not off the mark. A few years later (by the time Madhavrao was long gone), former union secretary, R.D. Pradhan, Sonia Gandhi's close aide, head of the AICC's coordination department, and former union home secretary, corroborated Madhavrao's hunch in his book, *My Years with Rajiv and Sonia*.[15] Giving an account of the events of 1999 – when the then president, K.R. Narayanan, had invited Sonia to explore the possibilities of forming an alternative government after the fall of the Vajpayee regime – Pradhan wrote that Sonia had informed him and Fotedar about her decision to not accept the prime minister's post shortly before her meeting with the president in April. 'She had told me even then that she had in mind the name of Manmohan Singh,' Pradhan wrote. He observed that what happened in 2004 (Sonia Gandhi's act of renunciation of the prime minister-ship) was consistent with her stand in 1999.

Fate Intervenes

Madhavrao's death came in the midst of the Congress's attempts to find its feet in Uttar Pradesh through its *parivartan* yatras (campaign seeking change of government in Uttar Pradesh). He was to be the star attraction at one such rally in Kanpur. But he never made it. Around 1.30 p.m. on 30 September 2001, the Cessna C-90 – supposed to be one of the safest 'all-weather' small planes – carrying Madhavrao, lost contact with the Lucknow air traffic control (ATC). Because of bad weather, the pilot, Ray Gautam, had asked the ATC for 'direction'. That was the last contact. The ten-seater aircraft crashed soon after in a waterlogged field in Motta village in Mainpuri, 160 km from Kanpur. Apart from Gautam, six others were accompanying Madhavrao: his personal secretary Rupinder Singh aka Rippy; co-pilot Ritu Mallik; *Indian Express* journalist Sanjiv Sinha; *Aaj Tak* correspondent Ranjan Jha; cameraman Gopal Singh Bisht; and Anju Sharma of the *Hindustan Times*. There were no survivors.[16]

The bodies were taken to Agra by road and then flown to New Delhi by a special air force plane. Union Minister Arun Jaitley accompanied the bodies. Prime Minister Vajpayee wrote in the condolence book: 'Lightning has fallen. Can fate be so cruel. My salute.'

Months after the fatal air crash, the *Hindustan Times* accessed a secret report that contained the results of the investigation the Directorate General of Civil Aviation (DGCA) had conducted into the crash. The report raised several crucial questions relating to weather conditions, pilot error and the age of the aircraft. There were many questions as the Cessna C-90 did not have a black box since aircraft below a certain weight don't require black boxes on board. Aviation experts have also commented on the behaviour of the pilot, Captain Gautam. According to the ATC at Lucknow, Captain Gautam had requested permission to deviate 10 miles because of bad weather on that fateful afternoon. Eyewitnesses recalled it was raining heavily and there was a strong wind too. Satellite pictures also confirmed the weather conditions. The most likely cause of the crash was sudden engine failure. A senior official was quoted as saying, 'If that happens, you get something like six seconds before the situation blows up in your face.' What was most remarkable, according to the investigation, was that the pilot did not use any emergency channel, the normal operational procedure, to transmit a distress signal. Had the channel been used, all overflying aircraft and control towers in Agra, Kanpur and Lucknow would have picked up the message.

Did Madhavrao have any premonition of his death? It seems unlikely. However, days before his death, Madhavrao had reportedly planned for his son, Jyotiraditya, a grand civic reception that was to have taken place on 6 October 2001. Local BJP leaders, however, saw in it a plan to formally launch his son into politics. Dr. H.M. Purohit, a BJP activist in the Gwalior Municipal Corporation, claims that when Jyotiraditya returned with an MBA degree from Stanford, Madhavrao had got in touch with the local organizers close to the Congress to arrange a public felicitation for his son. 'What is so great about getting an MBA degree and that too when you are 30 years old? This was done just to create an atmosphere for Jyotiraditya to contest from

Gwalior,' Purohit recalls having commented in an conversation with the author.

But this event would never come to pass. Posters and banners for a marathon that was to have been organized as part of Jyotiraditya's civic reception were plastered all over Gwalior, along the route that Madhavrao's cortege took into the town on 2 October 2001. Former union minister, Dr. Karan Singh, who had seen the Scindias from close quarters, said that Jyotiraditya's political choice at that time was limited to the Congress. 'Jyotiraditya was not close to his grandmother or his aunts. As a result, the BJP as a political choice did not exist,' Karan Singh told Sanghvi, pointing out that Madhavrao perhaps wanted his son to deny any political space to his sister Yashodhara Raje who had joined the BJP.

~

On 10 March 1945, when Madhavrao was born in Bombay, the infant had a title that read, 'Ali Jah, Umdat ul Umrah, Hisam-us saltanat, Mukhtar ul Mulk, Azim ul Iqtedar, Rafi-us Shan Wala Shukoh, Muhtashim-i-Dauran, Maharajadhiraja Maharaja Madhavrao Scindia Bahadur, Shrinath, Mansur-i-Zaman, Fidvi-I-Hazrat-i-Malikha-Muzzam-i-Rafi-ud-Darjah-i-inglistan, Maharaja Scindia of Gwalior'. He was born at Bikaner House, a prime property on Bombay's Nepean Sea Road belonging to the maharaja of Bikaner.

The infant was named after his illustrious grandfather Madhav Rao (October 1876–June 1925), though his name was spelt as Madho Rao Scindia by aunt Asha Devi Phalke, in keeping with the Scindia family tradition of giving the maharaja's sister the honour of naming the newborn prince. Madhavrao was the third child of Jiwajirao and Vijaya Raje; Padma Raje and Usha Raje were his elder sisters while Vasundhara and Yashodhara were younger siblings.

The celebrations lasted over three months. When the child was born in Bombay, each and every person in the employ of the Scindia empire got a promotion while 21 guns blazed, signalling the arrival of the crown prince. Prisoners booked for minor crimes were set free.

Not to be left behind, A.B. Vajpayee, a lesser-known bard of Gwalior then, also rejoiced when sweets were freely distributed among one and all across the Scindia empire.

Three months later, a special train with elaborate saloons chugged into Gwalior station, carrying hundreds of personal attendants, porters, chefs, tailors, musicians, astrologers, gynaecologists, nurses, horse grooms and even dogs. A cynic had then described the arrival of the royal entourage as 'George's Circus'.[17] Another round of elaborate celebrations followed. This time, the focus was more on private dinners and lunches.

By the time Madhavrao was two-and-a-half years old, India had become independent. As mentioned earlier, Jiwajirao Maharaj was a pragmatic man and wasted no time in supporting a free and united India. In fact, as early as December 1946, Gwalior state had invited V.P. Menon, secretary in the ministry of states, to sign the Instrument of Accession, a legal document which gave the princely states certain privileges and rights.

Vijaya Raje and Jiwajirao hired an American nanny, Norma Mackay, soon to be replaced by Nurse Beatrice Barbara Castellino, to attend to Madhavrao. The maharaja and maharani of Gwalior were, however, clear about the grooming of the crown prince – Marathi was to be treated as the first language for their son and he was to be groomed like a 'normal' child, without much pampering, favours and luxuries. For example, it was only when foreign dignitaries visited Gwalior that Madhavrao would enjoy elephant rides. The young prince did most things that children his age did. Thus, when Madhavrao's eldest sister staged a play, *Cinderella*, inside Usha Kiran Palace, Madhavrao played the role of a coachman.[18]

Madhavrao's grandfather, with whom he shared his name, had established the Scindia School (originally Sardars' School) in Gwalior in 1897. That was a time of turmoil for the Indian education system as the one introduced by Thomas Babington Macaulay, with English as the medium of instruction, was displacing the traditional pathshalas, madrasas and *gurukuls*. Madhav Rao I wished to combine the best of ancient Indian learning with modernity so that every 'Scindian' evolved into a leader with understanding, intelligence, sensitivity and an inclusive attitude. Oxfordian F.G. Pearce had joined Scindia School with a brief to shape it, based on a healthy Indian background.

By the time Madhavrao joined, it was a nationalistic boarding school situated inside the Gwalior fort, and thus, it offered a near perfect setting for him. But there was a problem. A Scindia crown prince could not have been treated just like another student of Scindia School. But the instructions from Jiwajirao were clear: Madhavrao would be given the same type of mattress, pillow and wooden bed allotted to the others and was not to be allowed special visits. It was followed to a tee as Madhavrao was not even given hot water to bathe in winter.

But it was not that Madhavrao never got any special treatment. When Madhavrao went to attend a National Cadet Corps (NCC) camp in Bombay, Jiwajirao paid a surprise visit. He was furious to see that Madhavrao had been given a soft, thick mattress with silk linen when other wards were sleeping on coarse cotton mattresses. Former union minister and diplomat, Natwar Singh, who too studied in Scindia School and later served on the board of governors, told Vir Sanghvi that Madhavrao was always served hot meals. The meal was the same that was served to other students but care was taken to ensure that cold chapatis were not given to him.[19]

In studies, Madhavrao's teachers rated him 'above average'.

But by the time Madhavrao rose to join Senior Cambridge (the Senior Cambridge examination certificate was equivalent to Class XII), he began performing badly in mathematics. Jiwajirao sought the help of a private tutor, G.K. Kapoor. Sanghvi has quoted Madhavrao as bluntly telling Kapoor at their first meeting that he did not want to study mathematics and science. Kapoor took it up as a challenge. This was the time Madhavrao had holidays and was in Bombay where Kapoor, much to the prince's discomfort, spent four hours teaching him techniques to solve previous years' questions. Madhavrao passed in both subjects with first division marks.

The decision to send Madhavrao abroad for further studies was his mother Vijaya Raje's. According to the prevailing requirements, Madhavrao had to first study at Winchester to get the number of A levels needed to qualify for admission to New College, Oxford. At Winchester, Madhavrao excelled in athletics and represented the school in the Hampshire county championships. He then went to New College, where he maintained princely traditions by taking a Third in PPE (philosophy, politics and economics) after five years rather than the usual three. The PPE course at the Oxford has served as a leadership factory of sorts producing many public figures like Bill Clinton, Benazir Bhutto, Michael Foot, Edward Heath, Harold Wilson, Aung San Suu Kyi and Bob Hawke. John Campbell, a British political biographer, goes to the extent of saying, 'It is overwhelmingly from the Oxford that the governing elite has produced itself, generation after generation.'[20]

During his Oxford days, Madhavrao would often visit London. On one occasion, he was caught speeding. When a policeman booked him and asked his name, Madhavrao is said to have replied: 'I am maharaja of Gwalior.' Quick came the policeman's retort: 'If you are maharaja of Gwalior, I am Shah of Iran.'

By the time Madhavrao was in his second year of college, he had a two-bedroom cottage of his own in the village of Old

Marston, near Oxford, and an ADC, Prabal Pratap Singh, who had been flown in from Gwalior. Singh, a former shikari, had studied at Scindia School and was four years senior to Madhavrao.

Madhavrao's reputation as a ladies' man continued all throughout his life. At Oxford, his taste for fast cars and nightclubs is said to have attracted many girls. According to Shatrujit aka Bapa Dhrangadhra, his closest friend at the Oxford who was a *yuvraj* (crown prince) of Dhrangadhra, a state in Gujarat, 'I once introduced him [Madhavrao] to a rather stunning blonde acquaintance of mine. That was the last I saw of her.'[21]

K. Natwar Singh viewed Madhavrao as a 'very sensual person'. In a piece written for the *Frontline* magazine, the diplomat-turned-politician observed, 'Women found him irresistable. While he did not flaunt his sensuality, neither did he hide it under a bushel.'[22]

Natwar Singh considered many of his contemporaries, politicians in particular, to be 'insufferable bores' but found Madhavrao to be an exception. 'Most present day politicians are rightly considered insufferable bores. Most are, because they have no other interest except for politics. And that too politics of the sleight of hand, stab in the back. Literature, sports, music, good conversation have no attraction for them. Most of us are time-servers, fair weather friends. Madhav never let friends down. Madhavrao had a multiplicity of interest. Thus, he was always a wonderful companion. I sometimes pulled his leg, calling him comrade maharaja. He found that amusing.'[23]

While Sanghvi insists Madhavrao was not a playboy during his Oxford days, his social circuit was wide and nightclub visits were frequent. Thousands of miles away, Vijaya Raje, now addressed as Rajmata after becoming a widow, began scouting for a suitable match for Madhavrao. Instead of a Maratha sardar's girl as her daughter-in-law, Rajmata zeroed in on a girl from Nepalese aristocracy, Kiran Rajya Laxmi Rana.

In August 1965, Madhavrao was in Delhi for his summer holidays when a meeting was arranged at Delhi's majestic Ashoka Hotel between the prospective bride and groom and their families. Madhavrao was amused to hear Kiran ordering ice cream and chips for herself and could not resist asking, 'You came all the way from Nepal to have ice cream and chips?'

His cousin, Meena, later told Sanghvi that Madhavrao had been swept off his feet by Kiran. 'All he could talk about was this beautiful girl he had met,' Meena, who was present at the dinner, recalled. Within a week, the wedding was fixed even though Madhavrao still had a year to complete his education at Oxford.

The wedding was planned in New Delhi in March 1966. The bride's family stayed at the Claridges Hotel and the celebrations continued for nineteen days. Prime Minister Indira Gandhi, President S. Radhakrishnan and a number of other VIPs attended the reception at Delhi's Imperial Hotel. By the time the bride moved to Gwalior as the new maharani, her maiden name had become a thing of the past. In keeping with Scindia family traditions, she was given a new name: Madhavi Raje Scindia. Soon, the newlyweds left for Switzerland to spend their honeymoon.

The Scindias celebrated another wedding soon after Madhavrao's. Usha Raje got married to Pashupati Shamsher Jung Bahadur, from the Rana family of Nepal. Shamsher was Madhavi Raje's cousin, so the family bond grew stronger among them.

Madhavrao returned to Oxford to resume his undergraduate studies. In February 1967, he was blessed with a daughter who was named as Chitrangada. Life for Madhavrao in Oxford changed drastically. He was living in a modest two bedroom cottage (without central heating) where the young couple would cook, mop the floors and chop wood in addition to looking after a young Chitrangada.

Madhavrao returned to India in May 1968. He began focussing on public life, cricket, business and horses shuttling between

Gwalior, Bombay and Pune. In Bombay, Madhavrao developed a friendship with Nusli Wadia (grandson of Mohammad Ali Jinnah) and Ram Batra, a Jan Sangh sympathizer who served as sheriff of Bombay. Together, they served as Madhavrao's closest advisors and financial consultants. This was a time when Nusli Wadia was having differences with his father, Neville. In a complex battle over shares, Madhavrao became the second largest shareholder in an investment company after the Wadia family and was named as a non-executive director of Bombay Dyeing. Soon after, the Samudra Mahal complex was converted into a clubhouse.

While Madhavrao was leading a somewhat hectic social and business life, politics in India was changing. His mother Rajmata had become a prominent face of the Indian opposition and even succeeded in toppling a Congress government in Madhya Pradesh (see Chapter 2 for details), Prime Minister Indira Gandhi had successfully overcome an internal revolt in the Congress to stay on as country's premier. Next, she had abolished the Privy Purses. Madhavrao and every erstwhile ruling family of India was outraged.

At this juncture, Madhavrao turned political and decided to contest from Gwalior as a Bhartiya Jan Sangh nominee. He won the parliamentary polls with ease, netting around 70 per cent of vote, even though the Indira-led Congress was riding high on her catchy *Garibi Hatao* slogan.

According to Natwar Singh, the princes had erred by deciding to confront the Indira regime head-on when popular sentiment was in her favour. Natwar was working in Indira's prime ministerial office then. Vir Sanghvi quotes Natwar as saying that Indira was working on an economic package and extended Privy Purses for another ten years but the princes did not want a compromise.[24]

Madhavrao's three-decade-long political career, spread from 1971 to 2001, was both eventful and challenging. He enjoyed peoples' affection and a relatively clean image. Madhavrao perhaps owed his clean image to his own ability to fund and fight electoral battles. He did not have to become a lobbyist of any big business house of their interest. Secondly, he was not a flamboyant politician and thus was able to manage his affairs without dipping into tainted or ill-gotten money.

When Madhavrao died, even some die-hard anti-Congress politicians grieved his death. Madhavrao was described as a decent, soft-spoken man with a popular base of his own.

In its obituary of him, the British daily *The Guardian* said of Madhavrao, 'His aristocratic lineage, personal charm, articulateness, youthful image and talent for the rough and tumble of democratic politics shaped his mass appeal. Sonia Gandhi may have had the charisma of leadership and the family name, but Scindia had the oratorical powers and was Congress's second-biggest crowd-puller.'[25]

Writing in *India Today* magazine, journalist Sumit Mitra had observed, 'In public functions, he wore the khadi dress with a tricolour scarf. In private, he preferred smart casuals and his cigar. In his several visits to the swankiest nightclubs of London and Paris, he was photographed in designer suits. At the back of these sartorial, and attitudinal, flip-flops, however, was an intention to capture the middle ground of the Congress which had been left bare by the death of Sanjay Gandhi in an aircrash in 1980 and the assassination of Rajiv in 1991.'

For Mitra, Madhavrao could never claim his pre-eminence because he was always overshadowed in the two decades of his life in the Congress by the Gandhi family. 'Nevertheless, he liked being at the centre of decision-making in matters of importance. But never at the top. He was the King who, somehow, never had the will to be a ruler,' wrote Mitra.[26]

FOUR

Vasundhara Raje Scindia: Princess in Public Life

Mars and Jupiter had exchanged houses: the ninth house of Mars and the tenth house of Jupiter. According to some astrologers, this foretold a 'Raj Yoga' for the girl child born to Maharaja Jiwajirao Scindia and Vijaya Raje on 6 March 1953. But another configuration relating to Venus–Venus during Vasundhara Raje's *vimshottari dasha* – the total number of years allotted to all the planets if one considered 120 years as the full life span of a person – did not augur well for her marriage. In the following pages we will find out if the stars had predicted the twists and turns of Vasundhara's life accurately.

Early Life

'My childhood was a fairy tale… a bit like reel life where everything was fascinating and fantastic. Traveling in luxury ships, mini train salons, races, living in palaces, eating in silver plates, etc., this was all a fairy tale… not a real life. Real life is different, challenging and full of adversity.'

This was Vasundhara – Vasu to her close friends and family – describing her childhood years to the BBC's Sanjeev Srivastava on her 64th birthday in 2017.[1]

However enchanting the young princess's life may have been, she did feel somewhat caged, trapped by gilded bars. In the same interview she mentioned, 'I wanted to break free and forced my mother to send me to a boarding school in Kodaikanal (Presentation Convent, Kodaikanal). I became house captain there on my own merit. Virtually nobody knew that I was a real-life princess.' Vasundhara was also educated at the Cathedral and John Connon School in Mumbai and her school education was completed at the Scindia Kanya Vidyalaya, a school founded by her mother in Gwalior. She graduated in economics and political science from Sophia College for Women, Mumbai University, in 1972.[2] Vasundhara told Srivastava, 'I had the freedom to choose my education but it was also in an all-girls' school. I travelled out but with my brother. I wanted all the freedom in the world which was not there.'

Vasundhara further told Srivastava that despite hailing from a privileged background, her life had been one of immense struggle and perseverance. The strong values and influence of her mother always remained a rock of support for Vasundhara and her siblings in trying times.

Rajmata Vijaya Raje Scindia also made sure that her children – son Madhavrao and four daughters, Padma Raje, Usha Raje, Vasundhara and Yashodhara – were brought up equally, without any discrimination based on their gender. For example, they were all taught to ride horses. Vasundhara, like her siblings, was made to ride bareback, graduating to the saddle only after she had learnt to ride the hard way. Similarly, Vasundhara, her *bhaiya* (Madhavrao) and sisters were taught to make the customary morning and evening *mujra* (bow) to their parents, elders and visitors. To Muslims, they were taught to offer *salaam*.

By the time Vasundhara turned eighteen, the Scindias had started looking for a suitable match for the Gwalior princess.

In her autobiography, Rajmata Scindia has narrated the story of Vasundhara's marriage with a tinge of regret (the reasons shall become clear soon), while owning the responsibility of accepting the alliance with the young prince of Dholpur, Hemant Singh.

Dholpur, located on the easternmost edge of Rajputana, beyond Agra, was infamous for its illegal stone quarries, bandits and distressingly depressed sex ratios. Founded by Udaibhan Singh, Dholpur was one of the two Jat princely states in Rajasthan which had acceded to the Indian Union in 1949. Hemant was Udaibhan's grandson (from his daughter's side), who was chosen as a successor when the Dholpur ruler died without a male heir in 1954. His widow, Malvinder Kaur, had adopted Hemant Singh.

Vasundhara's marriage to the young prince of Dholpur had surprised many, given that Gwalior and Dholpur had been bitter enemies since centuries.[3] When Vasundhara's match was sought with Hemant Singh, many royal watchers could not fathom how the two families could forget their traditional historical feud and think of a marital alliance. Their apprehensions proved to be right when the alliance turned out to be short-lived.

At the time of her marriage, Vasundhara was oblivious of the goings-on, believing that something wonderful was being planned for her future happiness and that all she had to do to make it come true was fall in line with the family's wishes. She told Srivastava that since her childhood it had been ingrained in her that women had no say in their marriages.

Marriage and Separation

When the horoscopes of the future bride and groom were matched, the family priests pronounced them to be complementary. But something or the other kept propping up before the marriage was finally solemnized. There was talk that Hemant's mother was keen to marry him off to her close relative. In fact, Hemant himself met Madhavrao and the Rajmata, complaining about his mother's reported interference in his affairs. He admitted that she was not in favour of him marrying Vasundhara, but assured the Scindias that he would not be swayed from his decision to go ahead with the alliance.[4]

Vasundhara's marriage was a grand affair. It took place on 17 November 1972. Within a year, Vasundhara gave birth to a boy, Dushyant Singh. But, it seems the happy times were already at an end. A few months later, Hemant abruptly left Dholpur. He took away with him as much of his moveable possessions as he could cram into a fleet of lorries – carpets, silver, clocks, expensive crockery and wall decorations of Chinese porcelain – leaving behind his wife, his newborn heir, and his hauntingly beautiful palace. The marriage was later annulled by a court at the behest of Hemant Singh, but the decree was challenged by Vasundhara who sought maintenance and legal rights as a former royal.

The Rajmata was particularly affected by the plight of Vasundhara and her young grandson, Dushyant. In her autobiography she recorded: 'As the months passed, we became reconciled to the finality of separation. Attitudes hardened on both sides, releasing a storm of recrimination and accusations. All I could do was to keep reminding myself that such adversities are visited on us to test our inner strength and to prepare us for a purer and nobler way of life, and also that it was as though history itself had rejected our puny efforts to span the breach between the two families.'

In 1978, the Rajmata filed a case against Hemant on the ground that Dushyant, then a minor, had a right to his ancestral property. It was only in 2007, almost three decades later, that a compromise was worked out, ending the dispute over property worth hundreds of crores of rupees.[5] The Rajmata did not live to see the settlement. But as a sympathetic mother who blamed herself for the failed marriage of her daughter, the Rajmata, throughout the latter part of the 1970s, kept trying to take responsibility for Vasundhara's life by introducing her to politics. It was at this very time that the Rajmata's differences with son Madhavrao became more and more public and increasingly bitter. The ties between Vasundhara and Madhavrao, however, remained cordial.

It was as if Madhavrao could sense her loneliness and Vasundhara could understand why her *bhaiya* did not like the overt interference of Bal Angre in the Rajmata's personal and political life. Vasundhara was somewhat familiar with the world of politics, having witnessed her mother's Lok Sabha contests from Guna and Gwalior in 1957–1962. She would often accompany the Rajmata to Delhi during Parliament sessions but her mother's political engagements across the then undivided Madhya Pradesh (including present-day Chhattisgarh) often kept her away from home for weeks at a stretch. Vasundhara would often ask the Rajmata why, as a 'normal' mother, she could not be with her daughter for even thirty days.[6]

Interestingly, a young Vasundhara had herself turned a campaigner in 1962 when voters in Gwalior were charmed to see a princess with folded hands, greeting them with a namaste, bowing before them and requesting votes.

The Emergency

When the Rajmata was imprisoned in Tihar jail during the Emergency, Vasundhara and her sisters, Usha Raje and Yashodhara, were not informed about their mother's whereabouts. In fact, when Usha Raje met Indira Gandhi, they learnt that the prime minister did not consider their mother a 'political prisoner' but a 'smuggler' and the Rajmata was being treated as a criminal.

Vasundhara describes the fortitude of her mother at this

adverse time and how she held the Rajmata in a high esteem all along. She claims she had seen the Rajmata make good use of her time in confinement in Tihar, talking to criminals and prostitutes about religious scriptures and teaching them how to sing bhajans (religious songs). 'Even in jail, she became a mother figure,' Vasundhara would later recall, pointing out that since her early days she had been exposed to instances such as these where politics and a sense of service came naturally to her because of the Rajmata's influence.

The year of 1975–1976, was a difficult time for the Scindias, particularly Vasundhara. Coping with a seemingly endless separation from Hemant Singh and raising a young Dushyant, Vasundhara also found herself torn between affection for brother and her mother. At this time, Madhavrao was in hiding in Kathmandu, Nepal, to escape Indira Gandhi's ire and had sent for his wife Madhavi and children. He had also sent a series of communications to sisters Vasundhara and Yashodhara requesting them to join him at Kathmandu. Although the Rajmata did not agree with Madhavrao's decision of fleeing to Nepal, the Scindia sisters greatly valued their brother's concern for them. 'I know he felt enormous anguish and he wanted us to join him,' she told Vir Sanghvi adding, 'But before I could act, raids [during the Emergency] began,' Vasundhara said while glossing over the Rajmata's disapproval for such a course of action.[7]

Vasundhara has vivid memories of the problems faced by the Scindias during the Emergency, beyond the family's separation. She recalls how the income tax authorities, while raiding the Jai Vilas Palace, had impounded even a toy walkie-talkie, seized as 'proof' of espionage.[8]

For the first time, the Scindias felt the pinch of the paucity of funds. Their bank accounts were frozen and Vasundhara and Yashodhara could not even pay the salaries of those working at the Gwalior palace. Yashodhara would later recall in conversation with the author: 'I had to sell old tents as scrap and few silver items that were not seized.' Their wide social circle in Gwalior, Delhi, Bombay, Pune and other places became cold and reserved as friends were apprehensive to even talk on the phone.

Amid all this, while trying to secure the release of her mother, Vasundhara had an unfortunate experience with a public official that she would neither talk about nor forget easily. The Rajmata, however, wrote about it in her memoirs. Vasundhara was meeting with several influential people to get more information about the Rajmata. 'One such person, with a particularly unsavoury reputation in his dealings with women, insisted on making appointments to see Vasu in the luxurious suite he seemed to have permanently at his disposal in the capital's two most prestigious and expensive hotels, where the table for two, in the authentic style of Hollywood assignments, seem(ed) to have (been) laid just as permanently. Exasperated by Vasu, who made a point of never showing up at this rendezvous without a servant trailing behind her, he took (her) aside: "Tell me, what sacrifices will you be prepared to make to have your mother set free?"' While Vasundhara chose to keep the identity of the politician a 'secret', many have conjectured that it was a senior minister in the Indira regime who was subsequently accused of curbing media freedom and harassing members of the Hindi cinema industry. Vasundhara snubbed him hard but she did find out where her mother was locked up. She and Yashodhara then sought a meeting with the Rajmata at the Tihar Jail, which materialized after a fortnight of legal wrangling. During this period, Vasundhara had also taken up her mother's case with Rajiv and Sonia Gandhi but that came to naught.[9]

After the Emergency, Vasundhara continued to have cordial ties with Rajiv, but her support for his estranged sister-in-law, Maneka Gandhi (Sanjay Gandhi's wife who had a bitter split with Indira after Sanjay's death in June 1980), cast a shadow on their friendship. Soon, Vasundhara's friendship with Sanjay and Maneka become a subject matter of media speculation.

A few months after Sanjay's death, the Vasundhara–Maneka friendship had provoked anger at Indira Gandhi's residence. This was in March 1981, when Vasundhara hosted Maneka's son Feroze Varun's first birthday. The year-long mourning period for Sanjay hadn't ended then. But Vasundhara stoutly defended Maneka saying, 'We had a party at our clay mines in Mehrauli. It was so innocuous – it was my way of wishing mother and son well.'

In the 15 May 1982 edition of *India Today*, journalist Chaitanya Kalbag claimed that Vasundhara was responsible for arranging the sale of the *Surya* magazine to Sardar Angre. This magazine was edited by Maneka and it had played a role in dividing Indira Gandhi's key opponents such as Morarji Desai and Choudury Charan Singh. Vasundhara had spoken to Kalbag admitting her friendship with Maneka. 'I find Maneka extremely bright, down-to-earth, and I enjoy being with her,' she said adding, 'I had found Sanjay extremely soft-spoken, very gentle, and not rude and crude as his enemies labelled him.' Vasundhara also told Kalbag that she knew Rajiv and Sonia much before she ever met the younger Gandhis. 'This was when Amma [Vijaya Raje] was in the Janata [Party]. Rajiv and Sonia wined and dined me.' She had remarked. The sale of *Surya* magazine to Angre was significant and considered a blow to Indira Gandhi. When Indira was out of power (1977–1980), *Surya* under Maneka had fought a spirited battle to defend Indira amid a general atmosphere of hostility and intimidation.[10]

Involvement in Politics

Vasundhara's first direct brush with politics came in 1978 when the Bhairon Singh Shekhawat-led Janata Party formed the government in Rajasthan. Shekhawat, who was a close associate of the Rajmata, could sense her desire to introduce Vasundhara to public life. Thus, it came to be that the young princess was made a member of the Rajasthan Social Welfare Board.[11] Vijay Nahar, who later became Vasundhara's biographer, was also a member of the social welfare board. He could sense the budding politician's sense of dissatisfaction with this board's activities that were technically outside the ambit of politics. After a few meetings, however, Vasundhara seemed to have lost interest in the board's activities although she availed herself of all the perks of office.[12]

A more direct political role was in the offing when the BJP was founded in 1980 and the Rajmata became its founder member and vice president. By 1984, Vasundhara had become a member of the BJP national executive. She was given a ticket to fight the assembly elections from Bhind in Madhya Pradesh as a BJP nominee but lost to Udayabhan Singh of the Congress in the sympathy wave that swept across the country in the immediate aftermath of Indira's assassination.

That defeat, however, would not be a hurdle to Vasundhara's meteoric rise in politics. She was appointed vice president of the Yuva Morcha of the Rajasthan BJP and won the Dholpur assembly seat in 1985. The choice of Dholpur at this time was an especially courageous one. It was here that she had got married and had been bestowed the title of the maharani of Dholpur, but she did not have any support from her in-laws. This did not stop Vasundhara from defeating Congress heavyweight Banwari Lal by over 23,000 votes. There would be no looking back after this as even her detractors acknowledged this victory, achieved despite various odds and perceived hostilities.

Vasundhara was, in 1987, appointed the vice president of the Rajasthan BJP. In 1989, she was asked to contest from the Jhalawar[13] parliamentary seat and she won this, polling more than 50 per cent – a margin of 146,000 votes – of the votes cast. In fact, she would win this seat four more times – in 1991, 1996, 1998 and 1999 – retaining the Lok Sabha seat till 2003 and polling over half the votes every time (except in 1996, when she got 49.89 per cent of the votes cast).

However, her electoral success from Jhalawar may not have been possible without the blessings of Atal Bihari Vajpayee, Bhairon Singh Shekhawat, L.K. Advani and, of course, the Rajmata. In 1989, when Vasundhara was first considered for the Jhalawar parliamentary seat, her first reaction had been one of disbelief. She had reportedly said that her lack of familiarity with Harauti, the local dialect,[14] could come in the way. But as just mentioned, she was highly successful in this constituency, that was later renamed Jhalarapatan, till she was made the chief minister of Rajasthan.

As Minister under Vajpayee

Vajpayee and Vasundhara shared a strong political connection. When Vajpayee took over as prime minister in 1998, he made Vasundhara a junior minister in the Ministry of External Affairs, a portfolio that Vajpayee had initially himself held. This gave Vasundhara an opportunity to work directly under the prime minister. Interestingly, she was also backed by Jaswant Singh in this role, who was seen as her rival in state politics. As the minister of state for external affairs, Vasundhara led the ministry in carrying forward a foreign policy of facilitating the creation of an external environment of peace, prosperity, security and development. She also had the opportunity to visit various countries and played an important part in strengthening their relations with India. She also gained valuable experience receiving delegations from across the world.

Within a few months of assuming office, Vajpayee had ordered the testing of India's nuclear capabilities. As India became a nuclear power and the nation rejoiced, the world community reacted adversely and imposed sanctions on India. At such a delicate time, Vasundhara became an effective voice for promoting India's foreign policy, expressing the country's stand with courage when engaging with large sections of the international community. The fact that the international community withdrew sanctions soon after indicate the hard work that had been put in, among many others, by the Ministry of External Affairs.

Thirteen months after Vajpayee became prime minister, fresh elections were called and once again Vajpayee donned the mantle of leadership. He rewarded Vasundhara's hard work in the previous tenure by giving her independent charge of small-scale industries and agro and rural industries even as she continued to assist the prime minister in the departments of Personnel and Training; Pensions and Pensioners' Welfare; Public Grievances; Atomic Energy; and Space.

With a budget of approximately US$300 million, the Ministry of Micro, Small & Medium Enterprises operated various programmes and schemes for the benefit of small enterprises. Vasundhara took several initiatives to help the Indian small-scale sector become competitive in the globalized economic environment. Various new schemes, such as the Credit Guarantee Scheme, Credit Rating Scheme for enhancing access of credit to SMEs, Credit Linked Technology Upgradation Scheme for modernizing technology and the Market Development Assistance Scheme for support to marketing, were launched during her tenure and proved to be immensely successful. As the minister for small-scale industries, Vasundhara initiated the phased removal of a policy that provided for reservation of certain items to be manufactured only by small industries to encourage greater competitiveness within the small-scale sector.

While assisting the prime minister in the other portfolios, Vasundhara was directly involved in providing leadership and direction to the bureaucracy. In order to enhance accountability and transparency, the NDA government drafted a bill that later became the foundation for the Right to Information Act, and Vasundhara was part of this historic process.

Back to Rajasthan

In 2002 Rajasthan was headed for assembly elections. By now, Bhairon Singh Shekhawat, the erstwhile chief minister of the state, had become the country's vice president and the BJP had a leadership vacuum in state politics. Vajpayee chose Vasundhara to lead the party in Rajasthan and, in November 2002, she was packed off to Jaipur as the state BJP chief.

This was a challenging assignment. The patriarchal order of Rajputs, Jats, Gujjars and other influential communities was reluctant to accept a woman as a potential chief minister. Moreover, Vasundhara was not a Rajasthani; she did not speak the local Marwari or Harauti dialects and she had been a resident of Delhi for many years. Despite these odds being stacked against her, Vasundhara proved to be a worthy leader as the BJP recorded its biggest ever victory in Rajasthan in December 2003, winning 120 seats in the 200-member legislative assembly. 'We did not expect to cross the figure of 91,' a beaming Vasundhara told a news conference on 4 December. 'Crossing the 100-mark was a dream and getting 120 was good,' gushed Pramod Mahajan, BJP national general secretary, who was by Vasundhara's side when she spoke to the press.

Chandraraj Singhvi, who had left the Congress to join the BJP at that time, credits Vasundhara for making new headway in the state. 'She has won the support of the Jat community, which never came to the BJP fold as long as the Rajputs [Shekhawat is a Rajput] dominated the Rajasthan BJP. We had put up 33 Jat candidates and 25 of them won their seats,' Singhvi told news portal *Rediff.com*. Vasundhara herself believed that the overwhelming support of women had ensured the party's emphatic victory. 'We have 61 per cent of the women voters behind us for this thumping win,' she told *Rediff.com*.[15]

Throughout the campaign, Vasundhara had acted and behaved like a commoner. She worked hard to project herself as one of them, eating and drinking water from their utensils. 'Once she had broken this barrier between the royalty and the commoner, we knew the party would win over 100 seats,' said Sheshadhari Chari, editor of the *Organiser*, a publication of the RSS, the BJP's ideological fulcrum.[16]

Writing for *The Telegraph*, senior journalist Radhika Ramaseshan, who toured extensively during the Rajasthan assembly polls of 2003, credited senior BJP leader Pramod Mahajan for teaming up with Vasundhara to ensure her win. Mahajan, who was BJP general secretary with overall charge of the elections in Delhi, Madhya Pradesh, Rajasthan and Chhattisgarh, decided to concentrate on Rajasthan and Chhattisgarh, leaving Madhya Pradesh to his party colleague Arun Jaitley. Ramaseshan felt that Rajasthan initially had appeared to be a tough state for the BJP to win because Vasundhara, in spite of being a five-time MP from Jhalawar in south-eastern Rajasthan, was not well-known in rest of the state. Thus, one of Mahajan's first moves was to organize a *parivartan* (change) rally to familiarize Vasundhara with the terrain and people.

As per a plan, Vasundhara got a blueprint of each district with geographical, social and political data from a polling agency. This 'familiarisation trip' helped her strike a chord with the people, building a rapport and making her a household name. 'In the penultimate phase of polling, Vasundhara was asked to focus on 37 constituencies,' Ramaseshan wrote in *The Telegraph*. She added: 'In the absence of a central issue and given the overriding importance of caste in the state, the BJP decided to project its candidate as a leader who did not represent any caste. She was actually a Maratha married into a Jat family and her son is married into the only Gujjar royal clan Rajasthan has.'[17]

The strategy to 'de-casteise' Vasundhara sprang from the

perception that the incumbent Congress chief minister Ashok Gehlot's backward caste origins had antagonized the upper castes, which were still powerful in Rajasthan unlike in Uttar Pradesh and Bihar. The Jats, who had traditionally voted for the Congress, also veered towards the BJP because they viewed the Gehlot–Samajik Nyaya Manch grouping with suspicion. The Manch had spearheaded a campaign for the upper-caste poor and challenged the inclusion of Jats in the OBC category, saying this would deprive the genuinely backward classes of the benefits of reservation. As a result, the Jats regarded the Congress–Manch grouping to be a 'conspiracy' to snatch away their new status.

The Vasundhara-led BJP cashed in on the disenchantment of the Jats with the Congress by stepping in to help the four candidates fielded by the Jat Mahasabha and used celebrity Jats in its campaign. The BJP roped in prominent Jats Sahib Singh Verma (who was a union minister then) and actors Dara Singh as well as Hema Malini, who is married to the Jat actor Dharmendra. But there were still many hurdles. Rajasthan state-level veterans refused to accept Vasundhara as their leader and secretly backed rebel candidates. Mahajan sensed this and brought as many as 175 BJP workers and MLAs from his home state, Maharashtra, and assigned each of them a constituency. He told Ramaseshan before the results came out that there was a 'youth upsurge' in Rajasthan in favour of Vasundhara where her sophisticated, no-nonsense image worked to the party's advantage.

On 8 December 2003, history was created when Vasundhara became the first woman chief minister of Rajasthan. It was significant on many counts. Rajasthan had never been a politically hospitable terrain for any woman politician, particularly for someone who was not a native of the state, and additionally her marriage with a former royal from the state had broken down, making it politically a potentially debilitating cocktail. More importantly, Vasundhara held on the job and proved her mettle.

This was a time when a more glamorous and politically potent Uma Bharti had taken over as Madhya Pradesh chief minister. But the fiery sanyasin did not last beyond nine months. Uma had to step down after an adverse court ruling, although, on the turf of realpolitik, her exit had more to do with the BJP's internal dynamics.

Thus, the win in Rajasthan did not come easy. 'Vasundhara had to sweat it out before earning her spurs,' Ramaseshan would write later. 'An air-conditioned SUV that used to take her around the state was rejected for a stodgy Ambassador after it was suggested sotto voce that the 'maharani' would not withstand the heat and dust. She kept a grueling schedule and nursed her calloused feet in warm water at day's end, sometimes caviling. At such moments, she was reminded about her mother, Rajmata Vijaya Raje Scindia, who once campaigned with a broken foot and never thought twice of breaking meals with the BJP workers at party conventions. That was when Vasundhara began dining in people's homes, unmindful of the water that was served.'[18]

A 'Strong' Chief Minister

As chief minister, Vasundhara introduced key changes to several laws – such as the Industrial Disputes Act, Apprentices Act, Factories Act, Contract Labour Act and Boilers Act – to make the state a preferred business destination. She simplified the process of land acquisition that earlier required compliance with tardy procedures extending over at least fifty-eight months. As Narendra Modi had done as chief minister of Gujarat, Vasundhara too rolled out the red carpet for private investors.

In 2015, Vasundhara hosted a 'Resurgent Rajasthan' investors' meet where she showcased the state's model of development on the 'triad of social justice, effective governance and job creation'. She launched the Bhamashah Scheme – a riff on the Aadhaar card that was named after Bhamashah, an aide and adviser to the legendary Rajput ruler Maharana Pratap – in 2014, which, for the first time, recognized women as the head of the household. It promised to transfer financial and non-financial benefits of central and state government schemes directly to women through an eponymous card, by allowing for direct disbursal of all subsidies to the bank accounts of women. It had the added benefit of Rs 30,000 as health insurance and a coverage Rs 300,000 in the event of serious illness. Another scheme, Annapurna Rasoi, modelled on Tamil Nadu's Amma Canteen, served subsidized meals in the state.[19] Vasundhara also executed reforms to unshackle the private sector from an obsolete labour law regime.

Vasundhara was a firm believer in the empowerment of women. She was convinced that any woman could become a politician. 'When girls go to college, interact with people, participate in the public discourse, they gain confidence. Politics is like any other career, and it is as easy and as difficult as it is to pursue any other career,' she told Rahul Kanwal of *India Today TV*.[20]

It is notable that Vasundhara emerged as a much stronger persona in her second stint as chief minister. Even state Congress leaders would acknowledge off the record that Vasundhara could not be faulted for being short on policies. 'Left to herself, without outside intervention and interference, she might have set a record for conceptualising and possibly implementing a range of schemes and reforms, imbued with some sort of a vision,' a retired civil engineer, who was with the Congress, told Ramaseshan.[21]

Throughout her political career, Vasundhara worked hard to act like a commoner and also to work for the common people of the state. During the 2014 Lok Sabha elections, she could be seen travelling by the Golden Temple Mail in non-AC coaches while speaking to *India Today's* Rohit Parihar. She told him that after being chief minister for several years, she understood what people expected from her: water, electricity, roads, drains, doctors, teachers and employment. 'People want delivery to uplift them and not doles,' she said. 'Every state has its own priority and one size given by the Centre does not fit them all. Instead of the Rs 80,000 crore NREGA [the rural job scheme] and The Food Security Bill, please give me Rs 1,000 crore or even Rs 800 crore for each of my districts and I will turn them around as the best ones in India. But I have to be allowed (to decide) on how and where that money has to be spent. Give me my money and not your schemes.'[22] It was evident that she had a mind of her own.

When Parihar asked if there was any other central scheme that she found flaws in, Vasundhara replied, 'There are many. The Centre promised 75 per cent aid in the Sarva Shiksha Abhiyan and some years later, demanded that much share from us! Where is that huge fund for education gone?'

Serving and retired bureaucrats, who did not wish to be named, told this author that as chief minister, Vasundhara often acted more like a CEO than a politician. 'She only wants original ideas,' said an IAS officer. 'She is relentless,' added another retired official, recalling how she would insist that so-called solutions which had failed for decades needed to be discarded.

Dogged by Controversy

Notwithstanding such successes, Vasundhara's two full five-year stints as chief minister of Rajasthan in 2003–2008 and 2013–2018 had their share of controversies. Perceived as a tough administrator, she did not shy away from contentious issues. The VHP, considered a BJP sympathizer and member of the loose-knit Sangh Parivar, often cried foul. It even dubbed Vasundhara 'pseudo secular' for targeting Hindu places of worship as, in September–October 2014, Vasundhara had personally monitored the removal of 1,050 structures, including twelve Hindu temples, during an unprecedented three-week demolition drive to clear land for the long-delayed Rs 870-crore Jaipur Ring Road project.

Some people in power in Rajasthan felt that Vasundhara was not very accessible. When India Today TV's Rahul Kanwal asked her about this, Vasundhara replied: 'Have to listen to many complaints about it. I am working for 10–15 hours. People say the work done now has not been done before, nor will it be (done) in the future. You can't just wander in.'[23]

In fact, this was not the first time that the Rajasthan chief minister had heard complains about her work life. In 2009, Congress MLA Raghu Sharma had brought up Vasundhara's alleged absence from work in the evenings. 'In your tenure you were known as no CM after 8 p.m.,' Sharma had said in the assembly. At this accusation, an agitated Vasundhara had rushed into the well of the House in protest. While nothing much could be heard in the din that followed, Sharma alleged that Vasundhara had asked how he would have felt if somebody had said that his wife had a drink every night and then danced on the streets. Sharma's allusion to the '8 pm' brand of whisky wasn't lost on anyone. It sought to amplify Vasundhara's purported failures and arrogance in the public mind and image of a woman who reportedly had a drink at leisure.

This was not the only time when Vasundhara's personal life was brought into the public domain in a rather distasteful way. In the early 1980s, there were rumours of Vasundhara marrying politician Akbar Ahmad 'Dumpy', a close Sanjay Gandhi associate, parliamentarian and a man with an active social life. When Kalbag asked her about this in 1982 for the *India Today* piece, she had flared up, 'My friendship with Dumpy is like my relationship with Maneka. I married in 1972 and separated in 1974. I haven't got my divorce yet, haven't started proceedings, and don't intend to. If I wanted to marry Dumpy would I have remained single for eight years?'

In her long and distinguished political career, Vasundhara, like many other women politicians, has often had to face subtle (and not so subtle) attempts at character assassination. In April 2017, Aatish Taseer, a well-known author and columnist, wrote a piece in *The New York Times* condemning the behaviour of Vasundhara's government in handling a controversy arising out of the lynching of a fifty-five-year-old Muslim dairy farmer, Pehlu Khan, who had been attacked by cow vigilantes. Taseer cited the growing support of most politicians to promote the BJP's ideology of Hindutva, a major aspect of which is the deification of the cow. 'BJP chief ministers across India are now falling over themselves in a quest to outdo one another in showing their love of the Indian cow, which, as Mr. Khan's killing demonstrates, is animated partly by a hatred of Muslims,' Taseer wrote.[24] But soon, it spiralled into a personal attack on the chief minister. 'Vasundhara Raje, the chief minister of Rajasthan, is someone I grew up around in Delhi and have known all my life. She is aristocratic and is educated. She had many Muslim friends and even a Muslim boyfriend. She was a single mother, like mine. She smoked, she drank; she is well read and widely traveled. She certainly seemed the beneficiary of liberal values. That someone like her would now refuse to speak up for a poor Muslim farmer with small children who was lynched in her state is an indication of how poisoned the air has become in three short years since the BJP came to power.' Whether Vasundhara's silence in the matter was justified is a topic that is outside the scope of the present book. What is, however, in bad taste is the reference to Vasundhara's habit of 'smoking' and 'drinking'.

Vasundhara had to weather several other storms too. In 2015, when Vasundhara was serving her second term as chief minister, a major political upheaval had shaken her government to the core. Before we delve deeper into the controversy, we have to take a long look at the man at the centre of the storm, Lalit Modi.

Lalit Modi had begun his career as president and managing

director of Modi Enterprises. In 1993, he ventured into the entertainment world, entering into a partnership with Walt Disney Pictures and brought the world-famous studio's programmes to millions of television screens in India. Soon, however, unsavoury information began to emerge about this media magnate. In 2010 a profile titled 'Captain Crony Capital' in the *Outlook* magazine claimed that the man had many dark sides; it even alleged that Lalit Modi had a history of cocaine possession.[25]

Lalit had reportedly met Vasundhara for the first time in the early 1990s when he was seeking clearance for a factory near Gwalior. By the time Vasundhara became Rajasthan chief minister, the bond of friendship between the two had become so visible that Lalit acquired the sobriquet of 'Super Chief Minister'. 'His arrogance was the talk of the town; his opulent suite at the luxury Rambagh Palace hotel (was) almost the centre of government, as officials were summoned to receive orders. Modi and Minal [Modi's wife] exploited their proximity to those in power to secure two havelis in Amer, near the famous fort, in contravention of Archaeological Survey of India rules.' A bigger stink was raised by the 90B scandal. Under this section of the Land Acquisition Act, farmers were allowed to reclassify agricultural land and put it to non-agricultural uses. Through misuse of this clause, much land was passed on to big builders.

It was as if 'corruption became the byword for the Vasundhara Raje government, and (Lalit) Modi became its public face, something the Congress exploited during the Assembly election of 2008,' reported Rohit Mahajan and Arindam Mukherjee in an investigative piece published in the 3 May 2010 issue of the *Outlook* magazine. Lalit Modi had also seen a fantastic rise in the world of cricket entertainment: the brain behind the incredibly successful Indian Premier League (IPL), he had come to occupy the post of the IPL Commissioner. But severe financial irregularities marred his legacy and his fall was finally as dramatic as his rise. A disciplinary committee of the Board of Cricket Control in India (BCCI), consisting of Arun Jaitley and Jyotiraditya Scindia, indicted Lalit on multiple counts, following which Lalit Modi was banned for life from the Indian cricket board in 2013. Lalit had by then fled the country and had taken refuge in the UK to evade arrest.[26]

Lalit was now a wanted man in India. It was in this context that a damning document dating back to 2011 was made public by the then *Times Now* editor-in-chief, Arnab Goswami, on the news channel. The document was signed by Vasundhara and endorsed Lalit Modi's application to stay on in the UK to avoid arrest in India. This exposé embarrassed the BJP and dealt a body blow to one of its core ideological platforms: patriotism. Egged on by Prime Minister Modi's silence on the matter, the controversy raged for days.

The document attributed to Vasundhara and released in the public domain had begun with the by-now infamous line: 'I make this statement in support of any immigration application that Lalit Modi makes, but do so on the strict condition that my assistance will not become known to the Indian authorities.' The witness statement contained several cringe-inducing paragraphs about the internal political situation of the country, which, even though no secret, went against the convention of not washing the nation's domestic dirty linen in front of foreign powers. At one point, the document even mentioned: 'A significant part of the Congress Party's election campaign [in 2008] was devoted to the propagation of a smear campaign against me [Vasundhara] and Lalit…'.[27]

Vasundhara's alleged nexus with Lalit Modi also brought under the spotlight Adil Ahmad, the nephew of politician Akbar Ahmad 'Dumpy', whom we have come across earlier. Adil had made his way into Vasundhara's close circle of associates and aides during her first term as Rajasthan chief minister in December

2003 at 8 Civil Lines, Jaipur, the official residence of the chief minister.

Since then, he had been a regular visitor at her residences in Jaipur. Adil had earned the reputation of being an 'interior designer to the royals' and had also designed some of Vasundhara's properties. Lalit Modi had soon developed a close working relationship with Ahmad and it was based on this connection that Lalit began to get development contracts, as many as twenty-two, from the Rajasthan state government.

This controversy involving Vasundhara proved to be a major dent in the reputation of the Narendra Modi establishment as a wave of moral outrage swept across the political landscape. Lalit Modi is considered both controversial and fugitive because he is wanted by Indian investigative agencies on several charges of corruption and money laundering. An RTI filed by activist Saurav Das reveals that a request for CBI probe against the London-based Modi has been pending since 2017 with a department headed by the prime minister of India.

In Recent Times

By the time the 2018 assembly elections for Rajasthan were announced, then BJP president Amit Shah had appointed central minister Prakash Javadekar as the *prabhari* (central minder) for the state and asked him to 'study' and explain Vasundhara's schemes to party workers and 'motivate' them to publicize them. The choice of Javadekar was interesting. He had a good equation with Vasundhara as she had known his family for long and both conversed in Marathi, which brought an informality to their association.

But by this time, Vasundhara's popularity had waned. A slogan heard throughout Rajasthan in 2018 is proof: it was 'Modi *tujhse vair nahin*, Vasundhara *teri khair nahin*.' An approximate translation would be that Vasundhara's detractors had nothing against Narendra Modi, but they wouldn't spare her. Narendra Modi himself heard this slogan at his Jhunjhunu rally in March 2018.

Vasundhara lost the November 2018 assembly elections but the BJP, written off as a has-been, put up a decent battle, depriving the Congress of a simple majority. Party chief Amit Shah had reportedly wanted many of the sitting 163 MLAs dropped to buck anti-incumbency but Vasundhara had put her foot down. A majority of the MLAs then were personally loyal to her. The BJP lost power in Rajasthan but Vasundhara survived. In the subsequent Lok Sabha polls in 2019, the BJP won all the parliamentary seats. While the victory was attributed to the Narendra Modi magic, as a seasoned campaigner, Vasundhara Raje often spoke like Narendra Modi, her speeches shorn of oratorical flourishes. But unlike Modi, Vasundhara seldom named her opponents. Journalists on the campaign trail, heard her say '*Woh log* [those people]', which was how she dismissed them. When she did refer to her rival, Ashok Gehlot, she described him as a '*kangal* [bankrupt]'.

Within the BJP, Vasundhara is seen and admired as a woman of substance. Post 2014, when Narendra Modi picked Amit Shah as the BJP's national president, Vasundhara remained as a person who could stand up to the latter. But 2018 saw a stalemate over the appointment of a new BJP state president. Incumbent Ashok Parnami's term had ended but no successor could be found even after meetings between Shah and Vasundhara. For Rohit Parihar, the Jaipur-based correspondent of *India Today* magazine, the episode did not reflect healthy democratic dissent, rather it highlighted indecisiveness, lack of a plan in place for Rajasthan and strong differences between Vasundhara on one side and Shah and Modi on the other. As the deadlock continued, the services of RSS supremo, Mohan Bhagwat, was reportedly sought. Vasundhara vetoed Arun Meghwal and Gajendra Singh Shekhawat's nomination as state party chief but had to accept the appointment of Satish Poonia, who had a strong Sangh background and was her open critic. This was the first time since 2003, when she became chief minister for the first time, that someone with an RSS background had got prominence and an official post as the head of the Rajasthan BJP.

In fact, in journalist D.K. Singh's view, many RSS leaders and senior party colleagues found her imperious, which prompted Vasundhara to establish a direct connect with the people and often resort to the politics of polarization to counter anti-incumbency and keep the RSS under check. This is probably why the RSS did not get a response from Vasundhara that satisfied them after the Pehlu Khan lynching case.[28]

Vasundhara was reportedly hurt by the criticism of her government following that incident. Thus, when a similar incident happened in Alwar in July 2018, she quickly condemned it and brought in a new inspector-general of police to take charge of the Jaipur range, under which Alwar district falls.

Vasundhara's political clout was on display once again in July 2020 when the Congress's Sachin Pilot, the deputy chief minister of Rajasthan, raised the banner of revolt against chief minister Ashok Gehlot. Political commentators had considered the development as a repeat of Jyotiraditya Scindia's defection from the Congress to the BJP, which brought down the Kamal Nath government in Madhya Pradesh. But Gehlot survived, largely because Vasundhara and BJP MLAs loyal to her (around thirty out of the seventy-five BJP MLAs) refused to accept Pilot as a chief ministerial candidate. Her radio silence on Pilot's rebellion made many believe that she was 'indifferent' to the idea of toppling the Gehlot government. At one point, union minister and senior BJP leader, Gajendra Singh Shekhawat, who was reportedly stoking the revolt in the Congress, told the media, 'Raje's silence could be a strategy that is sometimes louder than words,' indicating that the BJP high command could not make Vasundhara accept Pilot as a member of the Rajasthan BJP. Pilot subsequently beat a retreat and the political crisis in the state was defused.

Whether in or out of power, Vasundhara has always been a person of good taste, her three-bedroom cottage in New Delhi reflecting the influence of the West – a style that once marked Indian palaces. The house also has a touch of Adil Ahmad who catered to Vasundhara's tastes. A glance at her Delhi residence shows that more than big expenditure, it was a combination of personal legacy and complementary contemporary styles that had gone into planning the cottage. For instance, the walls have several ornithological prints – Vasundhara loves birds – while being an avid gardener, she has ensured that vistas of greenery surround the home. Fresh flowers are everywhere around the house.

A soundtrack of 'Om' chants is almost always playing in her home. Unnoticeable when you step inside, the music registers unobtrusively in your consciousness and eventually settles into it as part of the background, in keeping with the surroundings, just like the little mandir (temple) that sits in a niche right next to the front door. Vasundhara is intensely spiritual and the puja room is right at the starting point of her household within the bright 'lucky red' foyer.

'I hate houses that make you feel like you're a visitor in your own home,' says Vasundhara. 'The thing I love about this house is that it represents my personality so perfectly.' Just as a home should.[29]

Vasundhara is an avid reader too, her favourite author being Margaret Atwood. *The Edible Woman*, *The Circle Game*, *The Animals in That Country*, *Double Persephone* and *Expeditions* were among her favourite works during her school and college days when she would often read by torchlight, her blanket pulled over her head, to beat the early lights-off curfew at home and boarding school. Her passion for books has not diminished. Despite her busy schedule, she still finds time to read.

FIVE

Yashodhara Raje Scindia: Princess Crusader of Many Causes

Sometime in the summer of 1954, a part of the Gwalior royal household was transported to the UK. So much so that a section of the British media had called it 'George's Circus'. It was the birth of a 'princess' that had necessitated the temporary shift.

Yashodhara Raje Scindia was born in London on 19 June 1954, when Jiwajirao Scindia was visiting the UK. Gynaecologists, nurses, ADCs, guards, cooks, personal attendants and even dogs were brought to London so that Jiwajirao's queen, Vijaya Raje Scindia, and their older children could feel at home. Although the Scinidias had officially ceased to be monarchs, they still lived the opulent lives of the royalty, and this was the reason the term 'George's Circus' was repeatedly used – not for their wealth but for the pomp and show that went into flaunting that wealth.

This was still a time when the Scindias were fabulously wealthy. Jiwajirao was the *Rajya Pramukh* of Madhya Bharat, had more than thirty limousines, over 300 race horses and owned lucrative properties.

Yashodhara's early life, thus, was carefree, full of fun and frolic and extravagance – somewhat like a fairy tale, as she herself recounted to columnist Malavika Sangghvi during an interview. She grew up amidst 'unimaginable wealth and privilege; gourmet nursery food, garage filled with more than 30 limousines, a mother who sang mera lal dupatta malmal ka, playing hide-and-seek with her sister in magnificent palaces and a governess called Betty Barbara Beatrice Castellino.'[1]

But the fairy tale wouldn't last long. A short seven years later, Yashodhara lost her father. As Queen Mother, Vijaya Raje had to look after her daughters and assist the new maharaja of Gwalior, her son Madhavrao, who was barely sixteen then.

The 1962 general election saw Vijaya Raje, as the Rajmata of Gwalior, reaching out to the electorate and seeking votes and her youngest daughter was introduced to politics at that young age. Yashodhara would accompany her but would often doze off in the car as her mother made political speeches. 'I was not sure what was happening then but had a faint idea that elections are something important,' Yashodhara recounted to this author, sitting at her tastefully decorated official bungalow in Bhopal.

'Amma [the Rajmata] never sat down to enjoy our company or that of her friends; she was so convinced that her party would make a difference in the country,' Yashodhara said, repeating some of the comments she had made to Sangghvi. 'She always had her foot on the accelerator; if we wanted to meet her during the holidays, we would have to go on tour with her. I remember it used to be hot, sweaty and dusty. There was little fun. Cars would often break down in the heat.'

Yashodhara's first real brush with politics came as a rude jolt when she turned twenty-one according to the Hindu calendar. A surprise party had been organized for her at Gwalior House, the Scindia residence on Delhi's Rajpur Road, where close family friends and relatives had been invited. On 25 June 1971, a Jana

Sangh worker called up the Rajmata close to midnight when the birthday party was in full swing to inform her that Opposition leaders were being arrested by the government. The Rajmata returned to the party as if nothing had happened but the birthday girl could sense that all was not well. She heard her mother whispering to a maid to pack a bag and not to let any outsider enter Gwalior House. The Rajmata also visited her puja room before retiring for the night.

The next morning, the Rajmata left early. She no longer wore white. Minutes after she had left, Yashodhara heard police officials knocking on the door, asking about her mother's whereabouts.

A few months later, Yashodhara would have a more direct and difficult brush with the authorities when she was alone at Jai Vilas Palace, Gwalior. The Rajmata was under detention while Madhavrao was in Nepal trying to evade arrest. Her two elder sisters, Vasundhara and Usha, were in Rajasthan and Nepal, respectively. Madhavrao's Bombay-based buddies, Ram Batra and Nusli Wadia, stood by Yashodhara during this period, often even giving her money to settle bills and pay salaries to palace employees.

Then, one day, Yashodhara had an early-morning knock at Jai Vilas Palace. Teams from the Income Tax Department, Directorate of Revenue Intelligence and the Enforcement Directorate had arrived for search-and-seizure operations. They took control of the telephone line and demanded the keys of the *tosha khana* where gifts and expensive jewellery, precious stones, artefacts and silver utensils, etc., were stored in steel cupboards.[2] The sheer opulence of the palace is said to have rattled the officials.

The allegation against the Scindias was that they had withheld information regarding how much gold they had. The Rajmata has, however, insisted that she and her son regularly paid all taxes.

When the smartly clad confident Yashodhara feigned ignorance about the keys of the *tosha khana*, the income tax officials from Delhi became stern. They told Yashodhara in no uncertain terms that if she withheld information and obstructed government officials from performing their duties, she could be booked and arrested. This threat was enough to rattle the palace staff and a chambermaid blurted out that she had the keys.

Yashodhara, however, did not lose her calm. As the officials barged inside the *tosha khana*, she gently told them to take their shoes off as the Scindias considered the *tosha khana* their 'puja *ghar*' (prayer room). The tax officials kept talking in conflicting tones claiming huge seizures over the telephone when nothing was recovered. Yashodhara's freedom and privacy was severely curtailed as she had to take permission from tax officials (mostly men) to even shift from one room to another or to talk on phone. In the midst of the searches, a telegram arrived; this was impounded and searched as the tax officials suspected it to be carrying a 'coded' or encrypted message.

Sources close to the Scindias later revealed that the tax sleuths were reportedly looking for the '*beejak*', a secret code that would have led them to a chamber of secret treasures. The story of the *beejak* and the Scindias' wealth have been part of folklore. As mentioned in Chapter 1, by the latter half of the seventeenth century, the Scindias were virtually the leaders of the entirety of north and central India, and Gwalior fort was at the heart of this realm. In that era, there were no banks or strongrooms to stash assets or cash. In order to secure the assets, the Scindias used the *beejak* along with mystery vaults, known as the 'Gangajali' to protect the riches. Only the maharaja of Gwalior knew the secret code; and this was passed on from father to child. Nobody else in the Gwalior durbar knew about the *beejak* or the Gangajali's mystery chambers.

The Indira Gandhi regime perhaps believed that there were several such undiscovered chambers from which hidden riches could be recovered. Conflicting claims have been made about the 1975 raid. While the authorities asserted that huge chunks of gold and silver were seized, the Scindias believed nothing was found. Officials of the tax department and other law enforcement agencies reportedly destroyed material that was invaluable. One such item was a letter containing the notations of a raga composed by Indian classical music's greatest legend, Ustad Allauddin Khan (see Chapter 2) named after Vijaya Raje in 1953. The law enforcement officials conducting the raid mistook the notations for some kind of secret code and impounded the letter. Raga Vijaya was lost forever.

Low-key Wedding

By the time the Rajmata was granted parole on health grounds after spending a substantial period of time incarcerated, a lot had happened in her family. Her son, Madhavrao, had started leaning towards the Congress while her youngest daughter had become romantically involved with Siddharth Bhansali, son of a noted Bombay-based cardiologist Dr. Kiritlal Bhansali. Apparently, Yashodhara and Siddharth met frequently at the Racecourse's Turf Club. It was at one such rendezvous that Madhavrao spotted them sipping tea together at the Willingdon Club.

'Dada [Madhavrao] was furious; after all, he had taken on the role of our father, and (insisted that) Scindia girls maintained a strict code. He put me on the first plane to Gwalior,' reminisces Yashodhara in her conversation with Sangghvi.[3]

The Rajmata was caught in a bind as inter-caste marriages were not acceptable to the Scindias. Madhavrao was totally opposed to the alliance and mother and son started looking for a suitable match for the youngest princess of Gwalior. But Yashodhara had a mind of her own and remained adamant. According to a conversation reproduced by the Rajmata in her memoirs, Yashodhara told her that she would remain single if she could not marry Siddharth.

The Scindias did not attend the wedding, which turned out to be a low-key affair. Even the friends of the Scindias in Bombay stayed away. Yashodhara moved to New Orleans, USA, in 1977, where Dr. Siddharth Bhansali was earning an intern's salary. It would initially be a difficult life for a princess who had till then never had to bother about everyday chores. 'I used to cook, clean, wash the dishes and, every week, spend two hours at the local laundromat doing the linen.' The young princess would also often stand in queues in stores to buy groceries and carry home the items herself. 'I remember when my family would visit, we would rush downtown and rent a TV for them,' Yashodhara recalled.

Siddharth went on to become an accomplished cardiologist.

Soon, life at 7, Audubon Pl, New Orleans, settled into a rhythm. Three children were born. Akshay, born in 1982, became a producer at MTV Desi in New York; Abhishek, born in 1985, studied at NYU Stern School of Business, and Trishala, born in 1988, founded 'Lekha', named after her illustrious grandmother, to showcase the two rich cultures of India and USA, in her line of handmade dresses, blouses, pants, jackets and shoes. In fact, Trishala's love for Indian fabrics and textiles began virtually with her first breath, when her mother had wrapped her tiny wriggling body in a *dohar*, a traditional central Indian blanket made of three layers of fine soft muslin.

Between 1977 and the early 1990s, Yashodhara led an active social life. She became a board member of the Delta Festival Ballet, an advisory board member of the Contemporary Art Center, and a Fellow of the New Orleans Museum of Art. As an environment and wildlife enthusiast, Yashodhara is said to have raised a quarter of a million dollars for the Audubon zoological society (The Audubon Zoo is among the most visited and well-kept zoos in the USA). In addition to raising funds, Yashodhara conceptualized and supervised the making of an exhibition on

Indian crafts, made by craftsmen in India and then transported in small pieces by sea to be reassembled at New Orleans.

Siddharth himself had a passion for collecting bronze sculptures of Hindu, Buddhist and Jain deities. In fact, even now, the Bhansali collection at New Orleans contains numerous rare and noteworthy bronzes, including some of the earliest known metal representations of a deity. Among these is an extraordinary group of Gupta bronzes (320–550 CE). Few private or public collections anywhere can claim so many metal sculptures of this period of such variety. Bronzes from this period are rare, partly because metal images were easily melted down and reused.[4]

Nearly thirteen years after marrying a 'commoner', Yashodhara's marriage began to fall apart. Her children understood the problems and respected their parents' decision to separate. Yashodhara returned to India after restoring her Indian citizenship, and looked to join politics as a career.

Yashodhara didn't want to talk about the exact cause of her divorce during her interview with Sangghvi. All she would say was that she wanted to live a new life. 'I came back to start life all over again and to look after my mother,' she said. 'I wanted to see her alive, living well in the way she should be living with her family around her.' By her own admission, the Rajmata saw her as the 'man' in the family.

Life in Politics

When it came to politics, Yashodhara drew comfort in being in the BJP. There were feelers from the Congress but Yashodhara had her reasons for not joining the party that had her brother Madhavrao as an influential leader. In an interview she revealed why she did not join the party: 'I have really, really honestly come to the conclusion that the Congress party can never stay out of power. They lust for power. They cannot do without it, apart from a few like my brother or the Madhya Pradesh chief minister [Digvijaya Singh] who have integrity – there are literally a handful you can name.'[5]

Yashodhara chose the BJP, more so as the invite to serve the party came from no less a person than Atal Bihari Vajpayee. Thus, she contested the Madhya Pradesh Assembly elections in 1998 as a BJP nominee. That same year she had also been considered for the Lok Sabha seat from Guna, but her non-resident status posed some legal issues. According to the law, she had to be in India for over 180 days in the year to be eligible to contest the Lok Sabha elections, an eligibility criterion she had reportedly fallen short of.

Politics, she told Archana Masih of *Rediff.com*, came naturally and easily to her. 'It is quite amazing. My mother's whole career has been a role model for us children,' Yashodhara recalled while fighting the 1998 election.[6]

'Take my example, I was brought into the first election in 1989, when I went personally to ask for votes on behalf of my mother. While I was doing that I always thought I had to come back and that was how it first started. Don't call me Ma'am, call me Yasho – that becomes an equaliser,' Yashodhara added. Yashodhara, who has always fancied herself as a sort of fashionista, wore a classy crepe sari, a string of pearls, diamond earrings and gold anklets during the interview.

When did she start taking interest in politics? From 1989, Yashodhara said, when she was in India to campaign for the Rajmata. 'So, since '89 onwards, I have fought my mother's election while she has been elsewhere.'

Politics was in her 'blood', she told the *Rediff.com* interviewer. 'Even when I was in America, I got calls about what was happening here. And every third or fourth month, I was back to work in this area. It is nothing new. I have been doing it for a very long time, just that I have never bothered to highlight it to anybody.'

Archana Masih followed Yashodhara's campaign over several elections – 1998, 2003, 2007 (when she contested for the Lok Sabha seat from Gwalior), 2013 and 2018. She witnessed Yashodhara's journey as a seasoned campaigner, politician and minister. Unbeaten so far, Yashodhara makes sure that in every electoral battle, she holds anything between fifteen and twenty-five meetings a day over a fifteen-day campaign period. By the time Yashodhara had served two terms as a state minister, her political acumen had sharpened and she had understood the significance of the caste system, the need to judiciously utilize funds and how to negotiate local dynamics.

Yashodhara's children had to get used to her hectic schedule and political commitments. Her eldest born, Akshay, had visited his mother when she was contesting the Lok Sabha election from Gwalior and was seen flaunting his Scindia credentials and mingling with villagers.

Yashodhara said her children had got used to her political life just as she herself had got used to her mother's political life at the very young age of eight when her mother entered politics. 'If we had to see her when we were in boarding school, we had to go on tour with her. I use this as an anecdote in my meetings that as much as we were upset with my mother for giving up on her role as a mother for a bigger role – I tell people that when we used to get back to school from holidays, other children would say they went to Simla, Mussoorie – we would say we went to Durg or Bhilai.' Yadhodhara told this author.

However, Yashodhara's political journey was far from smooth. Apart from the unusual and inordinate delay in getting back her Indian citizenship, Yashodhara often found herself to be at the centre of controversies because of the 'Scindia' connection. By the end of 2003, when her elder sister Vasundhara Raje was all set to become chief minister of Rajasthan, Yashodhara had been left sulking in Madhya Pradesh's political scene.

Prior to the November 2003 assembly polls in Madhya Pradesh, Yashodhara had quit the BJP. Yashodhara's grouse was that the state unit, under the firebrand Sadhvi Uma Bharti (who became chief minister in December 2003), wanted her to give up the traditional Scindia seat of Shivpuri and contest from neighbouring Pichore, where state minister K.P. Singh, a known Scindia baiter, was the strongman. Yashodhara had till then been raising the issue of alleged illegal mining in Shivpuri by Singh's family. Yashodhara was also upset that despite being the state BJP secretary, she had been constantly 'ignored' and not consulted over key appointments made in the Gwalior–Chambal region.

In 2004, Yashodhara had claimed that under Uma Bharti's leadership, the BJP was heading towards a 'big zero'. The Shivpuri MLA had commented, 'I am tired of answering to BJP workers. There is lawlessness, drift all over. I guess the party would have to start afresh from the district level.'

Without naming Uma Bharti's brother, Swami Prasad Lodhi, who had unsuccessfully contested the assembly polls from the region, she had said, 'Outsiders are interfering in all aspects of governance and organisational affairs. Those given responsibility are not fulfilling their tasks.'

Political sources would say in hushed voices that Yashodhara's lifestyle in Delhi (she was a regular at parties) had been cited to discount her abilities as a BJP satrap. Yashodhara had reacted angrily to this whisper campaign, saying, 'When there is no concrete complaint, such trivialities are played up.'[7]

Her 'royal sulk', as *India Today* termed it,[8] became a major embarrassment for party chief L.K. Advani, who summoned Uma Bharti and directed her to patch things up with Yashodhara. The move to make Yashodhara shift from her seat was shelved. However, Uma Bharti had her way in not inducting her as a minister in her cabinet. Yashodhara had to wait for two more years before getting a ministerial berth in 2005. By then, Uma Bharti was out of the BJP and party veteran Shivraj Singh Chouhan had become chief minister.

Political trouble, however, continued to dog Yashodhara.

In 2007, the BJP leadership asked her to resign as a minister in Madhya Pradesh and contest a Lok Sabha by-election from Gwalior. There, Yashodhara defeated the Congress nominee, Ashok Singh, by over 90,000 votes. After winning, when Yashodhara was Gwalior MP between 2007 and 2009, a controversy arose. Suspecting that her movements were under watch, Yashodhara had to call up the state intelligence chief asking why she was being kept under surveillance, prompting a series of denials by Chief Minister Chouhan, director-general of police A.K. Puar and IG (Intelligence) Surinder Singh. 'Why should we do that,' Chouhan had said while inaugurating a state meet of kotwars, village-level government officials who keep records of births and deaths.

Apparently, the presence of two state intelligence officials at the otherwise well-guarded Rani Mahal in Gwalior, where the late Rajmata used to stay, had infuriated Yashodhara. According to the verbal complaint lodged with the state intelligence chief, Yashodhara had alleged that when she was discussing a water crisis with councillors in Gwalior, she had noticed the presence of two 'unauthorised' persons. When she checked with her ADC, she was told that they were from 'secret police'. Yashodhara had immediately ordered her security staff to nab them, but before they could do anything, the two had sped away on a motorcycle.

Family retainer Sardar Angre stood by Yashodhara. He said it was extraordinary that the BJP regime was keeping 'an eye' on one of its own MPs. 'Have they forgotten that she is Amma Saheb's daughter,' he said, referring to Rajmata Vijaya Raje Scindia. Angre said the state BJP organization secretary, Makhan Singh, owed an explanation to them for this. 'He must go beyond the routine bureaucratic denials,' Angre had said. 'Otherwise, the consequences will be grave.'

On another occasion, Yashodhara had expressed her unhappiness with the chief minister after Chouhan had made a rather sweeping and critical remark about the Scindia family while addressing a public meeting in Bhind district ahead of the Ater assembly by-polls in April 2017. Chouhan said that the Scindias had 'oppressed' the public in Bhind in connivance with the British before Independence.

Yashodhara quickly got even when she reminded state BJP leaders how her mother, the Rajmata, a founder member of the BJP, had to sell gold ornaments to arrange vehicles for the BJP during elections and even auctioned off jewellery to arrange for party funds.

Another issue that resurfaces time and again is linked to how the Scindias are sensitive about their past, particularly their role in the 1857 uprising (for more details, see Chapter 1). Any reference to Rani Lakshmibai touches a raw nerve among the present-day Scindias because their ancestors had fought against her on the side of the British during what is called India's first war of Independence. Because the Scindias appear a tad apologetic about this aspect of their family's past, local BJP leaders, hostile to the erstwhile royals, have often cited RSS ideologue Vinayak Damodar Savarkar's views on the Scindias (see Chapter 1).

Savarkar was not the only one to have put the present-day Scindias on the defensive. Noted Hindi poetess, Subhadra Kumari Chauhan, too, had made a scathing attack on the Scindia legacy in her poem *Jhansi Ki Rani*.

Angrezon ke mitra Scindia ne chhodi rajdhani thi
Bundelon harbolon ke muhn humne suni kahani thi
Khub ladi mardani woh toh Jhansiwali rani

Friends of the British, the Scindias, had abandoned their capital;
we have heard the story from Bundelon harbolon
[religious singers from Bundelkhand]
she fought with valour, she was the queen of Jhansi.

These lines from the famous Hindi poem were mysteriously dropped from school textbooks supplied by the Madhya Pradesh's BJP government in 2011 when Yashodhara was a Lok Sabha MP. Chief Minister Chouhan ordered a probe and asked officials to put back the lines '*Khub ladi mardani woh toh Jhansiwali rani* [Lakshmibai fought like a man]' on the 1857 uprising, even if it meant destroying thousands of Class VI textbooks already printed with the edited version for the subsequent academic sessions.

Sources close to Chouhan said he suspected an 'inside job' aimed at refurbishing the image of the Scindias as many political activists, academics and bureaucrats in the state are considered Scindia loyalists. Even among IAS and IPS officers, the term 'Gwalior Administrative Service' has informally been coined for officers known to be close to Gwalior's erstwhile rulers.

Chouhan, however, continued to shower praise on the Rajmata in public even when he had political differences with Yashodhara. He would often describe the Rajmata as a 'mother to lakhs of party workers like me'.

Again in 2019, Yashodhara had walked out of a BJP meeting in Bhopal because a portrait of her mother had not been put up. She rued that her mother, a founder member of the BJP, was being ignored when the party was supposedly celebrating her birth centenary by erecting statues, releasing postage stamps and naming government buildings after the Rajmata.

Another running feud Yashodhara had was with her party colleague, Jai Bhan Singh Pawaiya, who had served as an MLA and MP from Gwalior and was a bitter critic of the Scindias. During the 2014 Lok Sabha polls, Yashodhara had ticked off

Pawaiya, her ministerial colleague, in full public view. Speaking at an election rally, Yashodhara had turned to Pawaiya, who was seated on the dais, and remarked, 'Some persons have collected soil from Rani Lakshmibai's mausoleum. Such people ought to take soil even from the Rajmata's samadhi. The Rajmata was not only my mother but the entire BJP's mother.'

Pawaiya, who was contesting against Yashodhara's nephew, Jyotiraditya Scindia,[9] in Guna, was quick to retort: 'I have always respected Rajmata Scindia and never spoken flippantly regarding her. However, freedom fighters are accorded an exalted position by me. I make a clear distinction between politicians and those who selflessly sacrificed their lives during the country's freedom struggle.'

Earlier, in 1998, Pawaiya had contested against Yashodhara's brother, Madhavrao, in Gwalior and lost by a narrow margin. The scare had forced Madhavrao to shift to neighbouring Guna in 1999. Pawaiya won as a BJP nominee from Gwalior that year but in subsequent elections the ticket went to Yashodhara.

At the 2014 election rally, Pawaiya did not name Yashodhara, but went on to say that his opposition to the 'palace' was well known to everyone. 'In Guna–Shivpuri–Gwalior, I have been raising my voice against the mentality of "Shrimant" and "Maharaj". And I do not care if I get support from such quarters,' he said.

The public spat displeased Chouhan, who spoke in the presence of both. '*Janata ke beech mein pair me chakkar, munh mein shakkar, dil mein aag aur dimag shant kar jayen* [When leaders go to the masses, they should go with a burning zeal in their hearts, and a calm mind and a sweet tongue],' he had said.

Shift from Gwalior

As a politician, Yashodhara often had to change her constituency and fight assembly or parliamentary polls based on party diktats.

For instance, in 2007, Yashodhra had left her MLA seat and contested a Lok Sabha by-poll from Gwalior after the town's Congress MP was disqualified in the 'cash-for-query' scam.[10]

Yashodhara won the Gwalior seat in March 2007. But by mid-2008, Yashodhara had decided to contest the November 2008 state assembly polls when she still had almost a year to go as Lok Sabha MP from pocket borough Gwalior. This amounted to saying a political farewell to Gwalior by a Scindia after ruling it for over two centuries and then representing it for the better part of five decades after Independence. Perhaps the narrow victory of 35,000 votes in the 2007 Lok Sabha polls was a reason behind Yashodhara deciding to leave Gwalior just as a similar close shave in 1998 had led her late brother, Madhavrao Scindia, to abandon Gwalior for Guna in the 1999 election. The family's supporters had then blamed the dwindling votes on the people's unrealistically high expectations from the Scindias.

However, Yashodhara, just like Jyotiraditya, never gave up flaunting her 'emotional' link with Gwalior. In 2008, she and her nephew had crossed swords over the civic body's plan to build a 750-metre ropeway from Gwalior fort to the city's Phoolbagh Garden. Jyotiraditya had opposed the move, saying it would damage the environment at Gwalior fort, the family's ancestral home, but Yashodhara had challenged the claim. There had been other such skirmishes too earlier. In 2007, Union civil aviation minister, Praful Patel, had come to the city with Jyotiraditya to inaugurate a Delhi–Gwalior–Bhopal flight. Yashodhara, as Gwalior MP, had written a letter of protest to Lok Sabha Speaker Somnath Chatterjee against the 'gross injustice', wondering why the Guna MP had been made the guest of honour when he had 'nothing to do' with Gwalior.

Around the same time, a theft at the Gwalior royal palace had prompted Yashodhara's personal secretary Satish Jaiswal to point an accusing finger at Vijay Phalke, the personal secretary to Jyotiraditya. Jaiswal filed a complaint of alleged burglary at Jai Vilas Palace and listed ninety-one antiques and precious silver utensils as missing from the palace, which was run by a Scindia family trust. Police Officer Munish Rajoriya received another complaint, too, this time from Phalke, asking Rajoriya to investigate the burglary. He, however, did not submit any list of 'stolen items'. Both complaints claimed that the items were stolen from the eastern portion of the palace, better known as Rani Mahal.

Scindia insiders claimed that 'burglaries' at the royal palace were not uncommon and were aimed at clandestinely selling antiques. Moreover, police investigations have seldom made any headway lending some credibility to this claim.

Fight for Turf

From 2001 to 2020, Yashodhara and Jyotiraditya remained locked in a fight for their control over the political turf, each claiming to be the true inheritor of the Scindia legacy. When Yashodhara's son Akshay got married on 5 February 2017, at Bangalore, a wedding reception was planned at Rani Mahal, inside Jai Vilas Palace. But the venue had to be abruptly changed to Usha Kiran Palace Hotel as somebody had mischievously watered the lawns of Rani Mahal without Yashodhara's knowledge, making it unfit to hold a reception. Sources close to Yashodhara pointed a finger at Jyotiraditya, who, as the head of the Scindia family, has employees reporting directly to him.

During every assembly and parliamentary poll in Madhya Pradesh, Jyotiraditya would urge 'Gwalior *ki praja*' to vote for the Congress. Folklore has it that whenever a Scindia was asked to campaign against another, they would simply tell the crowds, '*meri izzat rakh lena* [protect my dignity]', leaving them confused as to what exactly they meant.

'Ship with a Leak'

Most residents of Gwalior still believe that the Scindias collectively possess a fortune. But in an interview, Yashodhara had once said the Scindia wealth was 'like a bottle with a hole or a ship with a permanent leak in the ocean'. 'I don't think there is a single one of us who had an easy life,' Yashodhara told Sangghvi, adding that the Scindias had little choice but to trust each other.

As a politician, Yashodhara turned out to be a crusader of sorts for many causes. One that stood out was her drive against illegal mining. Madhya Pradesh has a history of the sand mafia threatening, attacking and even killing police and forest officials. The sand business in the state is largely controlled by politicians and their close relatives and a huge black-money economy has emerged. According to anti-sand mining activist Sumaira Abdulali, the same politicians charged with enforcing environmental laws are actively engaged in destroying the environment and covering up their misdeeds through intimidation, threat and violence, including murder.

In 2012, an IPS officer, Narendra Kumar, was brutally killed in Morena district of the state. Six months later, Abhishek Singh, a trainee IAS officer posted at Morena, was attacked by members of a sand mafia when he tried to prevent sand mining in Bhavana village near the Chambal Gharial Sanctuary.

The Mumbai-based Abdulali said the menace can be curbed only when local people become vigilant and policies relating to sand mining are changed, both in the state and at the national level. 'For example, when the film *Sand Wars* premiered in Paris, it evoked a lot of reaction from citizens and the EU is now considering possible change in their sand mining laws,' Abdulali said, while suggesting the creation of an environmental police force. 'A trained environment police, with suitable powers to take penal action on the spot on the lines of customs authorities, might be an answer.'[11]

As a politician from the Gwalior–Chambal region, Yashodhara had to fight within and outside the BJP against illegal mining in Shivpuri by K.P. Singh's family. Yashodhara has also alleged that senior BJP functionaries were patronizing 'illegal mining' in the region and government agencies were turning a blind eye to what was happening. 'I have written several letters but, so far, there has been no effective response,' she had said.

Yashodhara has remained passionate about building sports complexes and roads, electrifying villages, and setting up polytechnics and computer centres. 'If you visit villages of India, you will weep at the poverty,' she once told an interviewer. 'I may not be a minister or Padma (award) recipient or even get voted back for the work I have done, but I have the satisfaction of knowing that I have made a few lives better.'[12]

Princesses are, perhaps, not known to say such things or take up such causes but that's what makes Yashodhara a different politician in the true mould of the Rajmata.

By the time Jyotiraditya joined the BJP in March 2020, the relationship between the two branches of the Scindias had become cordial. When Archana Masih asked Yashodhara if she had played a role in bringing her nephew to the BJP, the aunt had replied, 'I'm not going to let you in on whether I had a role or not. Sorry.'

After a pause, she added, 'I was seeing this unfold and I had a feeling that this was going to happen because this was the only way he [Jyotiraditya] could have moved forward.'

When asked if it was due to Congress leader Rahul Gandhi's failure to match Prime Minister Narendra Modi's political prowess, Yashodhara was measured in her response. 'It is not a question of being close to Rahul Gandhi. He had 16 MLAs and a government can be formed with those MLAs in a very dignified way. He approached us; we approached him – and he decided to come to our party.'

Would the late Madhavrao Scindia have approved of his son joining the BJP?

'It is a hypothetical question,' Yashodhara replied. 'He was a Congressman in another time and that time has changed. One has to change with the times. A politician always moves forward taking the time with him. If one is unhappy and dissatisfied with the role one is playing within a certain area, then you do look to see how you can improve the role so that the efficacy of doing work for the constituency can also improve. So everything is in the moment.'

Among the Scindia sisters, Yashodhara was the closest to Madhavrao. In fact, around 2000–2001, when the Rajmata was ailing and Madhavrao would visit them frequently, he had told Yashodhara, 'I will be a changed person and fulfil all rights and duties of a brother.' But 'before he could do all that, he was gone', she told this author in 2020, while recalling that conversation with her brother.

Columnist and television anchor, Priya Sahgal, claimed that a family friend had brokered Jyotiraditya's entry into the BJP. 'Though this was something the late Arun Jaitley had also been pushing for, it took Scindia a while to finally take this step as the decision to leave the party his father had been associated with was an emotional one,' Sahgal wrote in *The Sunday Guardian*.[13] 'The differences between the aunts and the nephew weren't just political. At stake is the vast family inheritance that includes the Jai Vilas Palace in Gwalior and others such as Kuleth Kothi, Sakhya Vilas, Takenpore retreat. There are properties scattered all over India – from neighbouring Shivpuri to Maharashtra, Ujjain and Pune. Not to mention more than 200 acres of prime real estate in Delhi.'

According to Sahgal, in politics, nothing is what it seems

like. 'A fact that the Scindias know all too well. For, displayed in the public section of the Jai Vilas Palace in Gwalior are a set of green dining plates that turn red if served with poisoned food,' she wrote in her characteristic style.

SIX

Jyotiraditya Scindia: The Ambitious Gwalior Royal

Just like his grandmother and father, Jyotiraditya Scindia turned a rebel after failing to find a foothold in politics in his home state Madhya Pradesh.

Jyotiraditya (Bal or Aditya to close friends and family) had been restless and edgy since May 2018, when the Congress leadership (Sonia Gandhi and Rahul Gandhi) picked the veteran Kamal Nath as state party chief. Six months later, when the Congress wrested the state, ending fifteen years of BJP rule, Sonia and Rahul chose Nath as chief minister.

Jyotiraditya, who had till then fancied himself as a contender, went into a prolonged sulk but sources close to Sonia said an informal headcount conducted among the newly elected Congress MLAs had given Nath the thumbs-up.

Maharaja Bhanu Pratap of Narsingarh, a subject of the erstwhile Gwalior empire, had succinctly explained why Jyotiraditya lost the battle for the chief minister's post to Nath. 'There are two reasons for it,' Bhanu Pratap, a former parliamentarian, told veteran journalist, Nirmal Pathak, and a few others when he met them in the Central Hall of Parliament. 'Everyone knows Maharaj Jyotiraditya Scindia in Madhya Pradesh but he knows very few of them there. Secondly, the maharaja's kurta reportedly does not have pockets.'[1]

The reference to kurta and pockets was an allusion to the Scindias' (in)famous ability to spend money and extend patronage. Nath, on the other hand, has the reputation of being a generous patron of all those who are fond of worldly possessions.

The 70-plus veteran was also credited with funding the Congress campaign in Karnataka, where assembly polls were held in May 2018, coinciding with his appointment as Madhya Pradesh Congress chief.

According to informal convention within the Congress, a party unit chief is perceived as the chief ministerial face in a poll-bound state. But Jyotiraditya, forty-seven then, had fought hard to dispel such an impression. He was the chairman of the Congress campaign in Madhya Pradesh and had projected himself as a young and 'credible face' to take on the then BJP chief minister, Shivraj Singh Chouhan.

Chouhan himself ran a rather personal and intense campaign against Jyotiraditya with the tagline '*maaf karo maharaj* [excuse us, maharaj!]' while labelling the contest as a battle between the 'palace and the people'.

Till May 2018, Jyotiraditya and Nath were on the same page and often spoke with a sense of camaraderie. 'We are one. You can check with Jyoti…,' Nath would often tell this author. Jyotiraditya, a little more guarded, would say he was open to the idea of supporting anyone the party high command chooses. At that juncture, these regional satraps seemed to be making a concerted bid to keep out the third player in the race, Digvijaya Singh, who was busy with his 1,100-mile-long Narmada river parikrama on foot.

In December 2018, the Congress emerged victorious in Madhya Pradesh, Rajasthan and Chhattisgarh. Virtually everyone in the Congress and outside had expected Rahul, who had been crowned the 87th president of the grand old party around the same time, to usher in young blood.

It was not to be, as Nath, Ashok Gehlot and Bhupesh Baghel earned their jobs in Bhopal, Jaipur and Raipur, respectively, not just through grit and hard work, but also because of some last-minute, behind the scenes deliberations. There was some arm-twisting and a fair bit of cajoling, as well.

The three-act play belied expectations of a change in approach, most glaringly in the case of Madhya Pradesh than the other two states. But I'll come back to that after dealing with Chhattisgarh first and then Rajasthan, as the political decision-making process was linked and had a long-term bearing on internal Congress politics, affecting Jyotiraditya, Sachin Pilot and Rahul Gandhi.

Chhattisgarh

The selection of the chief ministerial candidate for Chhattisgarh proved to be the trickiest. It is possible that the Congress high command had not anticipated a landslide victory in the state and so had made little preparations for the change. The 11 December 2018 verdict offered Rahul four options.

Tribhuvaneshwar Saran Singh Deo was a suave and experienced hand but his feudal background stood against the former Sarguja ruler.

Tamradhwaj Sahu, the Congress MP from Durg, was backed by AICC point man, P.L. Punia, but had been fielded at the last minute to win over the influential Sahu *samaj*.

The resourceful and worldly-wise Charan Das Mahant, a former union minister, was among the contenders, too.

And then there was Baghel, Chhattisgarh's Congress unit chief.

Baghel, who had dropped out of college while doing his BSc, had convinced his father to allow him to join the uncertain world of politics by promising him that he would become a chief minister one day. Thirty-seven years later, in December 2018, Baghel's father Nand Kumar Baghel would proudly narrate to the media the conversation he had with his son.

Baghel was, however, not the first choice of the top brass, despite being the state unit chief. On 13 December, the four contenders were summoned to Delhi for a meeting with Rahul. The Congress president tried to hammer out a consensus for three hours and decided that Sahu would be the next chief minister. But the AICC chief met with a full-blown rebellion. The other three satraps said they would not work under Sahu.

Another round of consultations followed. This time, Singh Deo was the favourite, but now Sahu was ready to revolt. Motilal Vora, a former chief minister and the All India Congress Committee general secretary in-charge of administration, was brought in for the negotiations. When the deadlock continued, AICC treasurer, Ahmed Patel, intervened. Patel backed Baghel and, to Rahul's astonishment, everyone agreed, with Mahant putting in a condition that he should be made the speaker of the assembly.

Rajasthan

Rajasthan was not easy either. When former minister Sachin Pilot landed in New Delhi from Jaipur after winning the Tonk seat, he went to meet Rahul at his residence. Around the same time, Gehlot, who had won from Sardarpura, was confabulating with Patel at his residence. Hectic lobbying followed. It led to a see-saw battle, which first saw Pilot on top and then Gehlot as the likely contender, with the former Rajasthan chief minister having nearly twice the number of MLAs backing him compared to those supporting Pilot.

Rahul had all along been keen to appoint a 'young face' in one of the three newly acquired states, but Gehlot, who comes from a family of magicians, proved to be a crafty customer. It was difficult to convince Pilot. Finally, it was Rahul's sister, Priyanka – who has known Pilot since he was a boy – along with their mother, Sonia, who prevailed upon him to accept the deputy chief minister's post.

Eighteen months later, Pilot would run out of patience and, for nearly a month, turn rebellious, almost on the brink of quitting the party and then emerging as Rahul's answer to counter Jyotiraditya.

Madhya Pradesh

After the chief ministerial candidates for Chhattisgarh and Rajasthan were selected on 14 December, all eyes turned to Madhya Pradesh, where Jyotiraditya was counting on his friend Rahul. The two had known each other from the age of four and had gone to Doon School and St. Stephen's College together – Jyotiraditya as a BA pass course student and Rahul as a student of history honours. Both had left midway, gone abroad and then returned to India, one as an investment banker and the other as a management consultant.

Rahul, however, turned a tad neutral when it came to friends like Jyotiraditya and Pilot. Perhaps it was the weighty office of Congress president that deprived him of an avenue to bestow favours, but this neutrality was crucial to the events that unfolded in early March 2020.

Minutes after Nath was picked as chief minister of Madhya Pradesh on 14 December 2018, Rahul, who was the Congress president then, tweeted a picture of him with Nath and Jyotiraditya Scindia and quoted Leo Tolstoy to say that the 'two most powerful warriors are patience and time'.

It is said that friendship is the most beautiful gift of God. If you have a loyal best friend, you are the happiest person in this world. But if that one loyal friend betrayed you, then you get disappointed and hurt. Dispassionate observers would later say it was a curious mix of promises not honoured and Jyotiraditya creating his own heartbreak through expectations.

The choice of Madhya Pradesh chief minister had moved to the stage of number crunching. Jyotiraditya's supporters still claim they had won twenty-six of the thirty-four seats in the Gwalior–Chambal region (the Scindias' political citadel accounts for only 15 per cent of Madhya Pradesh's voters) as against Nath's twenty-four out of thirty-eight assembly seats in the Mahakaushal region.

That was when former chief minister Digvijaya took centre stage, sharing a photograph of thirty-one newly elected MLAs calling on his son, Jaivardhan, who had won from the Raghogarh principality that was part of the erstwhile Gwalior empire. The subtle message was that Jyotiraditya's support of twenty-six MLAs meant little when a 'non-contender' had thirty-one MLAs behind him.

While this battle carried on, Nath, in Bhopal, messaged party bigwigs to say that over eighty MLAs from various Congress factions, smaller parties and independents were with him.

Rahul went public, demonstrating his figurative confidence in Jyotiraditya by ensuring that he was by his side when he travelled from Delhi to Jaipur, Bhopal and Raipur for the three swearing-in ceremonies. The idea was to showcase the 'young face' of the party when, in effect, the old guard was calling the shots. The chief ministerial selections of December 2018 once again underlined the old guard's grip on the Congress and palace intrigue.

By the time the 2019 Lok Sabha polls were announced,

Jyotiraditya had been given a political role in Uttar Pradesh. He was appointed AICC general secretary in charge of western Uttar Pradesh while Priyanka manned eastern and central Uttar Pradesh. Jyotiraditya spent a lot of time and energy in trying to revive the party but nothing worked.

In some ways, Jyotiraditya parting ways with the Gandhis was similar to the saga of the Gandhis and the Bachchans, largely a story of friendship that turned sour. And just like much of the real cause(s) of the split between the Bachchans and the Gandhis has remained in the realm of speculation – ranging from tussle over finances, ego, one-upmanship and infatuation with astrology – the real reasons for Jyotiraditya‘s devastating goodbye has not come out in the public domain yet.

One guess is that Sonia and Rahul failed to fulfil some of the informal promises that had been made to Jyotiraditya in 2018 and then 2019, the year the Lok Sabha polls were held.

In 2018, Jyotiraditya was in high spirits, eager to lead from the front, but after the assembly election results came out in December, Rahul, Priyanka and Sonia tried to convince him, pointing out that age was on his side and that a bigger role lay ahead.

Defeat in Guna

Jyotiraditya was reportedly reluctant to contest the Lok Sabha polls from Guna, as he was working full-time in Uttar Pradesh as an AICC general secretary, but Rahul and Priyanka forced his hand. Rahul reportedly advised him to let his wife Priyadarshini Raje campaign. Even son Mahanaaryaman was pressed into action. The duo drew good crowds but failed to bring home the votes. Jyotiraditya lost the Guna Lok Sabha seat to his one-time associate, Krishna Pal Singh Yadav, suffering his first electoral defeat.

Krishna Pal had reportedly fallen out with the Scindias ahead of the 2018 assembly polls after being denied a ticket. When the general election was announced, the BJP fielded him from Guna. Priyadarshini Raje had then reportedly shared on social media a photograph of Krishna Pal with her husband and ridiculed him, saying that a man who once stood in queues waiting to click a selfie with the erstwhile maharaja was now the BJP's nominee.

Krishna Pal, a doctor by profession, used to look after the Ashok Nagar assembly seat for Jyotiraditya.

Once the results were announced on 23 May 2019, Jyotiraditya took to Twitter to congratulate Krishna Pal. 'I humbly accept the people's mandate. For me, politics is a medium to serve the people and I am committed to serving the people. I thank all the voters, Congress workers who worked for me. Congratulations to Dr KP Yadav on his win,' he said.

For the first time, a Scindia had lost in their home turf. (Jyotiraditya's grandmother Vijaya Raje Scindia, too, had lost but in Raebareli, Uttar Pradesh, against Indira Gandhi in 1980.)

Sources close to Jyotiraditya maintain that the Gwalior scion held Rahul responsible for his defeat in Guna – a point of view based on the rather simplistic assumption that the 2019 Lok Sabha elections were a personality battle between the Congress leader and Prime Minister Narendra Modi, where individual party nominees such as Jyotiraditya were inconsequential. Jyotiraditya believed that many of his supporters voted for Modi as he was representing a 'loser' in Rahul.

The defeat created a deep wedge between Jyotiraditya and the Gandhis as the former could not reconcile with his electoral defeat. However, he put a façade of sorts when he became one of the most vocal supporters for buddy Rahul when the Congress Working Committee met in New Delhi on 25 May 2019, where Rahul dramatically announced his resignation as the 87th president of the AICC. Jyotiraditya, according to a section of

Congress leaders, was still expecting Rahul to use his authority (as outgoing party chief) to usher in change, hold people responsible for the 2019 Lok Sabha defeat and introduce a generational shift in the organization.

But Rahul's frame of mind was drastically different from many of his party colleagues. He stubbornly refused to withdraw his resignation and even made it clear that neither him nor his family members, Priyanaka and Sonia, would play any role in the matter of choosing a successor. Years of high command culture had made the Congress too submissive and timid to look for a party president on its own. What was more bizarre amid the inertia was that Rahul opted for a foreign holiday, leaving the party's decision-making apparatus in a lurch. This was not something Jyotiraditya and many other 'young' leaders were expecting.

Some senior Congress leaders think the seeds of discord between Jyotiraditya and the Gandhis date back to UPA I, when the younger lot of MPs were not made ministers despite Prime Minister Dr. Manmohan Singh's eagerness to induct fresh blood. In 2014, the year the Congress lost power at the Centre, Jyotiraditya had not been made party leader in the Lok Sabha. The job had gone to a rather listless Mallikarjun Kharge with Captain Amarinder Singh as his deputy.

In 2017, Amarinder became the chief minister of Punjab but, for some unexplained reason, the post of deputy leader was kept vacant in spite of Jyotiraditya's obvious and legitimate claim. During many crucial debates on issues such as Rafale, the farm crisis and national security, the party preferred other speakers over him.

On the national political scene, sweeping changes were being made, resulting in the abrogation of Article 370 and the introduction of the Citizenship Amendment Bill, the National Register of Citizens and the National Population Register, while the Ram temple verdict capped the virtual vertical divide among citizens. Popular sentiments, particularly in the northern, central and western parts of the country, were often contrary to the stand taken by the Congress.

Jyotiraditya was seen as taking a contrarian line on most of these issues but, each time, he was prevailed upon by Sonia, Priyanka and Rahul to make amends. On one occasion, Priyanka is said to have chastened Jyotiraditya in a rather affectionate manner, similar to the way she deals with Rahul, when she is known to put personal prestige at risk. Jyotiraditya is said to have obliged, albeit with a degree of reluctance.[2]

The Gandhis erred in not holding 'free and frank' in-house debates or fine-tuning their position in keeping with popular sentiments. Jyotiraditya kept throwing signals, once even removing the word 'Congress' from his Twitter handle. This was the time when Jyotiraditya had called on Shivraj Singh Chouhan to let everyone know that he was unhappy with the Nath regime's survey of the damage caused by the 2019 floods and claimed that the Congress's poll promises were not honoured.

Sources close to Jyotiraditya said that while he had easy access to the Gandhis, their repeated promise to intervene in Madhya Pradesh politics seldom translated into action. Increasingly, Jyotiraditya felt that either the Gandhis were complacent about the functioning of the Nath government or were unable to intervene. Either way, his sense of disillusionment was complete.

The Gandhis, on their part, failed to fathom why Jyotiraditya could not be a bit more patient or loyal, or both. After all, there was very little that Sonia or Rahul could have done. The informal headcount among the newly elected party MLAs in Rajasthan and Madhya Pradesh had clearly gone against Pilot and Jyotiraditya.

Rahul Gandhi broke his silence after almost a year over Scindia's decision to leave the party and join the BJP. Interacting with young party leaders during Indian Youth Congress (IYC) national executive meeting in New Delhi on 8 March 2021, Rahul

Gandhi said Congress has always given importance to patience and ideology. 'I had advised him [Jyotiraditya Scindia] to wait for his time. You will definitely be made the CM (of Madhya Pradesh). However, he decided to join the BJP. He should know that he would never be made CM by that [BJP] party,' Rahul Gandhi said. Responding to a question from a youth leader, the former Congress president said he was of the opinion that people who leave the Congress and come back after sometime should not be given any important role in the party.

Jyotiraditya responded wistfully commenting how Rahul Gandhi wasn't so concerned about this particular topic at the time and that it could have been a different situation had that been the case. 'It would have been a different situation had Rahul Gandhi been concerned the same way as he is now when I was in Congress,' Jyotiraditya told media on 9 March 2021.[3]

Rahul's bid to democratize such selections has been a story the party failed to communicate and more importantly, there are few takers even now. There was an acute dearth of resources and some members of the old guard had helped generate funds for assembly elections in Karnataka and other states. Political compulsions were such that the Gandhis, in spite of their notional authority, did not want to punch beyond their weight. They expected Jyotiraditya to make certain sacrifices while the young maharaja was weighing many other factors.

According to party insiders, the Income Tax Department and Enforcement Directorate notices served to the Congress in December 2019 had the potential to cause big upheavals. In such a grim scenario, party leaders were expected to close ranks, and not look for 'greener pastures'.

It is an open secret that the Gandhis are private persons. Their inner circle consists of those who are prepared to observe the code of 'Omerta' and make necessary sacrifices. The list of those who have fallen by the wayside include the Bachchans, Maneka Gandhi and son Varun, Natwar Singh, Hansraj Bhardwaj and M.L. Fotedar. The list is exhaustive and requires a separate chapter. In almost all the cases, the Gandhis shut the door without assigning too many opportunities.

In Jyotiraditya's case, they possibly viewed him as a tad too ambitious and saw little merit in going out of the way to cajole him. Perhaps, the very idea of someone dear and close to them crossing over to Modi–Amit Shah's brand of Hindutva foreclosed all options of conciliation.

In retrospect, it appears that by the time the Rajya Sabha polls were announced in early March 2020, Jyotiraditya had already negotiated his political future with the BJP. According to the numbers in the state assembly then, the Congress was in a position to win two Rajya Sabha seats and the BJP one.

Jyotiraditya, perhaps, expected Sonia and Rahul to nominate him as the first candidate ahead of Digvijaya. But Nath, who was both chief minister and state Congress president, indicated that a majority of party MLAs wanted Digvijaya to be the first nominee.

The tussle over the first and the second nominee was significant as the BJP under Modi and Shah had made a habit of queering the pitch for its opponents even in indirect elections like the Rajya Sabha, where open ballot and adherence to the party whip are mandatory to prevent cross-voting. It is believed that when Sonia came to know about this informal tussle between Jyotiraditya and Digvijaya, she offered the Gwalior scion a seat in Chhattisgarh. The idea of moving out of Madhya Pradesh as a Rajya Sabha nominee is said to have further infuriated Jyotiraditya and firmed up his resolve to quit the party.

The Stanford-educated MBA graduate turned out to be far more pragmatic than his father Madhavrao Scindia, who, despite having lived a large part of his life under Jana Sangh influence, had chosen to chart his own destiny. As authors Vir Sanghvi and Namita Bhandare wrote in their biography of Madhavrao, the late titular maharaja of Gwalior was one of the most liberal and secular politicians in the country.

It is interesting to note that until Jyotiraditya switched to the BJP, he, too, had remained a firm believer in his father's concept of secularism. Sometime in 2018, author-journalist Priya Sahgal had asked him why he had chosen the Congress, considering that the ideologies of both the BJP and the Congress were part of his family legacy.

Jyotiraditya had replied, 'I think that when you decide your course, you must understand what your core values and beliefs are. Then there must be a synergy between your value system and that of the institution you choose to be part of; if there isn't, then there will be dissonance, may not be today but somewhere down the road. Therefore, for me, my core values are clearly liberal, a secular outlook, an agenda of social empowerment and a model of economic growth. All of these find a great deal of resonance with the values of the Congress party.'[4]

This was not the only time Jyotiraditya had spoken about his 'core belief' in secularism. Jyotiraditya had told Sahgal in another interview, that for him, the most important political concern was the growing cult of intolerance. 'The Congress has always stood for secularism, stood for every faith, whether you are a Hindu, Muslim, Sikh, Issai (Christian). It has to be an amalgam. The word "secularism" has unfortunately been corrupted to sometime mean everything but Hinduism,' Jyotiraditya had said, adding, 'Hinduism is a part of secularism because Hinduism – my religion – is a philosophy. It is not even a Religion – it's a Darshan Shastra [philosophy]. It is only in this great country that we have given birth to four religions – Hinduism, Sikhism, Buddhism and Jainism. I am very proud of being a Hindu and my Hinduism certainly comes under the umbrella of secularism.'

The famed tale of friendship between Rahul and Jyotiraditya turned sour within hours of his defection. Jyotiraditya's supporters claimed that their leader did try to reach out to Rahul but could not meet him.

Sources close to Rahul denied this. Rahul himself went on record to describe Jyotiraditya as someone who could walk into his room without an appointment. K. Natwar Singh, a diplomat-turned-politician, told the *Sunday Guardian* newspaper how even the late Sheila Dikshit had to wait for days before being granted a meeting with Rahul.[5]

The charge against Rahul's inability to act swiftly or grant appointments to his party colleagues has been regular. The Jyotiraditya episode provided further credence to claims made by other Congress rebels who had quit the party. One such leader, Himanta Biswa Sarma, deputy chief minister in BJP-ruled Assam, insisted that when he was in the Congress, Rahul, as party president, had not given him an audience.

Stirrings of Rebellion

The BJP became interested in Jyotiraditya after a failed bid to topple the Nath regime in the first week of March 2020. This was a time when Jyotiraditya was merely a spectator, watching from the sidelines the BJP's bid to win over twelve disgruntled Congress and independent MLAs who were airlifted to the ITC Grand Bharat in Gurugram. Nath came to know of the plot early and deputed Digvijaya and MP Vivek Tankha to defuse the crisis.

Tankha, a former additional solicitor general and Congress Rajya Sabha member, was known for his proximity to Jyotiraditya, Nath and Digvijaya. On many occasions in the past, he had acted as a 'peacemaker'. But this time around, Tankha's persuasive skills failed when he reportedly sought Jyotiraditya's help to rein in the disgruntled Congress MLAs, who is said to have sarcastically told Tankha that Chief Minister Nath and Digvijaya were capable of tiding the party over the crisis. Subsequently, in a cloak and dagger manner, Digvijaya's politician son and minister under Nath, Jaivardhan Singh, Jitu Patwari and Kunal Choudhury checked into the ITC Grand Bharat to 'rescue' some of the dissident MLAs.

According to eyewitness accounts of the dramatic events that unfolded in the hotel's room number 307, some state-level Congress and BJP leaders got into heated arguments and even fist fights over the custody of the Congress MLAs.

Before the attempted poaching, Digvijaya had made a serious bid for rapprochement between Nath and Jyotiraditya. A Delhi-based newspaper baroness who had a considerable influence on Jyotiraditya was requested to play peacemaker. A lunch was organized where she, Nath, Digvijaya and Jyotiraditya were present. Nath kept agreeing to and accepting whatever Jyotiraditya sought, mostly in terms of transfers and postings in the Gwalior–Chambal region, but apparently most of these promises were not kept when Nath returned to Bhopal.

Digvijaya had sensed the disquiet in Jyotiraditya's words, deeds and body language but a course correction did not come to pass as Nath was unwilling to leave the entire Gwalior–Chambal region to the 'whims and fancy' of the former maharaja of Gwalior. AICC General Secretary Deepak Bawaria, too, tried his bit, but neither side accorded him any importance.

Many moons ago, Theodore Roosevelt had said, 'Comparison is the thief of joy.' But in politics, comparisons are inevitable and often play a crucial role. As a reporter, I had got a taste of it.

Sometime in 1994, when senior Congress leader, Arjun Singh, was locked in a titanic battle for supremacy with then prime minister and AICC chief, P.V. Narasimha Rao, I remember running into AICC General Secretary Buddha Priya Maurya. Maurya, a Dalit, was from Uttar Pradesh, where a large number of Congress leaders and workers had turned against Rao. I had asked Maurya why he was not supporting Arjun.

Maurya was not offended by the provocative query. In his measured voice he said, 'I hail from Utrauli, Aligarh, where there is a saying that one wishes for son-in-law or leader better than self. And I do not consider Arjun to be better than me.'

A cursory look at contemporary Congress politics would show that friends, peer group or white-collar professionals do not last long in the party. Megastar Amitabh Bachchan's parting with his childhood friend Rajiv Gandhi had singularly contributed to the prime minister's downfall as the Allahabad Lok Sabha by-election in 1988 spurred the fragmented opposition to unite and humble the Congress in the general election that followed. The Congress, which had 413 MPs in the 543-member Lok Sabha, was voted out in 1989.

Arun Nehru and Arun Singh – who were successful corporate and business honchos selling paint and shoe polish – deserted Rajiv when the beleaguered prime minister needed them the most.

In contrast, 'blue collar' political aides like Yashpal Kapoor, R.K. Dhawan, M.L. Fotedar and Vincent George had stood by Indira Gandhi, Rajiv and Sonia like a rock, even after experiencing neglect and humiliation.

The rebellion of the MLAs from the Congress stable in March 2020 also highlighted the endemic problem of defection and elected representatives' quest to become ministers. As per the 91st constitutional amendment of 2003, only 15 per cent of the elected representatives can become ministers. In Madhya Pradesh, for instance, in the house of 230, there is an outer limit of thirty-four in the council of ministers. Any political party having a majority of 116 MLAs is constantly confronted with a problem of 100-plus aspirants for ministerial berths which are non-existent.

Political grapevine has it that Nath did try to keep the disgruntled party MLAs in good humour. Those who could not become ministers were reportedly compensated adequately from the party funds to care for their constituency. Each month, they would go to Indira Gandhi Bhawan, the state party office, to sign a register and get funds. But when poaching season began, the monetary offer at the Indira Gandhi Bhawan appeared to be 'loose change' as compared to a figure allegedly running into eight zeroes and more for every willing player.

Exit from Party

Jyotiraditya carefully chose the day of his rebellion: his father's seventy-fifth birth anniversary 10 March. Jyotiraditya posted a letter on Twitter that was addressed to Sonia, the Congress's interim chief. The letter announced his resignation from the Congress.

Minutes after he posted his resignation, the Congress expelled Jyotiraditya for 'anti-party activities' – just as P.V. Narasimha Rao had expelled Madhavrao in 1996 when he had resigned from the Congress.

Madhavrao had formed his own party, the Madhya Pradesh Vikas Congress, and even managed to defeat a few Congress candidates in the 1996 general elections.

This was not the first time that a Scindia had joined the BJP. As chapters in this book have mentioned, Jyotiraditya's grandmother, Rajmata Vijaya Raje Scindia had left the Congress in 1967 to join the Jana Sangh and later in 1980, became the founder of the BJP while Jyotiraditya's aunts, Vasundhara Raje and Yashodhara Raje, rose to become senior BJP leaders.

Both the aunts welcomed his entry into the party. Moments after her nephew joined the BJP, Yashodhara, who served as a minister in Chouhan's cabinet, said that she hoped aunt and nephew would prove to be a good combination in Madhya Pradesh politics. 'Very happy today. Govt will be formed under SS Chouhan's leadership. We're happy as I've worked under him; I know what wonderful schemes we had for people; today we don't have those,' Yashodhara tweeted minutes after Jyotiraditya joined the BJP in a brief ceremony at the party headquarters in Delhi. 'Best wishes to my nephew, hope we'll have a good aunt–nephew combination,' she added.[6]

Yashodhara, who had described her nephew's move to join the BJP as *ghar vapsi* (homecoming), added that the political differences among the Scindia family members were a thing of the past now. 'Family was divided into two as there were two different political parties. It's natural that if you have political differences, it seeps into the family too. This step has made all small issues of differences to go away. We're on one stage now,' she was quoted as saying by news agency ANI.[7]

Jyotiraditya's other aunt, former Rajasthan chief minister, Vasundhara Raje, echoed similar sentiments while welcoming him into the BJP. 'Good to be on the same team,' she remarked, while lauding her nephew's strength of character and courage to put 'the nation first'. 'If Rajmata Sahab was here today, she would be elated to see you put the #NationFirst. I admire your strength of character and courage. It's good to be on the same team. Welcome to the BJP.' Vasundhara tweeted.

However, noted columnist, Coomi Kapoor, was not convinced that the reunion between the aunts and the nephew was all hunky-dory. Writing in the *Sunday Express*, Kapoor, author of an immensely readable book on the Emergency, observed, 'Whatever their public posturing, Jyotiraditya Scindia's two aunts in the BJP, Vasundhara Raje and Yashodhara, are not exactly thrilled about their nephew joining the party. The longstanding family feud is not about different political ideologies but over the inheritance of the vast Scindia estate. It was not Scindia's aunts but his in-laws from the Gaekwad royal family of Baroda, Gujarat, who opened a channel for him with Narendra Modi. Amit Shah backs the anti-Vasundhara Raje faction in Rajasthan, while Yashodhara was marginalised as a minister by Shivraj Singh Chouhan in Madhya Pradesh.'[8]

Jyotiraditya and his otherwise media-savvy aunts chose not to react to Coomi's observations, as if deliberately.

Chouhan welcomed Jyotiraditya once the Congress rebel had been formally drafted into the BJP, but his speech did not go unnoticed when he referred to Jyotiraditya as 'Vibhishan' – Ravan's younger brother in the Ramayana who deserted his brother to join the rival camp.

At the state BJP office in Bhopal, Chouhan, known to measure his words, remarked while welcoming Jyotiraditya, 'Kamal Nath, till we don't destroy your Lanka of terror and corruption, we will not sit in peace. To destroy Lanka, one needs Vibhishan. Today Jyotiraditya Scindia is with us,' Chouhan said.

The reference to Vibhishan, someone who turned against his own family, is not the most flattering and for the 'maharaj of Gwalior', the tag of a betrayer can hardly be desirable, said Rakesh Dixit, a Bhopal-based political commentator.[9]

Earlier in February 2020, the acrimony between Jyotiraditya and Nath had become visible when the former threatened to take to the streets if the Madhya Pradesh government failed to fulfil its promise to waive farm loans. His comment in Hindi, '*man sadak par utar jayon ga* [I will hit the streets]', received a quick retort, '*to utar jayein* [do it]'.

Nath had many times tried to reason with Jyotiraditya, pointing out that poll manifesto promises were meant to be fulfilled in five years, not in a few months.

Jyotiraditya's exit led to the fall of the fifteen-month-old Nath government. When the elections were held in Madhya Pradesh in November–December 2018, the margin of the Congress's victory was extremely thin. In the 230-member assembly, the Congress had won 114 seats and the BJP 109. The BSP won two, the Samajwadi Party one and independents four seats. The number required to form the government was 116. The Congress was two short, but managed to cobble up an alliance with the BSP, SP and independents. This is how Nath's government survived for fifteen months. But when Jyotiraditya defected, twenty-two Congress MLAs walked out and took shelter in a resort in BJP-ruled Karnataka. They tendered their resignations from the Madhya Pradesh Assembly, reducing the Nath regime to a minority. Nath tried hard to bring back the disgruntled lot and even offered them ministerial posts, but the MLAs bluntly refused.

The strength of the Congress in Madhya Pradesh has been due to regional satraps. Traditionally, Nath held sway in Mahakaushal while Digvijaya was a leader from Madhya Bharat. Arjun Singh and, later, his son, Ajay Singh, aka Rahul Bhaiya, were leading lights from the Vindhya region. The others hailed from Bundelkhand and Malwa. For decades, each regional satrap had focussed on a region of his influence, contributing to the party's strength. But in March 2020, the strength of regional satraps became a huge liability.

Towards the end of his association with the Congress, Jyotiraditya's feud was not so much with Nath but with another regional satrap, Digvijaya. The rivalry between Digvijaya and the Scindias goes back several decades. Jyotiraditya's father, Madhavrao, resented Digvijaya's spectacular rise that saw the former raja of Raghogarh twice become the chief minister, from 1993 to 2003. The Raghogarh principality falls under the erstwhile Gwalior empire of the Scindias. Senior Congress leaders of that era felt that Madhavrao could not stomach someone hailing from their turf going on to rule all of Madhya Pradesh.

When Madhavrao died in an air crash on 30 September 2001, some felt that his lifelong ambition of becoming chief minister had remained unfulfilled. Madhavrao's death had initially brought a young Jyotiraditya close to Digvijaya, albeit briefly.

Speaking in Jyotiraditya's parliamentary constituency Guna

in 2008, Digvijaya had described the then MP as a 'polished diamond' and himself as an 'astute' judge of gems.

However, the temporary truce had ended abruptly. At one point, Digvijaya even went to the extent of propping up Jyotiraditya's rival, Sachin Pilot, within the party as a counterbalance to the young maharaja. For instance, as chief minister of Madhya Pradesh, Digvijaya had once invited Pilot to tour the Gwalior belt, knowing that this wouldn't go down well with Jyotiraditya.

Nath too did the same during 3 November 2020 by-polls in twenty-eight assembly seats, inviting Pilot to campaign in seventeen assembly segments in the Gwalior–Chambal region. The outcome was these assembly polls were not encouraging for the Congress. The BJP won nineteen out of the twenty-eight assembly constituencies, consolidating Chief Minister Shivraj Singh Chouhan's hold over the state.

Going back to Digvijaya, the former chief minister had cemented his equation with Nath during his 1993–2003 tenure as the Congress chief minister of Madhya Pradesh. He would often tell his colleagues in a lighter vein, 'Of the 45 districts in the state, I rule over 44 while the 45th is Nath's.'[10]

All the postings in Nath's district, Chhindwara, were subject to his approval and he was known as the *Bada Bhai* [elder brother] and one whose writ ran large in the state. By the time Nath became chief minister in December 2018, the buzz in Bhopal was, 'Kamal Nath is Digvijaya Singh by another name'.

It would be an exaggeration to say that Jyotiraditya was not given enough chance to excel in Madhya Pradesh politics. In the 2008, 2013 and 2018 assembly polls, he was made head of the Congress campaign committee. However, often his campaign meals turned out to be far more lip-smacking than the electoral outcome. In the 2008 polls, none of the candidates fielded by the Congress MP from Guna, his constituency, tasted victory. While Chief Minister Chouhan and other Madhya Pradesh BJP leaders toiled day and night, some felt Jyotiraditya's focus wavered towards the dinner table.

Reporters covering his campaign recalled that before the former royal would fly to a campaign site, his family cook, Ravi Thapa, would be there, preparing his meal. If it was spaghetti with ginger chicken in Chanderi, it was chicken in tartar sauce at some other venue. Once the elections were over, sumptuous meals gave way to food for thought on whether the maharaja was cut out for a full-time role in state politics.

The Safdarjung Angle

Some Congress leaders attach considerable importance to a house in Lutyens' Delhi as playing a role in Jyotiraditya's exit from the Congress. Jyotiraditya was made to exit from 27 Safdarjung Road in July 2019 after losing the Guna parliamentary seat. The house was then allotted to union human resource development minister, Ramesh Pokhriyal.

For Jyotiraditya, 27 Safdarjung Road had a deep emotional bond. This was the house where his father, Madhavrao, had lived for decades. Madhavrao was the Congress's link to the great Indian middle class. He wore several hats – cricketer, golfer, connoisseur of art, culture and films and a prized celebrity among Delhi's glitterati. Yet, he would find time to pursue politics for at least twelve hours a day.

It was Madhavrao's passion for politics that got him on the ill-fated aircraft which crashed near Mainpuri on the fateful day. Jyotiraditya was in Mumbai then as part of a four-member team that was setting up Morgan Stanley's investment banking practice in India.

At 27 Safdarjung Road, Madhavrao would often invite a select group of media persons for drinks, meal and 'gupshup' and narrate anecdotes.

Madhavrao was elected to Parliament in 1971 as an independent and joined the Congress during the Emergency. He had moved into 27 Safdarjung Road after becoming a minister in the Rajiv Gandhi cabinet when Jyotiraditya was barely thirteen.

Shades of Politicking

A number of political commentators saw various shades of politics and politicking in Jyotiraditya's move to change sides. Rakesh Dixit, the Bhopal-based political analyst, felt Jyotiraditya's induction into the BJP pleased many ordinary party workers in Madhya Pradesh and 'Modi *bhakts*' as the late Vijaya Raje Scindia's grandson had finally joined the party he ideologically belonged to. 'As if he [Jyotiraditya] has atoned for the sins of his wayward father late Madhavrao Scindia who defied his mother and died in a wrong party...,' Dixit wrote in *Gfiles*.[11]

According to him, once disillusioned with the Congress, Jyotiraditya carefully decided to join the BJP rather than launch a separate party like his father had done. 'Maybe because MP Vikas Congress, the party Madhavrao had floated, managed to win just two Lok Sabha seats, unlike parties of other Congress rebel heavyweights such as Arjun Singh, N.D. Tiwari, Sharad Pawar, Mamata Banerjee, K. Karunakaran, A.K. Antony, G.K. Moopanar and Jaganmohan Reddy who had a much higher degree of success. Having lost the Guna Lok Sabha (seat), Jyotiraditya Scindia took an easy way to topple the Congress government and make a beginning in the BJP,' Dixit concluded.

Some Jyotiraditya supporters saw a bright future for their leader in the BJP, which had emerged as a pan-Indian and vibrant political outfit deeply steeped in the country's cultural and religious ethos. The healthy regard that the RSS, Hindu Mahasabha and the BJP have for the former rulers of Gwalior, along with the Rajmata's iconic position in the *parivar*, was seen as the passport for Jyotiraditya's entry.

Earlier, as minister of state for communications and information technology (2008), commerce and industry (2009) and minister for power (independent charge in 2012), Jyotiraditya had shown flashes of promise. Prime Minister Manmohan Singh had praised him for initiating Project Arrow, under which post offices across the country were to be modernized to provide the common man with a window to the world. Started with an investment of Rs 900 crore, post offices were sought to be converted into local retail centres. The idea was to use post office buildings, that had begun to wear a deserted look after the popularity of email services, to profitably sell other services, such as off-the-counter medicine, education schemes, auto loans and healthcare services. Under the scheme, some post offices sold text books, ayurvedic medicines, gold coins and railway tickets. Jyotiraditya had hired two consultants, Ogilvy & Mather and McKinsey, to give India Post a completely new corporate identity with a restructuring plan. The new logo, in bright red and yellow, is the shape of a bird about to take flight. The tagline reads, 'Giving Wings to Your Dreams'.

There were awkward moments, too, such as the incident when dacoits attacked Jyotiraditya's convoy when the newly appointed minister was on the first visit to his constituency since taking charge in April 2008. Jyotiraditya was travelling from Guna to Shivpuri around 10.30 p.m. on a Sunday in a cavalcade of twenty cars, when the dacoit gang struck. His additional private secretary, Purushottam Parashar, was thrashed and robbed.

Local people later claimed it was the first time a Scindia motorcade had been attacked in the Gwalior region the family once ruled. The incident enraged Malkhan Singh, a reformed dacoit from the Chambal region. 'I will soon find out who is responsible. I will also ensure that the law catches up with the culprits,' Malkhan had reportedly told Jyotiraditya when he met the minister later, adding that Jyotiraditya should have taken him along during the journey.

A gang, belonging to the local Kanjar community, had reportedly spread *ranpi* (sharp nails covered in cow dung) on the road his convoy was taking. Jyotiraditya escaped but a Toyota Innova carrying five persons, including his private secretary, was trapped. The driver had stopped, suspecting a flat tyre, but asked the other cars to keep pace with the minister's car. Within minutes, however, a gang of seven or eight appeared from nowhere and demanded money, mobile phones and watches. The Kanjars believe that they must work for their living and not take anything for free. So, the robbers were not content with snatching the valuables; they also thrashed their victims.

Parashar bore the brunt as he had reportedly called Jyotiraditya on speakerphone, hoping that hearing the 'Maharaj' at the other end, the robbers would flee. But the move backfired, and the dacoits attacked the private secretary with a sharp weapon and greater animosity. By the time a local Congress MLA and police reached the spot, the miscreants had fled. Parashar and the others had to be rushed to hospital in Shivpuri.

Malkhan, who was sarpanch of Oraon village in Guna, told this author that had he been around, nobody would have dared attack the convoy. 'The local dacoits seem to be out of their mind. These are not the kind of dacoits we used to have. How dare they try to belittle the Maharaja of Scindia, the most benevolent public servant of our times?' he fumed.

Malkhan, a legendary Chambal dacoit along with Man Singh and Mohar Singh till his surrender in 1972, was in the Congress then. 'We were baghis (rebels) who fought against social inequalities. We never snatched chains or insulted women. Chambal is indeed a changed place now,' he said.

Jyotiraditya's hands-on approach was evident in the power

ministry, too, where he was instrumental in setting up a council, consisting of retired bureaucrats, power producers and financiers to accelerate power-generation projects. A corporate-like approach was adopted where an inter-ministerial panel would meet every month to monitor the progress. For himself, Jyotiraditya had formed strict norms: 'Every six months, I judge myself, on what I have achieved and what new things I can do.'

In private conversations, Jyotiraditya's camp followers visualized a future where they saw him in the same league with the BJP's in-house leaders like Smriti Irani, Piyush Goyal, Devendra Fadnavis, Yogi Adityanath, and even Amit Shah, an optimism that currently has few takers in the party.

A reality check for the supporters came during the October campaign for the 2020 Madhya Pradesh by-polls. Among the 'star BJP campaigners', Jyotiraditya was slotted at number ten instead of his number one position in the state Congress campaign panels of 2008, 2013 and 2018. His photograph, too, was often not on BJP posters.

The Congress, on its part, levelled serious allegations against him, constantly dubbing Jyotiraditya as a 'traitor'. His family's past record of allegedly betraying the Maratha Peshwa to Rani Lakshmibai were raked up (see Chapter 1 for details).

Senior ministers and key bureaucrats during the Nath regime recalled how Jyotiraditya managed to get some old legal cases and disputes with the local administration settled between December 2018 and March 2020, when the Congress was in power in Madhya Pradesh. It was more baffling to them how Jyotiraditya managed to get some key appointments in cooperatives as late as 29 February 2020. By then, he had probably already made up his mind to ditch the Congress, although WhatsApp messages between him and Nath were both frequent and cordial.

The Congress, which levelled many allegations at Jyotiraditya during the 3 November 2020 by-polls, accused him of selling some ancestral properties in Gwalior. Congress state vice-president, Murari Lal Dubey, and spokesperson, K.K. Mishra, held a press conference and handed out some documents to claim that a tomb built in the memory of a dog had been sold off (details of the dog Hussu's tomb are in Chapter 1).

The Congress also hurled allegations of illegal sale and construction related to a property worth Rs 360 crore in Gwalior.

Reacting to the allegations of land grab and illegal sale of property, Jyotiraditya said his family properties dated back to over 300 years. He also mockingly said if it was a mistake to be born in an erstwhile princely family, he would accept the mistake.

Moreover, Jyotiraditya said those who had recently become 'maharajas' (kings) should answer such questions, in what appeared to be a dig at former chief minister Nath.

The Congress also targeted the Chouhan regime, with state leaders Sajjan Singh Verma and Jitu Patwari alleging that the government had shelved a probe initiated by the state police's economic offences wing (EOW) in March 2020. The probe, based on complaints by some Gwalior-based individuals, had been directed by the Nath government after Jyotiraditya left the Congress to join the BJP. When the Chouhan government was formed, the EOW said it had found no grounds to conduct a probe into the allegations.

A Different Role Then

Back in February 2016, however, it was Jyotiraditya who had been vocal as a Congress leader when he locked horns in the Lok Sabha with then HRD minister, Smriti Irani, over Dalit scholar Rohith Vemula's suicide and developments in Jawaharlal Nehru University (JNU).

Rohith was one of five PhD scholars from Ambedkar Students' Association (ASA), a pro-Dalit students' body, who were suspended from the hostels and certain campus areas following charges of assaulting a member of ABVP (Akhil Bharatiya Vidyarthi Parishad), the Sangh's student arm. The Hyderabad University researcher committed suicide on 17 January.

Initiating the debate, Jyotiraditya had alleged 'undue interference' by Irani's ministry and Labour Minister Bandaru Dattatreya in the case. Dattatreya, in a letter, one of six that had surfaced in connection with the case, had called Rohith casteist and anti-national.

Student protesters had alleged that the letter had played a part in the university expelling the five ASA members. 'Where in the world can you see an HRD minister writing five letters in any case,' Jyotiraditya had asked. He then went on to raise the issues from the Film and Television Institute of India, Indian Institute of Technology, Madras, and JNU, where Dalit students were targeted, and lambasted senior ministers in the Modi cabinet, namely Sushma Swaraj, Jual Oram and Irani, for emphasizing that Rohith was not a Dalit.

Criticizing the role of the Hyderabad varsity's administration on Vermula case, Jyotiraditya said protests and fights were common in academic institutions but, in this case, the vice chancellor should have tackled the controversy in a better way. 'But for the last two years, with an atmosphere of intolerance, no one feels secure,' Jyotiraditya had remarked.

Returning fire with fire, a visibly emotional Irani had cautioned Jyotiraditya against using 'education as a political battleground' and said, 'death of a child [Rohith Vemula] should not be used to do vote-bank politics'.

Irani had sought to rubbish allegations of discrimination against Rohith, saying, 'My name is Smriti Irani and I challenge you to tell my caste.' As Irani was concluding the debate, as per parliamentary convention, Jyotiraditya did not get a chance to retort further.

While Jyotiraditya remained tight-lipped about his future plans and why he parted ways with the Congress, except for making politically correct pronouncements, political commentators like Dixit felt he had reasons to feel acutely vulnerable after his shocking defeat in Guna.

Weighing heavily on his mind too was generation-next politics. In May 2019, while Jyotiraditya lost, Nath had succeeded in getting his son Nakul elected from Chhindwara. Digvijaya too got his son Jaivardhan a berth in the Congress ministry. 'Scindia perhaps felt that his future was bleak in the MP Congress as Nakul Nath and Jaivardhan have ascended in the state's firmament as two rising stars…,' Dixit wrote, while mentioning another youngster, Jitu Patwari.[12]

Rahul, in private conversations, had reportedly viewed Patwari, who is from Indore, as a future leader, better than some of the young dynasts.

Not the Only One

Prior to Jyotiraditya's exit from the grand old party, the period between 2013 and 2019 saw many Congress leaders leaving the party. In one particularly high-profile case, Jyotiraditya was himself responsible for the exit of Priyanka Chaturvedi, who was a young and suave Congress spokesperson and is currently a Rajya Sabha member from the Shiv Sena.

Jyotiraditya's 'inapt' handling of the Chaturvedi issue and his own subsequent move to leave the Congress made some senior party leaders bitter on grounds of depriving the party from a 'talented' Chaturvedi.

On 20 April 2019, Chaturvedi had stunned Congress leaders and virtually everyone in political circles when Sena supremo Uddhav Thackeray announced her induction as the Sena 'getting a new sister'.

Madho Maharaj Scindia (1876-1925) with son Jiwajirao 'George' Scindia (on his lap) and daughter Kamla 'Mary' Raje. © *Kedar Jain*

Lekha Divyeshwari Devi was married to the Maharaja of Gwalior, Jiwajirao Scindia, in 1941 at the age of 22. As per tradition a new name was chosen for her then – Vijaya Raje. Later, she was popularly known as Rajmata Scindia. © *Kedar Jain*

A young Vijaya Raje Scindia with her husband Jiwajirao Scindia, Maharaja of Gwalior, a state the size of Greece, that qualified for a 21-gun salute during the Raj. © *Kedar Jain*

Madhavrao Scindia at his wedding, 1966. He married Madhavi Raje (Kiran ajya Lakshmi Devi), the great-granddaughter of the Prime Minister of Nepal nd Maharaja of Kaski. He is flanked by his sisters, Vasundhara Raje to his right and Yashodhara Raje to his left. © *Kedar Jain*

Vasundhara Raje Scindi
and her husband Mahar
Rana Hemant Singh
of Dholpur on their
wedding in November
1972. Also seen in the
picture are Madhavrao
and Rajmata Scindia.
© *Kedar Jain*

Madhavrao Scindia with his mother Rajmata Scindia at an official function.
© *Kedar Jain*

Rajmata Scindia with her mother Chuda Devashwari Devi (seated next to her). Also in the picture are the Rajmata's daughters Yashodhara Raje (left) and Usha Raje (right). © *Kedar Jain*

The Rajmata with her grandsons, Dushyant Singh (Vasundhara Raje's only son) left and Akshay Bhansali (Yashodhara Raje's eldest son). © *Kedar Jain*

Rajmata Scindia with L.K. Advani and Dr Murli Manohar Joshi in Ayodhya. Along with Atal Bihari Vajpayee and L.K. Advani the Rajmata emerged as the BJP's all powerful trinity who shot into controversial national prominence after championing the Ram temple cause in Ayodhya. © *Parveen Jain*

Madhavrao with his sister Vasundhara Raje. © *Kedar Jain*

Madhavrao Scindia watches Sonia and Priyanka Gandhi pay homage to Rajiv Gandhi on his death anniversary at his samadhi, Vir Bhoomi.

© *Parveen Jain*

A procession in Gwalior on the occasion of the wedding of Jyotiraditya Scindia (standing) and Priyadarshani Raje Gaekwad of Baroda (seated), December 1994. Also in the picture is Madhavrao (seated, right). © *Kedar Jain*

Madhavrao Scindia performs the last rites of his mother Rajmata Scindia, January 2001. Mother and son did not make amends during her lifetime and a bitter property battle ensued after her death as she had written her only son out of her will. Eight months later, in September 2001, Madhavrao died in a plane crash.

© Kedar Jain

On 10 March 2020, the day of his father Madhavrao Scindia's 75th birth anniversary, Jyotiraditya quit the Congress to join the BJP. His aunt, Yashodhara Raje, praised his move and called it a *'gharwaapsi'*. *© Alamy*

Chaturvedi, who is from Mathura, Uttar Pradesh, and lives in Mumbai, had a rather meteoric rise in the grand old party. She had become visible in 2010 when she attended the Indian School of Business's 10,000 Women Entrepreneurs Certificate programme, a global initiative supported by the Goldman Sachs Foundation for women entrepreneurs. By 2012, the 1979-born Chaturvedi was the general secretary of the Mumbai north-west wing of the Indian Youth Congress.

Gurudas Kamat, a veteran and respectable Congress leader who was himself the Indian Youth Congress chief during the Rajiv Gandhi era, was said to have spotted her talent and remained her mentor till he was alive. The period between 2012 and 2014 was the most challenging for the Congress when Chaturvedi took a stand in television news debates and on social media, defending Sonia, Rahul and the party in the most spirited manner.

From May 2014 to April 2019, Chaturvedi became one of the most visible faces of the party on TV and social media.

At a time when Priyanka appeared as formidable and dependable as Rahul Dravid in Team India, her defection eight days before the 2019 Lok Sabha polls in Mumbai shocked everyone, including Jyotiraditya who was AICC general secretary in charge of Uttar Pradesh West.

A closer scrutiny showed that Jyotiraditya was the prime cause why Chaturvedi left the party. She was already unhappy over the party's refusal to give her a ticket from Mumbai North, where actress Urmila Matondkar was fielded. Chaturvedi was in Mathura in September 2018 to hold a media briefing on Rafale, as per Rahul's directive to hold press conferences across the nation on the deal. During her media interaction in Mathura, some local Congress leaders had misbehaved with her, allegedly at the behest of a local party leader who viewed her as some kind of a threat as Chaturvedi had deep roots in Mathura.

In fact, before the 2019 parliamentary polls were announced, there was a buzz that Chaturvedi might be fielded to take on BJP MP and actress Hema Malini. The alleged misbehaviour, a mix of physical and verbal abuse, was so ugly that Chaturvedi left the scheduled press conference in a huff but her tormentors followed her to a room where she had sought refuge.

The matter was taken up with the higher-ups in the party. Jyotiraditya, as AICC general secretary in charge of western Uttar Pradesh, was directly responsible for protecting the dignity of a woman leader of the party. It was said that when Chaturvedi sought Rahul's intervention, Rahul was both sympathetic and in a mood to take action against the culprits. He reportedly did talk to Jyotiraditya, urging him to act swiftly.

According to newspaper reports then, the people allegedly involved in the Mathura incident were Ashok Chakleshwar, Umesh Pandit, Pratap Singh, Abdul Jabbar, Girdhari Lal Pathak, Bhuri Singh Jayas, Pravin Thakur and Yatindra Mukadam. Jyotiraditya did act against them, suspending and serving show-cause notices to all eight. But within days, a volte-face followed. On 15 April, all of them were reinstated after being given a strict warning. The leaders gave a written apology.

Sources close to Jyotiraditya said the eight were reinstated on the recommendation of Uttar Pradesh Congress Committee chief, Raj Babbar, after they expressed regret and promised not to misbehave in the future.

Chaturvedi was outraged. Describing them as 'lumpen goons', she wrote on her Twitter handle, 'Deeply saddened that lumpen goons get preference in @incindia over those who have given their sweat and blood. Having faced brickbats and abuse across board (sic) for the party but yet those who threatened me within the party getting away with not even a rap on their knuckles is unfortunate.'

At this stage, Priyanka Gandhi Vadra and Sonia tried to intervene but Jyotiraditya and Raj Babbar reportedly cited 'delicate' political equations in Mathura, while declining to reverse the order to reinstate the culprits. The Gandhis wished Chaturvedi good luck even as she left the Congress.

A few months later, actress Matondkar, who had lost from Mumbai North, also left the Congress, levelling similar charges of inaction. Matondkar had accused local party leaders, Sandesh Kondvilkar and Bhushan Patil, close associates of Sanjay Nirupam, a former Mumbai Congress president, of misbehaving with her, but no action was taken. Jyotiraditya, however, had no active role to play in the episode.

The abrupt exit of Chaturvedi, Matondkar and many others showed how the Congress central leadership (read the Gandhis) handled party affairs, allowing mangers such as Jyotiraditya and Nirupam to let a sense of despondency set in within the ranks.

Defection and After

Post defection, Jyotiraditya emerged in a new avatar – more assertive, religious and confident. Amid whispers that his mother Madhavi Raje was not too pleased with his move to desert the Congress, Jyotiraditya began taking potshots at the Congress but avoided naming Sonia, Rahul or Priyanka, perhaps in keeping with his mother's sentiments. But he could not resist attacking Indira Gandhi's Emergency, a period that had seen his grandmother getting imprisoned, father fleeing to Nepal and officials from the Income Tax Department and the Enforcement Directorate harassing everyone at Jai Vilas Palace.

Jyotiraditya was barely five then but seemed to have an adult's memory while hitting out at his former party for imposing the Emergency in 1975.

Speaking at an event in Bhopal to mark 100 days of Chouhan's regime on 3 July 2020, Jyotiraditya spoke with flair claiming that even when he was in the Congress, he had taken a stand against the Emergency.

He also praised Prime Minister Modi's handling of the COVID-19 pandemic, 'The Congress in 1975 imposed the Emergency to cling to power, while PM Modi appealed for a lockdown to save lives and people obeyed the "pradhan sevak's" appeal wholeheartedly,' he said. 'While in the Congress, I always sided with the truth and always opposed the Emergency because what is wrong is wrong and what is right is right.'

Human Side

In September 2017, Jyotiraditya's quick thinking saved a fellow passenger travelling by the Shatabdi Express. Doctors later said had he not intervened, the passenger would have died.

Jyotiraditya was on the Delhi-bound Shatabdi Express from Bhopal when he saw the lady, Vandana Sharma, in the berth across his writhing in pain. The Congress MP realized something was seriously wrong.

It was past midnight and no medical help seemed at hand on the train that had stopped somewhere on a deserted stretch on Delhi's outskirts, waiting for signal clearance. Jyotiraditya pulled out his smartphone and called up Railway Minister Piyush Goyal, who woke up senior officials. The Congress MP's next call was to Ranjan Yadav, the Agra-based divisional manager of North-Central Railways. An ambulance arrived around 1.45 a.m. and Jyotiraditya accompanied Sharma, who was travelling alone, to the Northern Railways Central Hospital, Delhi, where doctors said the seventy-year-old had suffered a cardiac arrest. Many passengers and doctors felt that Vandana Sharma may not have survived had Jyotiraditya not acted fast.

Jyotiraditya reached his 27 Safdarjung Road residence in New Delhi around 4 a.m. He had boarded from Gwalior around 8 p.m. while Sharma had boarded from Agra an hour and a half later. The 12001 Shatabdi Express reached New Delhi station at 2.20 a.m., two hours and fifty minutes late.

Jyotiraditya said he was appalled that there were no emergency or medical services available on the premier train. 'There should be some kind of arrangement. If there are doctors travelling in the train, then the ticket examiner or ticket collector should have that information. The travelling doctors should be requested to carry some emergency medicines,' he had told this author while underplaying his role in saving Sharma's life.

The erstwhile Congress leader has inherited his passion for the railways from his father, who was minister for railways in the Rajiv Gandhi government. Running Shatabdi Express trains linking New Delhi with various state capitals, such as Bhopal, Jaipur, Lucknow and Chandigarh, was his brainchild. As mentioned in the earlier chapters, in the pre-Independence days, the royal family of the Scindias used to own the 'Scindia State Railways' that operated trains between Agra, Gwalior, Ujjain, Bhind and Sabalgarh.

Jyotiraditya's quick thinking drew praise from the Agra Tourist Welfare Chamber. Its secretary, Vishal Sharma, said that had it not been for Scindia or a 'VIP train' like the Shatabdi, medical assistance to a seriously ill passenger may not have arrived on time.

Early Life

Jyotiraditya was born on 1 January 1971, after two sisters. The arrival of a male heir in Bombay (now Mumbai) led to celebrations and festivities that went on for months. Madhavrao wanted his son to be called Vikramaditya but the Rajmata had overruled that and settled for Jyotiraditya, named after the family deity, Jyotiba.

Mother Madhavi Raje told authors Vir Sanghvi and Namita Bhandare, 'We had a series of parties for him. There were separate parties for business community, for the Maratha community, for our circle of political friends and so on.'

When the proud parents and grandmother returned to Gwalior, Jai Vilas Palace was illuminated, thousands were fed and offerings were sent to all city temples.

Jyotiraditya's initial years were spent in Nepal, where he was home schooled. When post-Emergency, Madhavrao returned to India, he made it a point not to send his son to the family-owned Scindia School in Gwalior. Madhavrao must have been conscious of the 'preferential treatment' he himself had received in Scindia School despite father Jiwajirao Scindia's specific instructions not to treat his son differently.

Jiwajirao would often conduct surprise 'inspections' and 'impounded' a thick, softer mattress that was reportedly given to Madhavrao. Vir Sanghvi has quoted diplomat-turned-politician Natwar Singh as saying that Madhavrao was seldom served a cold chapatti. 'He [Madhavrao] never sought preferential treatment. But in subtle ways, he was treated differently. I suppose it was inevitable,' said Natwar, who was a recipient of the first Madhav Award as an Old Boy of Distinction for the year 1984.

In their biography of Madhavrao Scindia, Sanghvi and Bhandare have given an extensive account of how an attentive Madhavrao had groomed his son for real-life challenges, even while on 'shikar'.

'He tried to instil in me a sense of fearlessness. He [Madhavrao] did not want me to be scared of the unknown,' Jyotiraditya said, recalling one instance.

The father and son were passing through a jungle in Shivpuri and night was about to fall when Madhavrao pretended his jeep had stalled. Madhavrao, sensing that his young son was frightened that tigers might be approaching them, made him walk ahead in the wild while keeping the jeep headlights on. After a few moments, he started the jeep and asked Jyotiraditya to hop on.

Madhavrao is said to have told Jyotiraditya that he did not want his son to be a cry baby.

The Scindias had many fancy cars but Madhavrao made sure that his son went to school in a twelve-year-old Ambassador. Both Jyotiraditya and sister Chitrangada were made to memorize *shlokas*. In school, Jyotiraditya paid special attention to learning the Hindi language, making him a much better speaker in Hindi than any public school product in public life. Jyotiraditya told Priya Sahgal that he was able to pick nuances of Hindi each time he accompanied his father on the election campaign. '*UP mein aur is samay ke Uttrakhand* [where Doon School is located] *mein bahut klisht Hindi boli jaati thi. Hamare Hindi ke adhyapak badi klisht Hindi mein charcha karte the* [in UP and in the present day Uttrakhand, chaste Hindi is spoken. My Hindi teacher used to converse in chaste Hindi].'

A Lavish Wedding

Jyotiraditya was barely sixteen when Chitrangada got married to Vikramaditya, son of former Kashmir *sadr-e-riyasat* (president), Dr. Karan Singh. Maharajahs, industrialists, foreign leaders, officials, journalists and villagers watched in drizzling rain, considered a sign of good fortune, as the bejewelled groom and the bride, diamonds glistening on her wrists, ears and nose, met under the silk canopy. And when they exchanged the symbolic garlands, enthusiastic cheers spread across the palace.

Inderjit Badhwar, *India Today* magazine's features editor, was present in Gwalior to cover the event when at 11.40 a.m. sharp on 11 December 1987, the Taj Express rumbled to a halt at Gwalior railway station and marked the beginning of a pageant. The all-male baraat of 113 – packed into two reserved carriages – wore brocade achkans and yellow turbans, while the receiving party, led by Jyotiraditya, were in their conical Shinde Shahi topis, bedecked with gold *todas* (multi-layered crescents), brocade dupattas and *madakhals* (gold brocade epaulettes). A Border Security Force band struck up *Sare jahan se achchha*, *Hindustan hamara*. The crowds cheered, and the groom's party wound its way to a cavalcade of thirty-five cars that took them to the Usha Kiran Palace Hotel, owned by the Scindias, where the *baraatis* were lodged in luxurious suites.

Badhwar observed that the Jai Vilas Palace complex resounded to a cacophony of music. 'A 15-piece brass band and shehnai players, dressed in gold achkans, played in the archways of buildings and on different hotel lawns. The music never stopped. Not even when Madhavrao Scindia took off in a helicopter to receive King Birendra of Nepal at the airport that afternoon.'

The women from the Scindia family: Madhavrao's wife Madhavi and his sisters, then arrived at the hotel for the groom's *haldi* ceremony, Badhwar recorded.

'They were dressed in ornate brocade saris, sporting kardanis of basra pearls and diamonds on their hips, four-tiered pearl and diamond bracelets and chokers. Accompanying them were the former maharanis of Jhabua, Jaipur and Badwani, among others.'

The canopied mandap, designed by Rajiv Sethi, built of clay and adorned with banana leaves, was in open view for a crowd of over 50,000.

At exactly 6.30 p.m., Badhwar noticed, the baraat arrived, led by an auspicious elephant painted a deep blue. The groom, his father, the former maharaja of Jaipur and Farooq Abdullah arrived in two carriages drawn by white horses, while a band played *Mera mehboob aya hai* from the 1966 movie *Suraj*.

The crowd went into a tizzy. The marriage ceremony was an extravagant affair, performed according to the 300-year-old Maratha tradition. 'It started with the singing of the Manaalashtak – an eight-stanza verse, sung in Raag Des, Marwah and Bhairavi – celebrating the history of the two 21-gun salute royal families now being united in matrimony. As the Vedic chants continue over loudspeakers, the couple sits face to face on low wooden stools separated by a hand-held veil,' Badhwar wrote.

'Just before the kanyadaan ceremony, the veil is dropped. And, as if by an eerie command, the skies respond with rain and a high wind causes the crowd to shiver. The physical barricade between the VIPs and the commoners is suddenly obliterated.'[13]

Dr. Karan Singh, a noted Hindu scholar, performed some rituals himself.

Swedish Radio correspondent, Gisela Widmer, who was part of the large foreign press corps present at the occasion, said: 'It is amazing how such a large crowd retained its enthusiasm in spite of being confronted with such differences in wealth.'[14]

Sheila Tefft, who was present at Gwalior, wrote in the *Chicago Tribune* that three days of lavish festivities reportedly cost US$4 million and stirred a national controversy because India, at that point of time, was grappling with economic hard times and the worst drought in years. 'But it also captured the attention of the country, which, although a modernizing Third World force and the world's largest democracy, is still enthralled by its feudal roots,' she wrote while quoting Narinder Singh, the Maharaja of Panna, who was among the more than 100,000 people who watched the palace wedding. 'This is an occasion to relive our glorious past.'[15]

Badhwar could not help noticing that there was no public feast, and only tea was served to the guests. The dinners where champagne flowed were strictly private affairs, attended by close friends and the *baraatis*. 'We wanted to keep this a dignified affair. And that's what it was,' Karan Singh told him.

The Scion Takes a Wife

When Jyotiraditya got married in December 1994, the celebrations were low key. Family insiders whispered that Madhavrao had become conscious of rumours of 'vulgar display of wealth', which had forced Sonia not to attend the wedding at Gwalior.

The 1975-born Priyadarshini Raje, daughter of a former Baroda royal, Kumar Sangramsinh Gaekwad, son of Pratap Singh

Rao Gaekwad, the last ruler of the erstwhile Baroda state, met Jyotiraditya sometime in December 1991 in Delhi. 'Our first meeting was an arranged affair – a dinner at a social gathering. From then on, it was up to us. But I knew from day one that Priyadarshini was the one for me. We were finally married in December 1994,' Jyotiraditya told *The Times of India*. 'Baba describes best [in an email message] what Priyadarshini means to me.

He wrote to her saying that she was the bulwark of his son. In terms of emotional strength, the foundation of our home, the interests of our children, Priyadarshini means everything to me. However, politics is not for her, she is keen on writing and will pen a novel someday.'[16]

The couple believe that theirs was a love marriage solemnized as an arranged marriage.

Along with son, Mahanaaryaman, and daughter, Ananya Raje, Priyadarshini Raje is a permanent fixture in high society glossies. Known for her innate style, she regularly tops the list of India's best dressed women and is widely viewed as a modern-day standard bearer of the Scindia family's longstanding style legacy. She was voted among Verve's 'Best dressed – 2008' hall of fame list and among 'India's 50 Most Beautiful Women' list by Femina. 'I was just 20 when my son was born and for a few years I just wanted to get to know the family better,' she once told the *DNA* newspaper. The couple had a two-year stint in the US, where Jyotiraditya worked for Merrill Lynch, the UN and Morgan Stanley in New York; then Hong Kong, and later shifted to Mumbai.

Sanghvi recalls Madhavrao turning emotional when Jyotiraditya was getting married. In the past 300 years, no Scindia had lived to see the wedding of his heir. Jiwajirao had died when Madhavrao was in school while Madho Maharaj had expired when Jiwajirao was barely nine. A historical jinx had been broken.

Like Father, Like Son

Like father Madhavrao, Jyotiraditya too dabbled in cricket administration. He rose to become the head of the BCCI's finance committee but left in a huff over differences with CEO, Rahul Johri. However, his hold over the Madhya Pradesh Cricket Association was total and he twice won the president's post, beating senior BJP leader, Kailash Vijayvargiya. The contest, held in Indore, used to be a no-holds-barred battle, with Vijayvargiya and his supporters leaving no stone unturned to win. In 2012, a last-minute judicial intervention helped Jyotiraditya score a convincing win over Vijayvargiya. In 2010, Vijayvargiya had lost to Jyotiraditya by seventy votes in an electoral college that consisted of 232 voters.

Interestingly, in private conversations, Vijayvargiya's supporters would point an accusing finger at a Delhi-based influential BJP leader (now deceased) for helping out Jyotiraditya.

At fifty, Jyotiraditya may not have achieved the political stature of his father in cricket or in politics but the titular head of Gwalior seems every bit determined and ready to fulfil the unfinished agenda of the Scindias to 'conquer' Delhi, which his forefathers had failed to do.

Will he be a bigger success story than grandmother Rajmata Vijaya Raje or father Madhavrao? As the eleventh titular maharaja of Gwalior, will Jyotiraditya's politics and actions live for that future?

SEVEN

Next Generation: Royals and their Political Future

At any other time, his presence at high-profile social gatherings would have been seen as de rigueur for someone with a background as his. Unfortunately for Dushyant Singh, the royal scion found himself in the middle of a raging controversy this time.

The four-time BJP MP from Jhalawar-Baran, Rajasthan, had attended a party thrown by Bollywood singer Kanika Kapoor in Lucknow. In a dramatic and worrying turn of events, the crooner of *Baby Doll* fame, later tested positive for COVID-19.

Kanika had thrown the party after her return from the UK, and many others, including Dushyant's mother, Vasundhara Raje Scindia, father-in-law Ranjeet Singh Judev, politicians Jitin Prasada and Akbar Ahmad 'Dumpy', and Ahmad's interior-designer nephew, Adil Ahmad, were present at the gathering.

It was still early days of the pandemic but Dushyant, who usually maintains a low profile, came under the glare because he attended parliamentary proceedings right after the party. At a parliamentary standing committee meeting, he sat next to the

Trinamool Congress's Derek O'Brien and had even visited the Rashtrapati Bhawan for a breakfast with President Ram Nath Kovind.

Nearly 100 MPs, including Defence Minister Rajnath Singh and Women and Child Development Minister Smriti Irani, had also attended the breakfast meeting.

While Kanika angered many – an FIR was filed against her amid allegations that she concealed her travel history and therefore put others at risk – Dushyant faced a greater social media backlash.

O'Brien had later taken to Twitter to voice his displeasure. 'This Govt [Modi government] is putting us all at risk,' O'Brien had tweeted after it emerged that Dushyant had attended Kanika's party. 'The PM says self isolate yourself but the Parliament is on. I was sitting next to Dushyant the other day for 2.5 hours. There are two more MPs who are in self-isolation. The session should be deferred.'

Dushyant's mother had leapt to her son's defence. 'As a matter of abundant caution, my son and I have immediately self-quarantined and we're taking all necessary precautions,' she had tweeted then.

This was not the first time that Dushyant, a 1991-batch Doon School student, had come under public glare. His name had earlier hit the headlines when the controversy involving disgraced cricket czar Lalit Modi had sucked Vasundhara into a snowballing scandal sometime after she had returned to power as Rajasthan's chief minister in 2013 (see Chapter 4 for details).

Vasundhara had gone into a shell following revelations that she had lobbied the British government in 2011 to extend Lalit Modi's stay in Britain, where the former IPL commissioner had fled. A document, which endorsed Lalit's application to stay on in the UK, said Vasundhara's 'assistance' should not 'become known' to Indian authorities.

It was common knowledge that Lalit Modi and Vasundhara's 'partnership' was quite strong and allegations surfaced that Dushyant had clinched a 'sweetheart deal' with Lalit Modi, who had reportedly invested Rs 11.63 crore in his hospitality company.

On 23 June 2015, the then Union finance minister, Arun Jaitley, admitted that the Narendra Modi government was investigating links between Dushyant and Lalit Modi. The BJP, at that point of time, had left both Vasundhara and Dushyant to fend for themselves. A hawkish Congress and a well-known television anchor had pressed for Vasundhara's resignation as chief minister of Rajasthan.

At that time it was the son's turn to stand by his mother. Dushyant, often called a 'mama's boy', a pejorative term that does not seem to offend the polite and reticent father of two, has always defended his mother every time she faced a crisis.

Sources close to the Scindias point out that Dushyant has been at his mother's side like a 'shadow' since 1978, when he was barely five. That was the time when Vasundhara, who was raising him as a single mother, got into a protracted legal battle with her husband Hemant Singh over their son's right to the family properties in the Dholpur principality. The case was eventually settled in 2007, with Hemant getting the family properties in Delhi, and the Dholpur Palace and several other properties in Rajasthan going to Dushyant.

Three years earlier, in 2004, Dushyant had cut his teeth in electoral politics following the footsteps of his mother, maternal uncle Madhavrao Scindia and maternal grandmother Vijaya Raje, continuing the Scindia family's involvement with politics. The St. Stephen's graduate who studied hotel management in the United States and Switzerland, won the Lok Sabha elections from Jhalawar-Baran, a constituency his mother had represented in five elections since 1989 before stepping down as an MP to take over as Rajasthan's chief minister in 2003.

Dushyant's victory, and subsequent electoral successes, are largely credited to Vasundhara's clout, although the son claims to have done some work in the region too.

A Congress Link

While the BJP dominates Dushyant's political lineage, the Dholpur scion has married into a family with close links to the Congress. Few are aware that Judev, father of Dushyant' wife, Niharika, was a prominent Congress leader from Uttar Pradesh with personal connections to Indira Gandhi.

In 1969–1970, Indira had reportedly told Judev to stop bothering about privy purses and 'start working' when most ex-royals, including the Scindias, were cut up with the then prime minister's move to scrap the special privileges and allowances they enjoyed. Judev, in that sense, proved to be an exception as he continued to work with three generations of the Nehru–Gandhi family – Indira, Rajiv, Sonia and Rahul.

Journalist Radhika Ramaseshan had met Judev in April 2007 when she accompanied Rahul Gandhi to the Bundelkhand region of Uttar Pradesh during an election campaign. Rahul, who was then general secretary of the AICC, had braved temperatures of around 43°C as he sought votes for Dushyant's father-in-law at Gharota, about 100 km from Jhansi.

Judev, the former raja of Samtar, had told Ramaseshan that he agreed to contest the election after a phone call from the Congress high command. 'I had no choice. Madam Sonia and Rahul phoned me and said this is a winning seat. We need to pick up as many of such seats as possible and you have to contest. I tried telling them I will give another candidate. But they wouldn't listen,' Judev said in his polished, public-school English.

Indira, Rajiv and Sonia have reportedly stayed at Judev's imposing fortress-like Samtar Mahal, a vision in red with sprawling grounds and a moat, with a red-and-white striped flag with a tuft of black hair flying atop. Judev also considered the late Madhavrao Scindia as one of his 'best friends'. The two had studied together at the Scindia School in Gwalior.

Judev has another Scindia connection, too. His wife, known as Maharani Sahiba, is the sister of Pashupati Rana, president of Nepal's Rashtriya Prajatantrik Party. Rana's wife is Vasundhara's older sister, Usha Raje.

For a former royal – his ancestors ruled over the erstwhile Samtar principality, one of the largest in Uttar Pradesh's Bundelkhand region – Judev, however, comes across as very *aam aadmi* (down to earth) and is popular among the residents of Gharota, who have sent him to the assembly six times.

Niharika

If Judev was a man of the people, his daughter Niharika maintained a low profile till the Rajmata's granddaughter-in-law found herself pitchforked into the role of a 'star campaigner' for the BJP in Rajasthan, although she does not hold any official position in the party. In 2014, for instance, she figured on a list of forty star campaigners the party had submitted to the Election Commission. Others on that list included Narendra Modi and other senior leaders such as L.K. Advani, Amit Shah, Rajnath Singh, Jaitley, Sushma Swaraj and Vasundhara. Every time her husband, Dushyant, or mother-in-law, Vasundhara, contested elections, Niharika has dutifully played the role of an effective campaigner. The party has also made use of her Gujjar background in Nasirabad and Weir, two seats that have a sizeable presence of people from the community.

Niharika and her mother-in-law have often tried to reach out to various castes, pointing to the heterogeneity they themselves represented. While Vasundhara was born in a Rajput family

– being the daughter of the former Maratha princely state of Gwalior – she married into a Jat family of the former princely state of Dholpur; on the other hand, Niharika was of Gujjar origin.

Niharika also played a pivotal role in ending a violent Gujjar agitation seeking caste-based reservation for the community, categorized as one of the OBCs. In 2008, after seven days of violence between the Gujjars and the Meenas that claimed over thirty lives, Vasundhara had managed to get the Gujjars to call off their stir with the help of her daughter-in-law. Her efforts were appreciated by then BJP national president, Rajnath Singh, the party's state in-charge, Gopinath Munde, and spokesperson, Prakash Javadekar.

The clash was over the OBC Gujjar community's demand for Scheduled Tribe (ST) status and its accompanying benefits, which the ST Meenas vehemently opposed. Niharika is said to have told prominent Gujjar leaders that the ground reality did not support their demand for ST status.

Akshay

With Madhavrao's son Jyotiraditya Scindia and Vasundhara's son Dushyant joining the family profession of politics, many thought that their first cousin Akshay, son of Yashodhara Raje Scindia, too, would enter politics. That has not happened so far. But the former MTV jockey and news producer with MTV Desi, a channel that celebrates South Asian and American pop culture and entertainment in the USA, has been a regular campaigner in the Gwalior-Shivpuri region.

Akshay, who holds a journalism degree from New York University, has had many 'familiarisation trips' to the Shivpuri Assembly constituency. And each time he arrived, it alarmed BJP as well as Congress circles in the region. A closer look explains why. In the past decade, many sons have risen on Madhya Pradesh's political turf, each threatening local aspirants and potential rivals. The state BJP leads the pack with nearly half a dozen second- and third-generation leaders taking up official positions in the party. But more on them later in this chapter.

Mahanaaryaman

Another Scindia scion, Mahanaaryaman, too, has been a visible presence on Madhya Pradesh's political terrain. During the 2019 Guna Lok Sabha elections, Mahanaaryaman, son of Jyotiraditya Scindia, was seen campaigning for his father in eight assembly segments that formed part of the parliamentary seat.

Earlier, Mahanaaryaman had accompanied his father when Jyotiraditya visited the Mahakal Temple in Ujjain, seeking divine blessings for the 2018 state polls. On 10 June 2018, Mahanaaryaman had delivered a political speech at Shivpuri. Dressed in kurta-pyjama and a *gamchha* draped around his neck, Mahanaaryaman had displayed his fine oratorical skills, avoiding any direct mention of the BJP while alleging that politics in Madhya Pradesh was dominated by lies. Jyotiraditya was still in the Congress then.

The November 1995-born Scindia scion has also displayed his ability to spontaneously connect with the masses. A day after his political speech, Mahanaaryaman was getting down from a car at Ashok Nagar in Jyotiraditya's Guna constituency when he spotted a roadside chaat vendor making aloo *tikki* on his handcart. Mahanaaryaman, who was headed towards the railway station, sought permission from the vendor to try his hand at making aloo *tikki* and then distributed the popular snack among curious bystanders. Before leaving, he gave the vendor Rs 350.

When Jyotiraditya defected from the Congress to the BJP in March 2020, his son was the first to welcome it. The Yale University graduate sent out two tweets. The first tweet, from the handle @ASCindia, said it took courage to 'resign from a legacy' and 'Sad it had to come to this'.

The second tweet read: 'I am proud of my father for taking a stand for himself. It takes courage to resign from a legacy. History can speak for itself when I say my family has never been power hungry. As promised we will make an impactful change in India and Madhya Pradesh wherever our future lies.'

Ananya

Mahanaaryaman's sister, Ananya, born in April 2002, has remained apolitical but, during the 2019 Lok Sabha elections, was often seen accompanying her mother and brother to various street corner meetings in the Guna constituency.

Ananya, who has studied at the British School, New Delhi, and learnt horse riding, is spotted in Gwalior during the annual Dussehra festival, performing *aarti* in full public view. However, it would be the rarefied ambience of glittering Paris where she would make her first splash in 2019. Ananya was invited to the prestigious Le Bal event that brings together youths from famous families across the globe who have a taste for fashion designing, dance and music. Only those who have been invited can take part in the couture event started by fashion designer Ophélie Renouard. Ananya's dance partner at the gathering was her brother, Mahanaaryaman.

A Tragedy

Not that the story of the younger generations of the Scindias is only about the inheritance of an opulent legacy. The arc lights haven't always been kind.

Nineteen years ago, a young Scindia had come under unwelcome glare when a drunken prince who loved her went berserk, killing his parents – Nepal's King Birendra Bir Bikram Shah and Queen Aishwarya – and several relatives at the sprawling Narayanhiti Palace before turning the gun on himself.

Birendra, who was extremely popular among his subjects, had opposed Prince Dipendra's love affair with Devyani Rana, daughter of Usha Raje Scindia. Usha Raje, Rajmata Vijaya Raje Scindia's eldest daughter, is married to Pashupati Shamsher Bahadur Rana of Nepal.

Historically and socially, the Shahs had been at loggerheads with the Ranas, who served as prime ministers and the real power behind the throne from 1743 till 2008, when the monarchy was abolished and Nepal was declared a federal democratic republic.

A section of Nepalese historians claim that the Ranas, who ruled the kingdom from 1846 until 1951, were oppressive, clamped down on political dissent, made little investment in health and education and ensured that power remained concentrated in the hands of a few.

Author Amish Raj Mulmi, however, says there is little historical evidence to suggest the Shah kings would have done any better. 'Indeed, if history tells us anything, it is that the Shahs were themselves prime autocrats,' he argues. The Ranas ruled Nepal until King Tribhuvan overthrew the oligarchy.

It is against this historical backdrop that Dipendra and Devyani fell in love with each other. Dipendra was a student at Eton when he met Devyani at the residence of their local guardians, Shelley and Charles. But King Birendra and Queen Aishwarya had another potential bride in mind for Dipendra, unaware of the love affair. In fact, both the families remained unaware of the affair for over two years.

Then, in 1995, according to a report in the *Nepali Times*, just before Devyani's older sister, Urvashi, married into a rich business family in India, Devyani's parents sent a proposal to the palace suggesting a matrimonial alliance between Devyani and

Dipendra. The offer was reportedly frowned upon.

According to the social grapevine, Devyani's mother Usha Raje was said to have mentioned the wealth of the House of Scindias when Shree Rajya Laxmi Rana, Dipendra's maternal grandmother, had met her once. The reported comparison between the wealth of the Scindias and the Shahs of Nepal apparently shut the door on a Dipendra–Devyani alliance.

While Narayanhiti Palace kept rejecting the relationship, Dipendra kept meeting Devyani. Their bond was intense. When Dipendra was training to be a parajumper, he had reportedly called up Devyani on the day of his first jump and told her he would do it only if she made breakfast for him. She did, and met him at the airport with his breakfast. He ate and went for his jump, while Devyani went to the banks of the Manahara river where he was supposed to land. Dipendra later drove her home.

Things got further complicated when Devyani's parents started getting marriage proposals from some ex-royals from India, such as the House of Bhagalpur, the House of Jaipur and the House of Baroda. Devyani asked Dipendra to take a call. The Palace, however, was set against their marriage. The denouement would be terrible – almost as if fate had been waiting to unleash its unfathomable ironies in an evening of madness.

Dipendra loved collecting guns. At eight, the crown prince had been gifted his first pistol. At fifteen, when he went to Eton, he would keep a loaded revolver with him. On 1 June 2001, as King Birendra and Queen Aishwarya chatted with other royals and friends at the luxurious Tribhuvan Sadan dining hall at Narayanhiti Palace, Dipendra burst into the room, dressed in army fatigues.

Eyewitness accounts said Dipendra carried an Uzi, an M16 assault rifle and a pistol. The prince raised one gun and fired two shots at the ceiling, then turned to his father and shot him dead. 'The king slid from his chair and collapsed on the floor,' *The*

Guardian reported. One report said doctors had found ten bullet holes in his body.

The guests ran for cover as the prince sprayed the room with bullets. He then ran into the garden to confront his mother but, according to an eyewitness, his younger brother Nirajan stepped into his path to stop him. 'Don't do it, please. Kill me if you want,' Nirajan implored his brother.

Seconds later, Nirajan too was dead, shot at least seventeen times, according to one report.

Dipendra then turned the gun on his mother, the queen, and shot her dead. The prince's uncle Dhirendra, sister Princess Shruti, two of the king's sisters as well as his brother-in-law and cousin were also among the dead. The massacre ended with Dipendra turning the pistol on himself, shooting himself in the temple. He was seriously injured and, after two days on a ventilator, died in hospital, after being declared the crown for barely forty-eight hours.

A day after the shootout, Devyani left for New Delhi to stay with her uncle Madhavrao.

An official probe later held Dipendra 'solely' responsible for the killing of King Birendra, Queen Aishwarya and seven other royals and confirmed that he had spoken to Devyani thrice on a mobile phone shortly before the shooting spree.

The two-member probe panel set up by King Gyanendra, in its report made public, mentioned that a 'drunk' Dipendra in army fatigues had fired indiscriminately at the royal family members who were relaxing in the billiard room of Narayanhiti Palace after dinner on 1 June.

The 200-page report said Devyani, in her telephonic tape-recorded interview to Nepal's envoy to India, B.B. Thapa, had spoken of a 'close relationship with Dipendra'.

Her parents told the committee that there was contact between Dipendra and Devyani. However, Devyani, in her twenties then, refused to disclose the details of her conversation with Dipendra, saying they were matters concerning her 'personal affair' and she did 'not want to say anything about them'.

A Different Angle

Other factors were at play too. Vivek Kumar Shah, who was serving as military secretary at the Narayanhiti Palace when the massacre took place, claims the royal family were against the crown price marrying someone with relatives in India.

Devyani's maternal side not only lived in India but was also deeply involved in the country's politics.

There was a time when the Rajiv Gandhi government had frosty ties with Nepal and Madhavrao was a minister, considered close to Rajiv and Sonia.

In 1989, Sonia had accompanied Rajiv to Kathmandu. The visit was billed as a mega event as the prime minister was expected to streamline relations with Nepal, the lone Hindu kingdom in the world. Rajiv and King Birendra got along well till the Indian prime minister decided to visit the historic Pashupatinath Temple. As at Tirupati and Puri, non-Hindus are debarred from entering the holy premises. Rajiv insisted upon taking Sonia with him, but the priests were in no mood to oblige and King Birendra expressed his inability to veto the representatives of God.

There was also talk that Queen Aishwarya, who had some influence over the temple trust, took a strong position not to let Sonia in.

Rajiv reportedly took it as a personal affront, thinking that it was the King's way of snubbing him. He returned without paying his respects at Pashupatinath. Needless to say, the relations between the two countries deteriorated further.

Dipendra's Personality

Accounts have also emerged of Dipendra's alleged personality problems. In his book, *Maile Dekheko Darbar*, Vivek Kumar Shah claims that Dipendra was brought up by nannies and orderlies, and was deprived of parental love, according to translated excerpts published in the *Nepali Times*.

Dipendra, Shah said, wasn't allowed to mingle much with other children, nor was he put under the care of experts to groom him to be the crown prince. He did not even get an opportunity to develop a normal personality, and used to beat people to the ground until they cried, Shah has claimed in his book, adding that Dipendra used to enjoy being sadistic.

'I couldn't help notice what was happening to him. Although mother–son relations should be warm, Dipendra was not on good terms with the queen as both were headstrong. Neither would concede defeat.... We had to escort him to school when he was in kindergarten. He did not want to go to school, but the queen forced him to. She used to shout at him and slap him often when he refused. Sometimes, he wanted to get off the car that was taking him to school.'

Shah also wrote that Dipendra caused a lot of trouble for his ADCs. 'He had a destructive streak and used to break glasses and pens in the ADC's office, and if an ADC refused to obey him, he used to kick and slap them. I had been at the receiving end of such treatment often.'

The King and Queen subsequently sent Dipendra off to boarding school at Budhanilkantha, where he reportedly took to drinking and smoking. 'The distance between Dipendra and his parents widened after he started going to school. The parents cut his allowance but he would borrow from others. Since childhood, he got pleasure from hurting others, he used to hunt pigeons with his catapult, and he would torture the wounded bird before it died. If he caught a mouse, he would set its tail on fire and leave it to die.'

Shah also saw a thoughtful side in the young prince. 'He loved travelling, wrote poetry, and Nepali literature teachers were hired to hone his talent,' Shah has said in his book. Shah later worked with the team that probed the palace massacre.

Author Jonathan Gregson, who attempted to unravel the mystery behind the massacre in his work, *Blood against the Snows*, claims the 1 June 2001, incident was the result of a generational conflict. 'His [Dipendra's] parents thought marriages should be arranged, he didn't. All those things were intensified and heightened because of the background. Marriage was not the only thing they had a control over: aged 29, Dipendra still had to hide the fact he was a smoker from his parents, although he had smoked since his teens,' Gregson writes.

After the massacre, Devyani had left Nepal and lived in exile in Delhi and London. In 2006, she got married to Aishwarya Singh, grandson of former Madhya Pradesh chief minister and Union minister Arjun Singh and heir to the erstwhile *riyasat* of Churhat in the state's Sidhi district. The marriage was attended by Devyani's maternal aunts, Vasundhara and Yashodhara, and first cousin, Jyotiraditya.

Devyani, who holds a master's degree from the London School of Economics and works as a consultant for the United Nations Development Programme, spoke to Murli Krishnan of the Australian Broadcasting Corporation in 2012.

'What royalty once did is what the state and central governments are doing, which is contributing towards development, education and the society,' she said, stressing the need for formal royals to meld with the times and work for the people. 'In today's day and age, I think, we should live with the times.'

She cited cousin Jyotiraditya's example to illustrate how former royals were making a name for themselves in all areas of contemporary India. 'These figureheads are putting themselves on the map,' she said.

Other Famous Progeny

The 'figureheads' are not the only ones. A different class of progeny, of non-royals, have also been busy carving out a place for themselves on the political map of Madhya Pradesh, which has traditionally been a fertile ground for what has been dubbed the 'dynasty culture'. While it has been a direct plunge for some, others have been playing a crucial background role.

Kartikey Singh Chouhan, son of BJP chief minister Shivraj Singh Chouhan, for instance, had campaigned for his father in the 2018 state elections. Kartikey, a law graduate from Symbiosis Law School, Pune, was often seen addressing public meetings, playing court to religious and spiritual leaders and selling flowers and milk in upmarket areas of Bhopal where ministers, bureaucrats and the affluent live.

His packaged milk brand came up with the name 'Sudhamrit' and the tagline '*Doodh ka dhula doodh, gai ka doodh* [fresh milk, cow's milk]'. Kartikey also runs Florica, which offers fresh flowers, bouquets and floral arrangements.

Kartikey's Facebook page introduces him as someone from the Bharatiya Janata Party Yuva Morcha.

Another son who has joined the list of political *babalog* is Nakul Nath. Nakul, forty-six, son of former Madhya Pradesh chief minister, Kamal Nath, won from Chhindwara in the 2019 general election when everyone else from his party, including Jyotiraditya who was then in the Congress, lost in the state.

Earlier, Nakul was often seen sitting right behind Kamal Nath at the Indira Gandhi Bhawan in Bhopal when the former Union minister took charge as state Congress chief on 1 May 2018. The Boston University graduate has been looking after Chhindwara, his father's pocket borough, for a long time, nursing the constituency from when he was in his thirties.

Away from the constituency, Nakul, who can mix with

everyone, leads a rather hectic social life in Delhi, at ease with a hep crowd in upscale places like Smoke House Grill at Greater Kailash. But back in Bhopal and Chhindwara, the Mandela shirt gets replaced with spotless white kurta and an *angawastram* of the Congress colours of saffron, white and green.

Even the language and gestures change for these next-generation politicians, trained to fold their hands in a namaste instead of the casual and urbane 'hi', while the faithful are allowed to touch their feet. A few words in the local dialect, Bundelkhandi, Baghelkandi or Gondi, before the start of a speech are considered a big draw.

The list of sons who have risen on Madhya Pradesh's political firmament is long. Among those who play an active role in state politics are Union Minister Narendra Singh Tomar's son, Devendra Pratap Singh, BJP National Vice President Prabhat Jha's son, Tushmul, party National General Secretary Kailash Vijayvargiya's son, Akash, former state BJP chief, Nand Kumar Chouhan's son, Harshvardhan Singh, and Sukaran and Abhishek, the sons of state ministers, Narottam Mishra and Gopal Bhargava.

Off the record, many politicians have justified the 'dynasty culture', saying it was both 'necessary' and 'practical'. Elections, one politician argued, require confidentiality. 'It is an open secret that even in Assembly polls, campaign expenditure is much more than the Election Commission ceiling of Rs 25 lakh. If a father is in the fray, the son's job entails interacting with influential caste leaders, thought influencers and keeping them in good humour. With rivals and law-enforcement agencies keeping a hawkish eye, use and distribution of resources require secrecy and confidentiality of the highest order. In such a situation, a family member, particularly a son, becomes an obvious choice.'

Another politician quoted from the, 'Bhagavad Gita' to say that a son is expected to deliver the father from the hellish condition of life.

In regional parties too, such as the DMK, Akali Dal, Rashtriya Lok Dal and the Samajwadi Party, several family members have held posts and positions without causing any disquiet. Party insiders say this has had a lot to do with the stature of the leaders concerned: M. Karunanidhi, Parkash Singh Badal, Ajit Singh and Mulayam Singh Yadav, within their parties.

However, it is the Congress, packed with young and not-so-young dynasts, that has come to be identified with dynastic politics more than any other, something that BJP leader Amit Shah has seldom failed to harp on.

At a party workers' convention in Delhi in July 2017, Shah, then the BJP's national chief, had made a strong point against dynastic politics. 'Who will become the party president after me?' he was quoted asking his audience.

When there was no immediate response, he asked: 'Now tell me who the next Congress president after Soniaji will be?' Many hands had reportedly gone up. Shah had then cited his own rise as an example of the party's 'internal democracy'. 'If dynasty instead of merit is the benchmark in a party, it can never take India forward,' he said.

Even as Vasundhara continued to be a major force to reckon with in Rajasthan, her presence as the BJP face in the state appeared inconsistent with the politics of Narendra Modi and Amit Shah. As part of his 2014 Lok Sabha poll campaign against the Sonia Gandhi-led Congress, Modi had roared and roared again dynastic politics, describing the UPA government as '*Maa-Bete ki Sarkar* [government of mother and son]'. Even then, Vasundhara went on to become the only BJP chief minister (2014–2018) with a dynastic history and is a contender for 2023 chief ministerial post. She and her son are perhaps the only Maa–*Beta* duo in the party that has survived in the Narendra Modi – Amit Shah raj.

EIGHT

Various Shades of Fortune and the Ugly Property Wars

Most of us have heard of the term million-dollar question. How about a 400-billion-rupee property dispute? Or, is the figure higher?

The answer is no, if one goes by the affidavits the Scindias have filed for parliamentary and assembly elections from 1957 till date. Their wealth appears to be far less than popular perceptions about what is being fought over in protracted legal battles across the country. According to some estimates – it is impossible to arrive at a definitive figure – these disputes are over properties worth around Rs 40,000 crore. Some of these disputes have been dragging on for thirty years among the former royals of the erstwhile Gwalior state, Jyotiraditya Scindia and his three aunts, amid speculation that the legal battle may be settled out of court.

On Jyotiraditya's side, Abhishek Manu Singhvi and Raian Karanjawala are said to be providing legal assistance while his aunts reportedly rely upon Rajiv Luthra's law firm. Neither side has denied or confirmed anything related to their legal battles, let alone reveal any details.

Going by his affidavit (filed at the time he contested elections), Jyotiraditya is the owner of properties worth over Rs 2 billion, including Jai Vilas Palace, which was part of his inheritance. He also owns a 1960 model BMW car,[1] again part of his inherited wealth; the Jai Vilas Palace in Gwalior, spread over 40 acres; 19 acres of land in Shrigonda and 43 acres in Limban village, both in Maharashtra.

Jyotiraditya also owns Rani Mahal, Hiranvan Kothi, Racquet Court, Shantiniketan, Choti Vishranti, Vijay Bhavan, Picnic Spot and other residential properties worth Rs 297 crore in the Gwalior-Shivpuri region of Madhya Pradesh.

The other assets declared in the affidavit are two properties in Mumbai's Samudra Mahal worth Rs 31.9 crore. Incidentally, he had rented out one of his duplex flats in the 'A' wing of the building to YES Bank co-founder, Rana Kapoor, now embroiled in a money-laundering controversy. Another lesser-known fact about the Samudra Mahal is that it was once the home of the now fugitive diamond merchant Nirav Modi.

Jyotiraditya also declared that he had fixed deposits amounting to Rs 30,187,000 and Rs 33,339,827 in movable assets. In his income tax return for 2019–2020, he declared an annual income of Rs 15,156,720, and his wife Priyadarshini Raje's income as Rs 250,400. The affidavit also stated that the annual income from his ancestral property was Rs 467,410 while he owned jewellery valued at Rs 86,853,219.

In her affidavit filed in November 2018, Vasundhara Raje had declared moveable and immovable assets worth Rs 5.5 crore. She said she owned jewellery worth over Rs 1 crore and gold worth Rs 1.2 crore. Her younger sister, Yashodhara Raje, while admitting ownership of a dinner set valued at Rs 1,54,19,938, had merely Rs 15,400 in cash. She had a bank balance of Rs 13.60 lakh across nine accounts and the market value of her investments in bonds and shares is estimated to be Rs 1,56,89,449, while her insurance policies are worth Rs 14 lakh. Yashodhara also said she possessed a diamond-encrusted ring worth Rs 6,66,704.

Royal Real Estate

From sons of the soil to wealthy landowners, the Scindias' stock has risen vastly over the years. Bhopal-based journalist Rakesh Dixit thinks the sprawling Jai Vilas Palace compound and other properties in Gwalior are worth over Rs 10,000 crore. There are also mansions such as the Sakhya Vilas, Susera Kothi, Kuleth Kothi, Cottage Hill and Takenpore retreat that the Scindias own.

In Gwalior, Jyotiraditya's grandfather, former Maharaja Jiwajirao Scindia, was also bequeathed properties by some sardars, such as a garden, plots, a house in Danaoli, another at Pichhadi Deodi, and a hilltop retreat. He also owned fifteen zamindari villages outside Gwalior.

The Scindias' properties elsewhere in the state are valued at Rs 1,000 crore. In Shivpuri, the properties include the Madhav Vilas Palace, Happy Vilas and George Castle. There is also the Kaliadeh Palace in Ujjain.

In Delhi, the family owns Gwalior House, a plot on Rajpur Road and Scindia Villa, whose value is estimated to be Rs 4,000 crore. The family also owns Padma Vilas Palace in Pune, Scindia Ghat in Varanasi and the Vithoba Temple, Sanquelim, in Goa.

The family controls four *inaam* (gifted) villages and land in ten other villages in the Deccan region. They also came to acquire properties such as the Rs 700 crore Vasundhara building on Peddar Road in Mumbai. The flat in Samudra Mahal in Mumbai where Madhavrao often stayed is valued at Rs 60 crore. In March 2020, these flats hit headlines when two disgraced business tycoons, Nirav Modi and Rana Kapoor, were discovered to be owning sprawling apartments in South Mumbai's Samudra Mahal.

Nirav Modi, his uncle, Mehul Choksi, and other family members are under the scanner of the Indian agencies for their involvment in the Rs 14,000 crore Punjab National Bank (PNB) scam. Modi fled the country after being charged for criminal conspiracy, criminal breach of trust, cheating and dishonesty including delivery of property, corruption, money laundering, fraud, embezzlement and breach of contract.

On 6 March 2020, the Enforcement Directorate conducted raids at Rana Kapoor's Mumbai residence. According to the *Hindustan Times*, the raids at Rana Kapoor's residence were linked to the agency's money laundering probe related to DHFL (Dewan Housing Finance Limited), which was accused of siphoning off around Rs 13,000 crore with the help of seventy-nine fictitious companies and one lakh fictitious customers.[2]

The Dispute

According to the journalist Dixit, the twenty-year-old Jyotiraditya was not in politics and his father Madhavrao Scindia was still alive when he filed a case in a Gwalior court in 1990, claiming to be the sole heir to the Scindia inheritance.

When Jyotiraditya's grandfather Jiwajirao Scindia, the erstwhile maharaja of Gwalior, died, he had not left instructions about how his immovable and movable properties were to be divided among his descendants. The properties were initially divided equally between his widow Vijaya Raje and his only son Madhavrao after she filed a suit in Bombay High Court, back in 1984. Mother and son both had 50 per cent share in the large number of immovable properties spread across India.

In his case, Jyotiraditya had invoked the Scindia custom of primogeniture, according to Amreesh Mishra of *India Today* magazine. 'According to his claim, the provisions of the Hindu Succession Act that normally divide property equally among the descendants do not apply to the princely line, given the exception under Section 5(2) of the Act for prevailing customs of inheritance in a family,' Mishra said.[3]

His aunts, Usha Raje (settled in Nepal), Vasundhara and Yashodhara, had contested their nephew's claim, citing the will of their late mother, dated 20 September 1985. Their lawyer, Deepak Khote, had told the court, 'We believe that the legal precedent of the Rajendra Singh (Dholpur) case, in which a Constitutional Bench of the Supreme Court had ruled in 1975 that personal rights will be ruled by personal law, applies here. Besides, it's hard to prove the primogeniture custom of inheritance in a family.'[4]

Amreesh Mishra quoted relatives of the late Sardar Sambhaji Rao Angre, a master of intrigue and former private secretary to Vijaya Raje, who had a fractious relationship with Madhavrao, to explain that the custom of the firstborn enjoying *jyeshthadhikar* (primogeniture) could not be established beyond doubt as almost everyone who had ascended the throne of Gwalior before Jyotiraditya's great-grandfather, Madhav Maharaj, did had been adopted. That was how the Scindias had managed to avoid the Doctrine of Lapse that eventually led to the 1857 rebellion by the Rani of Jhansi, Lakshmibai.

Mishra says this was not the only legal issue. Immediately after her death in 2001, Sardar Angre had produced Vijaya Raje's handwritten will drafted in 1985 that had disinherited her son and grandson while bequeathing two-thirds of the assets to her daughters and one-third to charity through a trust, which would in turn to cover the fifteen trusts she had formed in 1975 to manage the properties just before the Emergency.

Swadeshi Jagran Manch convener, S. Gurumurthy, and Angre were the executors of the Rajmata's will. While the legal feasibility of an umbrella trust is questionable, the will is being examined in a probate case by Delhi High Court and is currently in the stage of evidence.

Vijaya Raje's solicitors in Mumbai had produced another will in 2001. It excluded not just her son and grandson but the charities as well, leaving the entire block of properties that was under her control to her daughters. This will is also being examined under a probate case, this time by Bombay High Court, and is in the evidence stage. Her two wills are important because of an agreement in 1971 when Prime Minister Indira Gandhi had scrapped the system of privy purses. At that point, the Scindias were getting Rs 25 lakh annually, apart from incomes from various trusts.

Immediately after that, the Scindias had divided their assets through a verbal agreement: the immovable assets had gone to the mother and the cash, shares and debentures to the son. By 1975, through arbitrator D.M. Harish, the division was given legal shape in the form of a written document through a ruling of a Mumbai court. The next year, the immovable properties that came to Vijaya Raje were transferred to fifteen separate charitable trusts set up by her in the names of different members of the family.

In his 1990 suit, Jyotiraditya had also challenged the validity of the verbal agreement of 1971 and the subsequent court division of 1975 between his grandmother and father.

The case filed by Jyotiraditya dragged on for nearly twenty-seven years before he filed an application in October 2017 in the court of additional sessions judge, Gwalior, with his counsel Sachin Sharma expressing his desire for an out-of-court settlement of the property dispute. 'In view of the seriousness of the case and its far-reaching consequences, I am willing for disposal of the case through mutual consent,' the application said.[5]

The chances of a settlement by mutual consent increased when the judge reportedly asked the Scindias through their legal representatives if they were open to the idea of an amicable out-of-court solution. The judge pointed out that under Madhya

Pradesh High Court guidelines, all property disputes involving the Scindia family that were pending in various courts in the country, including Mumbai, Delhi, Pune, Jabalpur and Gwalior, were to be disposed of within a certain time frame. Therefore, 'the court expects both the parties to come up with a compromise formula as per the spirit of the Section 89 CPC,' Judge Sharma had said.[6]

Jyotiraditya's lawyer submitted before the court that his client had agreed to an out-of-court settlement earlier too, and deposited fees for the commissioner appointed by the court for this purpose. However, the commissioner had died during this period. Meanwhile, the lawyers for his aunts too had urged the court to consider appointing another commissioner and they also sought a copy of Jyotiraditya's application.

In June 2019, the prospect of a compromise suffered a setback when the Bombay High Court refused a request by Jyotiraditya to strike off a fresh written statement by his aunts, claiming that they had retracted from their earlier stance in the family's property dispute.

Jyotiraditya had petitioned a bench of Justice Ramesh Dhanuka, seeking to strike off this statement from the records of the trial court. He contended that this 'inconsistency' in the stand of his aunts was an abuse of the process of law.

Justice Dhanuka considered the submissions and noted that Vasundhara and her sisters were entitled to make such a statement, but would have to establish their claim. The court said all this would have to be tested at the stage of trial as the lower court in Pune was yet to commence trial in this dispute, pending since the 1980s.

'Striking of the written statement filed by the aunts would have serious adverse impact on their right to defend. Such powers can be exercised sparingly and in case of clear finding that such pleadings, if allowed to remain on record, would be an abuse of process of the court. In my view, since suit itself is pending since last 35 years, no case is made out by Jyotiraditya for striking off the written statements,' Justice Dhanuka said.

With Jyotiraditya joining the BJP in March 2020, many in Gwalior and Bhopal feel that the growing cordiality among the nephew and his aunts Vasundhara and Yashodhara will help resolve the property disputes. Dixit believes that Yashodhara stands to gain the most if the dispute is settled through mutual agreement. 'Her eldest sister, Usha Raje, is settled in Nepal and doesn't take any interest in the case, while the other sister, Vasundhara Raje, has her own vast properties which she inherited from the erstwhile Dholpur state that she was married into. She and her son, Dushyant, are reportedly not keen on fighting the case. Yashodhara, who was married but now divorced, has her eyes set on the Scindia properties in Gwalior, particularly the Jai Vilas Palace. Unlike her sisters, Yashodhara got no vast fortune from marriage,' Dixit told this author.

Other Assets

Before the 2014 Lok Sabha elections, Jyotiraditya Scindia and his family had disclosed that they owned shares in at least twenty-five companies. Besides holding a stake in Scindia Investments Pvt. Ltd, Jyotiraditya has shares in at least nine other companies: ARS Trustee Company, MJS Trustee Company, PRS Trustee Company, Ananya Raje Tavern, Mahanaaryaman Resort, Priyadarshini Raje Resort, Earth Financial Advisors, Moonrise Financial Advisors and Shivali Financial Advisors. Dixit said he had scanned data from the Registrar of Companies which showed that Jyotiraditya and his family have a 100 per cent stake (along with 100 per cent preference shares) in Scindia Investments Pvt. Ltd and, along with his wife Priyadarshini Raje Scindia, controls MJS Trustee Co. Pvt. Ltd, PRS Trustee Co. Pvt. Ltd and ARS Trustee Co. Pvt.

Ltd. Along with his mother Madhavi Raje Scindia, Jyotiraditya controls Indamsat Pvt. Ltd and Devvrata Investments Pvt. Ltd. Separately, Priyadarshini has a stake in Gaekwad Investment Corp. Pvt. Ltd.

At the time of Independence, the family owned shares in more than 100 companies, including 49 per cent stake in Bombay Dyeing.

Palaces of Woe

The history of the Scindias is best told through their lawsuits over property. The late Vijaya Raje had filed two suits in Pune in the additional district judge's court two decades ago, one each for possession of immovable and movable assets. The cases are still pending.

The charity commissioner in Mumbai is hearing a case of two trusts: the Sir Jiwajirao Trust and the Krishna Madhav Trust that own properties in Mumbai, in which the late Madhavrao had replaced the trustees appointed by his mother after her death in 2001.

In August 2006, the Madhya Pradesh government ordered supersession of the Jyotiraditya-controlled society that runs the Samrat Ashok Technology Institute, an engineering college in Vidisha district, and installed then minister Yashodhara as its chairperson. Jyotiraditya, however, returned to head the society in 2009 through a Gwalior High Court bench order after the government failed to hold elections to the society within the stipulated three-year period.

A case was registered in the Gwalior additional district judge's court in 1983 when Hiravan Kothi, a bungalow in Gwalior in which Vijaya Raje's confidant Sardar Angre used to live, was stormed by local goons allegedly acting at Madhavrao's behest. Angre and Rajmata were in London then. A case of loot, dacoity and forcible entry was filed and Madhavrao was charged under Section 120(b) of the Indian Penal Code for alleged conspiracy. While the Madhya Pradesh High Court quashed the FIR registered by the police upon the Gwalior court's order, a division bench of the Supreme Court in 2007 restored the FIR and ordered the additional district judge's court to proceed. The case is still pending.

In 1991, cases were filed in different courts in the country by the Scindias for the control of over fifty properties. Following an injunction from the Supreme Court, no property can be given to anyone in the Scindia family till the primogeniture case is settled.

While the extent of the Scindias' wealth defies speculation, the 1,240,771 sq ft Jai Vilas Palace's opulent interiors may give an idea. It leaves no doubt in our minds of the vast fortune at stake for the members of the erstwhile royal family.

Notes

Chapter 1

1. Crown Publishers Inc., First Edition, 1985.
2. Sarup & Sons.
3. Cambridge University Press.
4. Rathod, *The Great Maratha Mahadji Scindia*.
5. See https://www.tribuneindia.com/news/archive/features/-art-soul-825249.
6. A *tazia* is a replica of the tomb of Husain, the martyred grandson of Muhammad, that is carried in processions during the Shiite festival of Muharram.
7. Stewart Gordon, *New Cambridge History of India: The Marathas, 1600–1818* (Cambridge University Press).
8. 'The Scindias: A Brief History', a pamphlet published by the Scindia family.
9. One who holds land assignments in lieu of judicial and police duties without having to pay revenues.
10. R.V. Smith, 'Delhi's Affair With the Bais', available at https://www.thehindu.com/features/metroplus/Delhis-affair-with-the-Bais/article15718377.ece.
11. Penguin Books, 2009.
12. 1875, Reprint: Asian Educational Services 2005.
13. Mahadji's death is shrouded in mystery that led to conjectures about the possible use of black magic to end his life. The Scindia ruler had intermittent fever for over six months prior to his death for which the cause could never be ascertained.

14. Manu S. Pillai, 'The Shrewd Dowager of Gwalior', available at https://www.livemint.com/mint-lounge/features/the-shrewd-dowager-of-gwalior-11573194197290.html; Nandini Sengupta, 'The British Woman Traveller in India: Cultural Intimacy and Interracial Kinship in Fanny Parks's Wanderings of a Pilgrim in Search of the Picturesque', in *New Readings in the Literature of British India, c. 1780–1947 (Studies in English Literatures)*, ed. Shafquat Towheed (Columbia University Press, 2020).
15. Pillai, 'The Shrewd Dowager of Gwalior'.
16. Joyce Lebra-Chapman, *The Rani of Jhansi: A Study in Female Heroism in India*, 1st edition (University of Hawaii Press, 1986).
17. H.M. Bull and K.N. Haksar, *Madhav Rao Scindia of Gwalior 1876–1925* (Alijah Durbar Press, Gwalior).
18. This was the first land tenure system implemented in India by the East India Company. Under this system, the right of collecting revenue from a particular area was auctioned to the highest bidder. Peasants, shopkeepers and merchants had to pay taxes to the *ijardar* who eventually was also the highest bidder to the Company and established his own revenue collection department.
19. Where the breadth of the tracks was 2 feet, instead of the regular size of 2 feet 6 inches. Narrow gauge trains have a number of advantages over broader gauges. The narrow gauge enables tighter curves, especially in valleys and on difficult terrain, and requires less space at stations. The lower-cost narrow gauge was chosen for Gwalior in 1872 as the traffic potential there did not justify the cost of a standard- or broad-gauge line at that time.
20. V.D. Savarkar, *Indian War of Independence, 1857* (Abhishek Publications, 2019).
21. See https://www.telegraphindia.com/india/horse-haunts-scindias /cid/482276.
22. Bull and Haksar, *Madhav Rao Scindia of Gwalior.*
23. Allen and Dwivedi, *Lives of the Indian Princes.*
24. John Gaylor, *Sons of John Company: The Indian and Pakistan Armies, 1903–1991* (Parapress Ltd, Tunbridge Wells).
25. Bull and Haksar, *Madhav Rao Scindia of Gwalior.*
26. Unpublished but quoted by Bull and Haksar in *Madhav Rao Scindia of Gwalior.*
27. Madho Maharaj was so fiercely loyal to the crown that when his son, Jiwajirao, was born in June 1916, the infant was given the pet name 'George'. It was much more than a coincidence that George Frederick Ernest Albert or George V was also the emperor of India at that time.
28. Bull and Haksar, *Madhav Rao Scindia of Gwalior.*

29. Hill and Wang, 2013.
30. Some regiments of the Scindia army served the British and were largely drawn from outside the boundaries of Gwalior state. The state troops were recruited from within the limits of Gwalior. The native rulers bore the maintenance expenses of both troops.
31. Mary Leland, 'An Irishwoman's Diary', *The Irish Times*, available at https://www.irishtimes.com/opinion/an-irishwoman-s-diary-1.7 3171.
32. Bull and Haksar, *Madhav Rao Scindia of Gwalior.*
33. Babuji's father, Narayan Rao, was employed in the finance department of Madho Maharaj's court. Babuji too had served in the court of the Scindias.
34. Also mentioned in Bull and Haksar, *Madhav Rao Scindia of Gwalior.*
35. Maharani Chinkoo is remembered for her height. She was barely 4 feet 3 inches tall. It is said that Madho Maharaj was unaware of this until he saw her at the time of their wedding.
36. Orient Longman, 1985.
37. Jiwajirao and Sardar Vallabhbhai Patel shared a close friendship, particularly during 1947–1950. When Patel died in 1950, Jiwajirao had a painting of him commissioned, which hangs to this day in Parliament of India.
38. Sanghvi and Bhandare, *Madhavrao Scindia.*

Chapter 2

1. Vijaya Raje Scindia with Manohar Malgonkar, *Princess: The Autobiography of the Dowager Maharani Gwalior* (Century Publishing, London).
2. Kundan involves skillfully working highly refined strips of gold to secure gemstones to a metal framework through pressure rather than heat. This method of setting gems is unique to the subcontinent.
3. V.P. Menon, *Integration of the Indian States* (Orient BlackSwan.)
4. Seehttps://openthemagazine.com/features/history/savarkar-escaped-because-nobody-probed-how-godse-got-an-italian-revolver-from-a-gwalior-de aler/.
5. See https://scroll.in/video/341/nehru-asked-indians-to-give-jew ellery-to-fund-the-1962-war-and-some-of-it-is-still-in-rbi.
6. See https://www.theguardian.com/world/2001/feb/10/lukeharding.
7. See https://www.livemint.com/mint-lounge/features/opinion-th e-princes-in-a-socialist-republic-1549597446621.html.
8. Penguin Books Ltd.
9. Sunil Gupta and Sunetra Choudhury, *Black Warrant: Confessions of a Tihar Jailer* (Roli Books).
10. Taroon Coomar Bhaduri, *Off the Record* (Vikas Publishing House).

11. See https://www.indiatoday.in/magazine/special-report/story/19910930-domestic-battle-between-vijaya-raje-and-madhavrao-scindia-spills-into-national-politi cs-815619-1991-09-30.
12. Sanghvi and Bhandare, *Madhavrao Scindia.*
13. Sanghvi and Bhandare, *Madhavrao Scindia.*
14. See https://www.indiatoday.in/magazine/special-report/story/19 910930 -domestic-battle-between-vijaya-raje-and-madhavrao-scindia-spills-into-national-politics-815619-1991-09-30.
15. This fact has been recorded by the Rajmata in her memoirs and finds a mention in Vir Sanghvi's and Namita Bhandare's sympathetic biography of Madhavrao, too. Also see https://www.indiatoday.in/magazine/special-report/story/19910930-domestic-battle-between-vijaya-raje-and-madhavrao-scindia-spills-into-national-politics-815619-1991-09-30.
16. See https://magazine.outlookindia.com/story/they-call-me-rasp utin/210909.
17. A.G. Noorani, 'Indira Gandhi and Indian Muslims', *Economic and Political Weekly*, 25, no. 44 (November 3, 1990).
18. Cited by A.G. Noorani in the *EPW* on November 3, 1990.
19. The Hindu Inflexion, (November 30, 2017). See https://openth emagazine.com/cover-stories/ayodhya-25-years-later/the-hindu-inflexion/.
20. Sanghvi and Bhandare, *Madhavrao Scindi*a.
21. Sanghvi and Bhandare, *Madhavrao Scindi*a.

Chapter 3

1. See https://swarajyamag.com/insta/his-father-madhavrao-scindia-would-have -been-pm-if-he-had-lived-veteran-congress-leader-natwar-singh]
2. See https://www.thehindu.com/news/national/r-d-pradhan-sonia-made-up -her-mind-in-1999/article6281300.ece.
3. See https://frontline.thehindu.com/other/article30252286.ece.
4. In the long run, Advani was the one affected the most. In order to emphasise probity in public life, Advani did not contest the 1996 elections and missed the chance of becoming prime minister and Vajpayee was chosen to head the BJP government, which lasted for only thirteen days. Vajpayee became prime minister again in 1998 and ruled for thirteen months before winning the 1999 elections for a five-year term at the helm. By the time the BJP staged a comeback as the ruling party, Advani had been dethroned and replaced by the mighty Narendra Modi.
5. Penguin Books, 2009.
6. *Sunday Magazine*, April 14–20, 1996.

7. Rupa Publications, 2016.
8. See https://frontline.thehindu.com/other/obituary/article302522 84.ece.
9. In both the Lok Sabha and the Rajya Sabha, it is only the leader of the opposition who enjoys the status and perks of a cabinet rank minister.
10. Madhavrao was, however, careful not to be identified with the more radical elements of the Left.
11. See https://www.hindustantimes.com/india/remembering-scindia-a-leader-and-a-friend/story-oZYMpGMAaEB5c7QxCW xoFK.html.
12. Amar Singh continued to play an important role in relation to Madhavrao, Dalmiya and the BCCI. A decade after Madhavrao won the BCCI contest, he backed Dalmiya for the top post. Amar Singh is said to have played a key role in bringing Madhavrao and Dalmiya closer.
13. This incident was narrated to the author by a Bhopal-based cricketer.
14. See https://theprint.in/politics/a-1980s-cricket-match-that-gives-peek-into -how-ahmed-patel-tackled-party-politics-politicians /551798/.
15. Hay House, 2015.
16. Delhi chief minister, Sheila Dikshit, and Congress MP, Mani Shankar Aiyar, had providentially escaped the ill-fated flight after a last-minute change in travel plans. While Dikshit had fever, Aiyar was requested by Madhavrao to stay back to accommodate a journalist.
17. As the young prince had been nicknamed George.
18. Sanghvi and Bhandare, *Madhavrao Scindia.*
19. Sanghvi and Bhandare, *Madhavrao Scindia.*
20. Seehttps://www.theguardian.com/education/2017/feb/23/ppe-oxford-university-degree-that-rules-britain.
21. Sanghvi and Bhandare, *Madhavrao Scindia.*
22. See https://frontline.thehindu.com/other/article30252286.ece.
23. See https://frontline.thehindu.com/other/article30252286.ece.
24. See Sanghvi and Bhandare, *Madhavrao Scindia.*
25. https://www.theguardian.com/news/2001/oct/04/guardianobituaries1.
26. See https://www.indiatoday.in/magazine/obituary/story/200110 15-former-maharajah-of-gwalior-and-congress-leader-madhavrao-scindia-killed-in-aircrash-774413-2001-10-15.

Chapter 4

1. See https://www.youtube.com/watch?reload=9&v=xIwFrPqliTk.
2. By this time Vasundhara was a married woman.
3. The Scindias had been embroiled in conflict against the rulers of Dholpur

since the eighteenth century. To bring about an end to the hostilities between the two sides, the British intervened; Mahadji Scindia signed a treaty in October 1781 with the British government which stipulated that as long as the Ranas of Dholpur honoured the treaty, the Scindias would not interfere in Dholpur territory. However, there were frequent violations and the stipulation was subsequently removed. The bloody battles between the two principalities stopped when the British consolidated their hold over princely states. As part of the British-brokered truce after that, Jayajirao Scindia and Rana Nihal Singh of Dholpur are said to have hugged each other.

4. Scindia with Malgonkar, *Princess*.
5. The disputed property included the City Palace of Dholpur, a palatial home in Delhi's Panchsheel Marg, a number of vintage cars, farmland and a lodge in Shimla. The 2007 settlement gave Hemant the right to keep all the properties in Delhi while Dushyant became the owner of the Shimla lodge and the properties in Dholpur, including the City Palace, Dyodi Palace, Lodhi Palace, Motor Garage and the Ramsagar Gardens, some agricultural land, twenty-five vintage cars and jewels kept in the *shahi khazana* (royal treasury) of Dholpur Palace.
6. Scindia with Malgonkar, *Princess*.
7. Sanghvi and Bhandare, *Madhavrao Scindia*.
8. Scindia with Malgonkar, *Princess*.
9. Scindia with Malgonkar, *Princess*, p. 246.
10. See https://www.indiatoday.in/magazine/indiascope/story/19820515-scindias-accused-of-having-a-hand-in-feud-between-indira-gandhi-and-maneka-771774-2013-10-16.
11. In the Indian political system, membership to state-run boards and corporations indicates the occupant's political sympathies and is considered a parking place for beneficiaries.
12. Vijay Nahar, *Vasundhara Raje Aur Viksit Rajasthan* (Prabhat Books).
13. Jhalawar derives its name from the bells of temples, the most famous among the many here being the Sitalesvara Mahadeva shrine.
14. Harauti derived its name from the Hada Rajputs of the Bundi kingdom or the Harauti region of Rajasthan. The Hadas had ruled the region/kingdom after wresting it from the Meena rulers. In present-day Rajasthan, the Harauti region includes the districts Bundi, Baran, Jhalawar and Kota.
15. See https://www.rediff.com/election/2003/dec/08vasu.htm.
16. See https://www.rediff.com/election/2003/dec/08vasu.htm.

17. Radhika Ramaseshan, 'Wake Up and See the Sign, Vasundhara Defence Collapses, PM Still Silent', available at https://www.telegraphindia.com/india/wake-up-and-see-the-sign/cid/1478610.
18. Ramaseshan, 'Wake Up and See the Sign'.
19. In Tamil Nadu, Amma Canteens or Unavagam, are a big draw where a breakfast serving of idli costs just Re 1. A plate full of 'Pongal bath' (lemon rice) comes for Rs 5. In Chennai alone, there are some 200 low-cost restaurants that offer meals to itinerant workers, daily wage earners and many others at affordable, hygienic restaurants. The scheme, launched by then chief minister, Jayalalithaa, in 2015, benefited around 150,000 people a day and costing just about Rs 500,000.
20. See https://www.indiatoday.in/india/story/any-woman-can-become-a-politician-it-is-like-pursuing-any-other-career-vasundhara-raje-at-india-today-woman-summit-2018-1349934-2018-09-26.
21. Ramaseshan, 'Wake Up and See the Sign'.
22. See https://www.indiatoday.in/india/west/story/people-want-de livery-and-not-doles-vasundhara-raje-183191-2014-02-28.
23. See https://www.indiatoday.in/india/story/any-woman-can-become-a-politician-it-is-like-pursuing-any-other-career-vasundhara-raje-at-india-today-woman-summit-2018-1349934-2018-09-26.
24. See https://www.nytimes.com/2017/04/16/opinion/anatomy-of-a-lynching.html.
25. See https://magazine.outlookindia.com/story/captain-crony-cap ital/265185.
26. See https://magazine.outlookindia.com/story/captain-crony-capi tal/265185.
27. See https://economictimes.indiatimes.com/news/politics-and-nation/congress-affidavit-shows-rajasthan-cm-vasundhara-raj-commenting-on-the-political-equations-in-india/articleshow/4 7808604.cms?from=mdr.
28. See https://theprint.in/opinion/the-many-sins-of-vasundhara-ra je-that-are-coming-back-to-haunt-her/97460/.
29. See https://www.architecturaldigest.in/content/rajasthan-cm-vas undhara-raje-delhi-home/#s-cust0.

Chapter 5

1. See https://timesofindia.indiatimes.com/THE-PRIVATE-I-SE RIESThe-princess-diaries/articleshow/1125880.cms.
2. The allegation against the Scindias was that they had withheld information regarding how much gold they had. The Rajmata has, however, insisted that she and her son regularly paid all taxes.

•

3. See https://timesofindia.indiatimes.com/THE-PRIVATE-I-SE RIESThe-princess-diaries/articleshow/1125880.cms.
4. See https://www.thehindu.com/arts/crafts/figurines-from-antiquity/article 2458635.ece.
5. See https://www.rediff.com/news/1998/feb/28yasho.htm.
6. See https://www.rediff.com/news/1998/feb/28yasho.htm.
7. See https://www.indiatoday.in/magazine/indiascope/story/20030825-yashodhara-raje-spoils-bjp-hopes-in-madhya-pradesh-791929-2003-08-25.
8. See https://www.indiatoday.in/magazine/indiascope/story/20030825-yashodhara-raje-spoils-bjp-hopes-in-madhya-pradesh-791929-2003-08-25
9. Earlier, in 1998, Pawaiya had contested against Yashodhara's brother, Madhavrao, in Gwalior and lost by a narrow margin. The scare had forced Madhavrao to shift to neighbouring Guna in 1999. Pawaiya won as a BJP nominee from Gwalior that year in 1999 but in subsequent elections the ticket went to Yashodhara.
10. A sting operation by online news site *Cobrapost* that aired on a private television channel on 12 December 2005, showed eleven MPs accepting cash in exchange for raising questions in the Parliament. Out of the eleven MPs accused in the case, six were from the BJP, three from BSP, and one each from the RJD and Congress. They were Y.G. Mahajan (BJP), Chhatarpal Singh Lodha (BJP), Anna Saheb M.K. Patil (BJP), Manoj Kumar (RJD), Chandra Pratap Singh (BJP), Ram Sewak Singh (Congress), Narender Kumar Kushwaha (BSP), Pradeep Gandhi (BJP), Suresh Chandel (BJP), Lal Chandra Kol (BSP) and Raja Rampal (BSP). All of them, including Gwalior MP Ram Sewak, were expelled, necessitating Lok Sabha by-polls.
11. See https://www.news18.com/news/india/need-environment-police-for-tackling-sand-mafia-sumaira-abdulali-630744.html.
12. See https://timesofindia.indiatimes.com/the-private-i-seriesthe-princess-diaries/articleshow/1125880.cms.
13. See https://www.sundayguardianlive.com/news/house-scindias-family-saga.

Chapter 6

1. Based on the author's conversation with journalist Nirmal Pathak, editor of PTI-Bhasha.
2. See https://www.tribuneindia.com/news/archive/comment/amid-cong-turmoil -scindia-at-the-crossroads-826293.

3. See https://timesofindia.indiatimes.com/india/i-have-a-certain-level-jyotiraditya-scindias-response-to-rahul-gandhis-backbencher-remarks/articleshow/81408910.cms.
4. Priya Sahgal, *The Contenders* (Simon & Schuster India, 2018).
5. See https://www.sundayguardianlive.com/opinion/cool-breeze-series-missed-calls.
6. See https://twitter.com/ani/status/1237681490772684801.
7. See https://twitter.com/ani/status/1237681490772684801.
8. See https://indianexpress.com/article/opinion/columns/inside-track-jyotiraditya-scindia-vasundhara-raje-delhi-riots-6314649/.
9. See https://thewire.in/politics/madhya-pradesh-cabinet-shivraj-singh-chouhan-jyotiradtiya-scindia.
10. See https://www.sundayguardianlive.com/news/congress-troika-battle-party-fought-within-madhya-pradesh.
11. See https://www.gfilesindia.com/jyotiraditya-scindia-overrated-turncoat/.
12. See https://thewire.in/politics/madhya-pradesh-cabinet-shivraj-singh-chouhan-jyotiradtiya-scindia.
13. See https://www.indiatoday.in/magazine/living/story/19871231-history-came-to-life-at-the-wedding-of-chitrangada-raje-scindia-and-vikramaditya-singh-799642-1987-12-31.
14. See https://www.indiatoday.in/magazine/living/story/19871231-history-came-to-life-at-the-wedding-of-chitrangada-raje-scindia-and-vikramaditya-singh-799642-1987-12-31.
15. See https://www.csmonitor.com/1987/1217/owed.html
16. See https://timesofindia.indiatimes.com/delhi-times/the-evolut ion-of-jyotiraditya-scindia/articleshow/11710390.cms.

Chapter 8

1. The 1960 BMW Isetta, which runs on three wheels, is part of the vintage car collection that Jai Vilas Palace owns. The car makes appearances only on special occasions.
2. See https://mumbaimirror.indiatimes.com/mumbai/other/samudra-mahal-home-for-uber-rich-in-the-news-for-wrong-reasons/articleshow/74568142.cms
3. See https://www.indiatoday.in/magazine/the-big-story/story/201 01122-scindia-feud-castle-in-the-heir-744753-2010-11-13

4. See https://www.indiatoday.in/magazine/the-big-story/story/20101122-scindia-feud-castle-in-the-heir-744753-201 0-11-13
5. See https://www.indialegallive.com/special-story/scindia-family-dispute-over-property-worth-crores-battle-royale/.
6. See https://www.indialegallive.com/special-story/scindia-family-dispute-over-property-worth-crores-battle-royale/.

Bibliography

Abdulali, Sumaira. 'Need Environment Police for Tackling Sand Mafia'. https://www.news18.com/news/india/need-environment-police-for-tackling-sand-mafia-sumaira-abdulali-630744.html.

Advani, L.K. *My Country, My Life*. Rupa Publications, 2008.

Allen, Charles and Sharda Dwivedi. *Lives of the Indian Princes,* First Edition. Crown Publishers Inc., 1985.

Alva, Margaret. *Courage and Commitment: An Autobiography*. Rupa Publications, 2016.

Ashok, Sowmiya. 'At Delhi Stop, Amit Shah Takes Aim at 'Dynastic' Congress'. https://indianexpress.com/article/delhi/at-delhi-stopa mit-shah-takes-aim-at-dynastic-congress-4751179/.

Babuji, Kaudikar. Unpublished Memoirs. Cited by Vir Sanghvi and Namrata Bhandare. *Madhavrao Scindia – A Life*. Penguin Books, 2009.

Bhaduri, Taroon Coomar. *Off the Records*. Vikas Publishing House, 1989.

Bhatt, Sheela. 'Memoirs of a Hindutva Hawk'. https://www.rediff.com/news/2005/dec/27bjpspec.htm.

Bull, H.M. and K.N. Haksar. *Madhav Rao Scindia of Gwalior 1876–1925*. Alijah Durbar Press, Gwalior.

Chavan, Akshay. 'Tata Steel and Gwalior's Chamber of Secrets'. https://www.livehistoryindia.com/forgotten-treasures/20 17/07/14/tata-steel-and-gwaliors-chambers-of-secrets.

Dalrymple, William. *The Age of Kali: Travels and Encounters in India*. HarperCollins, 1998.

Dasgupta, Swapan. 'The Hindu Inflexion'. https://openthemagazine.com/cover-stories/ayodhya-25-years-later/the-hindu-inflexion/

Dixit, Rakesh. 'Jyotiraditya Scindia: Overrated Turncoat'. https://www.gfilesindia.com/jyotiraditya-scindia-overrated-turncoat/.

———. 'Madhya Pradesh: Small Shivraj Cabinet Spells Big Trouble for Scindia'. https://thewire.in/politics/madhya-pradesh-cabinet-shivraj-singh-chouhan-jyotiradtiya-scindia

———. 'Scindia Family Feud – Battle Royale'. https://www.indialega llive.com/special-story/scindia-family-dispute-over-property-worth-crores-battle-royale-38290.

Dutta, Anup. 'Kamal Nath's Son Makes a Silent Entry ahead of the Upcoming Lok Sabha Elections'. https://www.outlookindia.com/website/story/kamal-naths-son-makes-a-silent-entry-ahead-of-the-upcoming-lok-sabha-elections/311577.

Farooqui, Amar. 'From Baiza Bai to Lakshmi Bai: The Sindia State in the Early Nineteenth Century and the Roots of 1857'. In *Issues in Modern Indian History: For Sumit Sarkar,* edited by Biswamoy Pati. Popular Prakashan.

Mount, Ferdinand. *Tears of the Rajas: Mutiny, Money and Marriage in India 1805–1905*. Simon & Schuster.

Fotedar, M.L. *The Chinar Leaves*. HarperCollins, 2015.

Gaylor, John. *Sons of John Company: The Indian and Pakistan Armies 1903–1991*. Parapress Ltd, Tunbridge Wells.

Ghosh, Anirvan. 'How Lalit Modi Went From IPL King to Wanted Fugitive'. *Huffington Post* (June 15, 2015).

Gill, S.S. *The Dynasty*. New Delhi: HarperCollins, 1996.

Gordon, Stewart. *New Cambridge History of India: The Marathas, 1600-1818*. Cambridge University Press.

Goswamy, B.N. 'Lessons in Etiquette at Gwalior Court'. https://www.tribuneindia.com/news/archive/features/lessons-in-etiquette-at-gwalior-court-825249.

Gregson, Jonathan. *Blood against the Snows: The Tragic Story of Nepal's Royal Dynasty*. London: Fourth Estate, 2002.

Gupta, Sunil and Sunetra Choudhury. *Black Warrant: Confessions of a Tihar Jailer*. New Delhi: Roli Books.

Gyankosh. Maharashtra. http://ketkardnyankosh.com/index.php/20 12-09-06-10-43-51/8275-2013-02-13-04-37-25.

Harding, Luke. 'Indian Dynasty Aghast at £1bn 'Rasputin' Will'. https://www.theguardian.com/world/2001/feb/10/lukeharding.

Jana, Aastha. 'Dipendra and Devyani'. http://archive.nepalitimes.com/news.php?id=8217#.XoG2t4gzaCo.

Joshi, Manoj. 'Nehru Asked Indians to Give Jewellery to Fund The 1962 War – and

Some of It Is Still in RBI'. https://scroll.in/video/341/nehru-asked-indians-to-give-jewellery-to-fund-the-1962-war-and-some-of-it-is-still-in-rbi.

Kapoor, Coomi. *The Emergency: A Personal History*. Penguin Books Ltd, 2015.

———. 'Jyotiraditya Scindia's Two Aunts in BJP Are Not Exactly Thrilled about Their Nephew Joining the Party'. https://indianexpress.com/article/opinion/columns/inside-track-jyotiraditya-scindia-vasundhara-raje-delhi-riots-6314649/.

Kaye, M.M. *Far Pavilions,* Reprint edition. St. Martin's Griffin, 1997.

Kidwai, Rasheed. *24, Akbar Road: A Short History of the People Behind the Fall and Rise of the Congress*. New Delhi: Hachette India, 2011.

———. '45 Years after Its Dissolution, Here's What Opposition Parties Must Learn from Swatantra Party'. https://www.dailyo.in/politics/swatantra-party-indira-gandhi-indira-gandhi-politics-opposition-party-in-india-c-rajagopalachari-narendra-modi-jawaharlal-nehru/story/1/31526.html.

———. 'The Singaporean Who Took Indira Gandhi to Court'. https://www.orfonline.org/expert-speak/the-singaporean-who-took-indira-gandhi-to-court-53298/.

———. 'Royal Blood Is Thicker Than Party'. https://www.telegraphindi a.com/india/royal-blood-is-thicker-than-party/cid/201625.

Krishnan, Murli. 'Indian Royals Occupy New Place in Society'. https://www.abc.net.au/news/2012-10-10/an-life-changes-for-indian-royalty/4305026.

Lebra-Chapman, Joyce. *The Rani of Jhansi: A Study in Female Heroism in India*. University of Hawaii Press, 1986.

Leland, Mary. 'An Irish Woman's Diary'. https://www.irishtimes.com/opinion/an-irishwoman-s-diary-1.73171.

Mahajan, Rohit and Arindam Mukherjee. 'Captain Crony Capital'. https://www.outlookindia.com/magazine/story/captain-crony-capital/265185.

Malcolm, Sir John. *A Memoir of Central India: Including Malwa, and Adjoining Provinces*. Cambridge University Press.

Malhotra, Inder. *Dynasties of India and Beyond: Pakistan, Sri Lanka, Bangladesh*. New Delhi: HarperCollins, 2003.

Malleson, George Bruce. *An Historical Sketch of the Native States of India in Subsidiary Alliance with the British Government (1875)*. New Delhi: Asian Educational Services, 2005.

Masih, Archana. 'On the Campaign Trail with Maharaj'. https://www.rediff.com/news/2001/sep/30spec.htm.

———. 'The Rediff Election Interview/Yashodhara Raje Scindia'. https://www.rediff.com/news/1998/feb/28yasho.htm.

———. 'Scindia's BJP Entry: His Aunt Speaks'. https://www.rediff.com/news/interview/scindias-bjp-entry-his-aunt-speaks/20200312.htm.

McCarthy, Roy. 'Revealed: Secrets of Palace Massacre, Survivors Say Drunken Row Led to Shooting Spree by Crown Prince. https://www.theguardian.com/world/2001/jun/07/rorymccarthy

Menon, V.P. *Integration of the Indian States*. Orient Longman, 1985.

Mishra, Ambreesh. 'Scindia Feud: Castle in the Heir'. https://www.indiatoday.in/magazine/the-big-story/story/20101122-scindia-feud-castle-in-the-heir-744753-2010-11-13.

Mishra, Neeraj. 'Yashodhara Raje Spoils BJP's Hopes in Madhya Pradesh'. https://www.indiatoday.in/magazine/indiascope/story/ 20030825-yashodhara-raje-spoils-bjp-hopes-in-madhya-p radesh-791929-2003-08-25

Nahar, Vijay. *Vasundhara Raje aur Viksit Rajasthan*. Prabhat Paperbacks, 2016.

Naqvi, Saba. 'They Call me Rusputin'. https://magazine.outlookindia.com/story/they-call-me-rasputin/210909.

New York Times, The. 'A Somewhat Famous Historical Character, Passed Away – BHAESI-BHAE'. https://www.nytimes.com/ 1863/09/13/archives/spirit-of-the-paris-press-french-policy-in-mexico-american-affairs.html.

Noorani, A.G. 'Indira Gandhi and Indian Muslims'. *Economic and Political Weekly* 25 (1990): 44.

Pandey, Kirti. 'Love Story of Jyotiraditya Scindia and Priyadarshini Raje: Gwalior Ex-Royal Meets Baroda Former Royal'. https://www.timesnownews.com/india/article/love-story-of-jyotiraditya-scindia-and-priyadarshini-raje-gwalior-ex-royal-meets-baroda-former-royal/563485.

Parihar, Rohit. https://www.indiatoday.in/india/west/story/people-wa nt-delivery-and-not-doles-vasundhara-raje-183191-2014-02-28.

Pillai, Manu S. 'Opinion: The Princes in a Socialist Republic'. https://www.livemint.com/mint-lounge/features/opinion-the-princes-in-a-socialist-republic-1549597446621.html.

———. 'The Shrewd Dowager of Gwalior'. https://www.livemin t.com/mint-lounge/features/the-shrewd-dowager-of-gwalior- 11573194197290.html.

Ramaseshan, Radhika. 'Has Rajasthan CM Vasundhara Raje Been Good Administrator, Poor Politician?'. https://www.business-standard.com/article/elections/has-rajasthan-cm-vasundhara-raje-been-good-administrator-poor-politician-118120400122_1.html.

Rajput, Brajesh, "Wo Satrah Din" Shivna Prakashan; First edition (1 January 2020)

———. 'Indira to Rahul, Dynasty at Raja's Service'. https://www.telegraphindia.com/india/indira-to-rahul-dynasty-at-raja-s-service/cid/973215.

———. 'Princess and the Plebian'. *Ahmedabad Mirror*, February 5, 2018. https://ahmedabadmirror.indiatimes.com/columns/others/princess-and-the-plebeian/articleshow/62781181.cms.

———. 'Wake Up and See the Sign – Vasundhara Defence Collapses, PM Still Silent'. https://www.telegraphindia.com/india/wake-up-and-see-the-sign/cid/1478610.

Rathod, N.G. *The Great Maratha Mahadji Scindia*. Sarup & Sons.

Sahgal, Priya. *The Contenders*. Simon & Schuster India, 2018.

Sahgal, Priya. 'Cool Breeze – Series of Missed Calls'. https://www.sundayguardianlive.com/opinion/cool-breeze-series-missed-calls.

Sanghvi, Vir and Namita Bhandare. *Madhavrao Scindia: A Life*. Penguin Random House India, 2009.

Sangghvi, Malvika. 'THE PRIVATE I SERIES: The Princess Diaries'. https://timesofindia.indiatimes.com/THE-PRIVATE-I-SERIESThe-princess-diaries/articleshow/1125880.cms.

Savarkar, Vinayak Damodar. *Indian War of Independence, 1857*. Abhishek Publications, 2019.

Scindia, Jyotiraditya. 'People'. https://www.telegraphindia.com/opinion/people-jyotiraditya-scindia/cid/910719.

Scindia, Vijaya Raje and Manohar Malgonkar. *Princess: The Autobiography of the Dowager Maharani of Gwalior*. Century, 1988.

'The Scindias: A Brief History – A pamphlet'. Published by the Scindia family.

Sengupta, Nandini. 'The British Woman Traveller in India: Cultural Intimacy and Interracial Kinship in Fanny Parks's Wanderings of a Pilgrim in Search of the Picturesque'. In *New Readings in the Literature of British India*, edited by Shafquat Towheed. Columbia University Press.

Shah, Vivek Kumar. 'Maile Dekheko Darbar'. http://archive.nepalitimes.com/news.php?id=18247#.XoGU7ogzaCp.

Silbey, David J. *The Boxer Rebellion and The Great Game in China: A History*. Hill and Wang, 9 April 2013.

Singh, Onkar. 'A Royal Who Learnt to Be a Commoner'. https://www.rediff.com/election/2003/dec/08vasu.htm.

Singh, N.K. 'Angre Is a Vicious Man – Scindia'. https://www.indiatoday.in/magazine/special-report/story/19910930-angre-is-a-vicious-person-making-a-complete-fool-of-my-mother-madhavrao-scindia-814890-1991-09-30.

———. 'Domestic Battle between Vijaya Raje and Madhavrao Scindia Spills into National Politics'. https://www.indiatoday.in/magazine/special-report/

story/19910930-domestic-battle-between-vijaya-raje-and-madhavrao-scindia-spills-into-national-politics-815619-1991-09-30

———. "My Babu Caused the Rift' – Rajmata". https://www.indiatoday.in/magazine/special-report/story/19910930-i-must-have-committed-some-sin-in-my-previous-life-to-suffer-this-says-vijaya-raje-scindia-814880-1991-09-30.

Singh, Saghita. 'The Evolution of Jyotiraditya Scindia'. https://timesofindia.indiatimes.com/delhi-times/the-evolution-of-jyotiraditya-scindia/articleshow/11710390.cms.

Singh, Vertul. *Bhopalnama: Writing a City*. Amaryllis, 2020.

Sinha, Mridula. *Royal to Public Life.* New Delhi: Prabhat Prakashan, 2016.

Sowmiya, Ashok. 'At Delhi Stop, Amit Shah Takes Aim at 'Dynastic' Congress'. https://indianexpress.com/article/delhi/at-delhi-stopa mit-shah-takes-aim-at-dynastic-congress-4751179/.

Srivastava, Shruti. 'Truth behind the Hidden Treasure of the Gwalior Royal Family'. https://www.speakingtree.in/blog/gwalior-royal-family-treasure-secret.

Sultan, Abida. 'Memoirs of A Rebel Princess'. Oxford University Press.

Tefft, Sheila. 'India's Ex-Royalty Still Draws Crowds – and Votes'. https://www.csmonitor.com/1987/1217/owed.html.

Tiwari, Deepak, 'Rajnitinama Madhya Pradesh Rajnetaon Ke Kisse (1956-2003) Indra Publishing House; 1st Edition (1 January 2014)

Tiwari, Deepak, 'Peoples' King'. https://www.theweek.in/theweek/cover/peoples-kings.html.

Trevelyan, Humphrey. *The India We Left,* First Printing edition, 1972.

Smith, R.V. 'Delhi's Affair with the Bais'. https://www.thehindu.com/features/metroplus/Delhis-affair-with-the-Bais/article15718377.ece.

Ullekh, N.P. 'Savarkar Escaped Because Nobody Probed How Godse Got an Italian Revolver from a Gwalior Dealer'. https://openthemagazine.com/features/history/savarkar-escaped-because-nobody-probed-how-godse-got-an-italian-revolver-from-a-gwalior-dealer/.

Vajpayee, Atal Bihari. *Na Dainyam, Na Palayanam.* New Delhi: Kitabghar Prakashan, 2006.

Zarin, Anklesaria. 'Figurines from antiquity'. https://www.thehindu.com/arts/crafts/figurines-from-antiquity/article2458635.ece.

Index